# JOHN DUFFEY'S BLUEGRASS LIFE:
## FEATURING THE COUNTRY GENTLEMEN, SELDOM SCENE, AND WASHINGTON, D.C.

## STEPHEN MOORE
and G.T. KEPLINGER

### Foreword by TOM GRAY

BookLocker®

PAPERBACK ISBN: 978-1-63263-839-7
HARDCOVER ISBN: 978-1-63263-840-3

Published by BookLocker.com, Inc., St. Petersburg, Florida.

Printed on acid-free paper.

BookLocker.com, Inc.
2020

Second Edition

Library of Congress Cataloging in Publication Data
Moore, Stephen and Keplinger, G.T.
John Duffey's Bluegrass Life: Featuring The Country Gentlemen, Seldom Scene, and Washington, D.C. by Stephen Moore and G.T. Keplinger
MUSIC/Genres & Styles/Country & Bluegrass |
MUSIC/Genres & Styles/Folk & Traditional |
MUSIC/Ethnomusicology
Library of Congress Control Number: 2019904197

## Dedications

To Margaret, Charles, and Suzanna, with love.

Stephen Moore

To my family; my wife Jen, children Tommy, and Maddie. To my Mom, Helen Keplinger for indoctrinating me to the music of The Seldom Scene at an early age. To my Dad, I miss you. And to my brother Scott. Love to you all.

G.T. Keplinger

# Preface and Acknowledgements

It is clear from the interviews and stories gathered herein that John Duffey, the "Father of Modern Bluegrass" garnered unanimous acclaim and affection from audiences, reviewers, and journalists throughout an extraordinary life. His achievements warrant documentation.

This book sets down the facts of a career as preserved in scores of bluegrass books, magazines and recordings. We have had the pleasure and advantage of enriching these accounts with personal memories and reflections drawn from 1999, 2000, 2002, 2003, 2004, 2006, and 2018 interviews with John's fellow players, friends and family, including an unforgettable, 4-hour conversation in 1984 with Mr. Duffey himself. *These previously unpublished 1984 quotes by John are italicized throughout this book.* Many of the essential interviews with fellow players were video recorded by co-author, G. T. Keplinger for a forthcoming documentary film on The Seldom Scene based on this book.

The authors, with cool-headed scholarship but with warm-hearted devotion to John Duffey, his bandmates in both The Country Gentlemen and Seldom Scene, and their legion of admirers, have made every effort to create a complete and accurate history.

To the late John Duffey we express the deepest appreciation for his willing assistance with the foundation of this volume. Whenever the going was difficult, remembrance of his energetic and iconoclastic spirit enlivened the project.

We offer special thanks to John's close personal friend and omnipresent bass player, Mr. Tom Gray, for his enormous encouragement, memories, fact-checking, and Foreword, to Ms. Patty Johnson Cooper, for her expert editorial advice and ready help, to *Bluegrass Unlimited* writer and music producer Penny Parsons who provided early support and gravitas to this project, to writer Robert Kyle for researching and writing the Duffey genealogy, and sharing his Duffey moments, and to our friend and artist, Stilson Greene, for creating our beautiful book cover.

At the risk of omitting names, and with appreciation and apologies to anyone overlooked, we gratefully acknowledge everyone else whose contributions, photos and previously published work enriched our book, including Eddie Adcock, Martha Adcock, J.B. Allison, Ginger "Sam" Allred, Rick Allred, Dave Auldridge, Mike Auldridge, Mary Beth Aungier, Jim Beaver, Bill Blackburn, Bryan Bowers, Sam Bush, Joe Bussard, Tom Carrico, Laurie Williams Casey, Dick Cerri, Mary Cliff, Cerphe Colwell, Dudley Connell, Charles Cornett, Katy Daley, Lee Michael Demsey, Jonathan Edwards, Barbara Eldridge, Ben Eldridge, Sterling Ellsworth, Bill Emerson, Bill Emerson, Jr., John Fahey, Carl Fleischhauer, Jimmy Gaudreau, Frank Godbey, Marty Godbey, Jerry Gray, Tom Guidera, Richard Harrington, Rick Harmel, Emmylou Harris, Len Holsclaw, Mike Hurney, Chris Hayes, Cindy Howe, Len Jaffe, Becky Johnson, Pete Kennedy, Helen Keplinger, Moondi Klein, Pete Kuykendall, Robert Kyle, Kip Lornell, Bill C. Malone, George McCeney, John McEuen, Buzz McClain, Art Menius, Brian Murphy, Kay Mussel, Shawn Nycz, Gary Oelze, Akira Otsuka, Lou Reid, Neil Rosenberg, Phil Rosenthal, Rhonda Strickland, Linda Shaw, Ronnie Simpkins, Connie Brandt Smith, Butch Smith, Mike Southard, Cynthia Starling, John Starling, Richard Thompson, Fred Travers, Tom Travis, Laurent Vue, Cliff

Waldron, Boris Weintraub, Peter "Dr. Banjo" Wernick, Thelma Williams, Lou Ellen Wilkie, Billy Wolf, and Jesse Colin Young.

# Foreword by Tom Gray

It has been 24 years since we lost the great John Duffey, the father of modern bluegrass music. He still looms large in the minds of those who knew him and those who saw him perform. Those who came to love bluegrass since John's passing never got the chance to experience his power first-hand. Hopefully this book will give them an understanding of the unique larger-than-life character that was John Duffey. Fortunately, there are plenty of recordings and some videos still available to give a clue.

John's creative influence is heard and felt in the two main bands that he fronted, The Country Gentlemen and The Seldom Scene. These bands created the Washington sound, a newer, more cosmopolitan approach to a genre that had been invented by rural southern and Appalachian musicians in the 1940s. John co-founded The Country Gentlemen in 1957, stayed with them until 1969. Then in 1971, he was coaxed back into performing to help found The Seldom Scene. John remained with the Scene until his death in December 1996. I have been fortunate to have been a bandmate of John's in both of those bands.

There are so many Duffey stories that need to be retold lest they be lost. This book will help fill the void, and make him come alive to the readers.

**Tom Gray,** Bluegrass Hall of Famer in both The Country Gentlemen and The Seldom Scene.

# Table of Contents

# Chapter 1: Humbird in the Nest

*Well, I always thought the name of this business is show business. Hear that word 'show?' That's what I think is very important. The typical bluegrass band early on stood on the stage and looked like they all died last week. It was improper to smile or if you got a hand from the audience— anything—you didn't acknowledge it with a 'Gee, thanks a lot.' You sneered and walked off in a corner. I just thought no wonder this music can't get out of the closet. I was concerned.*

John Duffey, 1984

**T**he need to provide health care for Civil War wives and widows led to the construction of Washington, D.C.'s Columbia Hospital for Women in 1866. It was one of the first maternity hospitals to provide classes for expectant fathers and the first to establish nurseries for premature infants.

By 1925, a greatly improved Columbia Hospital started logging inked footprints of babies as a way to uniquely identify them. This practice soon became commonplace in hospital maternity wards throughout the country.

Bandleader, Duke Ellington, actress Katherine Heigl, D.C. Mayor Marion Barry, filmmaker Michael Dominic, and Vice-President Al Gore were born there as were some 250,000 other native Washingtonians until it closed its doors in 2002.

This is to Certify that John Humbird Duffey, Jr. was born at

Columbia Hospital for Women

at 8:46 o'clock P.M., on March 4, 1934.

S. O. B. Ragsdale M.D.
Superintendent

One set of fresh hospital footprints on March 4, 1934, belonged to John Humbird Duffey Jr., who would become a founder of two of the most influential bands in modern bluegrass music, The Country Gentlemen and The Seldom Scene. John's tribute in the 1997 *Congressional Record* described him as "a remarkable singer, possessed of a powerful vocal instrument, one that could soar to impossibly high notes or become the soul of harmony and touch the heart. He was an excellent performer with mandolin and guitar, and he was the prince of wit and laughter." He influenced string band musicians and singers across the Nation and around the world. Both of his bands helped bluegrass reach a wider audience. Like John Duffey, "Modern or Urban Bluegrass" was also born in Washington, D.C.

On stage Duffey was a dynamic force of nature, both irrepressible, engaging, and compelling. He sang in four octaves. His top note was the second F above middle C. That high note was recorded in The Country Gentlemen song, "New Freedom Bell." His lowest note was the second E below middle C.

Offstage he was surprisingly fascinating and complex. Enormously popular, he was a very private person with only a few close friends.

*"You can write that I was born in 1934 if you want, or you could make me younger,"* quipped John as he settled in his Arlington, VA home in 1984 to discuss his life story.

John was the only child of John Humbird Duffey Sr. (1879-1973) and mother, Florence (Ryan) Duffey (1899-1988). John Sr. was the son of a Methodist preacher who didn't approve of popular, secular music. John sang in his father's church choir as a youngster. When a new organ arrived in the church, John Sr. "borrowed" his father's keys and made duplicates so he and his pals could sneak in during the week and experiment with the various organ sounds they could produce.

By age 18, John Sr., secured a respectable job in a Washington, D.C. railroad office. He was probably smart enough to eventually become the railroad president, but one incident changed his life.

Operas didn't come to Washington, D.C. often in those days, so he was excited to see an ad promoting some glorious music on the way. He saved enough money to treat himself and his two "organ burglar" pals to this evening at the theatre.

John Humbird Duffey, Sr.
© G. Allred

However, with three tickets in hand on the afternoon of the opera, his boss told him he had to work overtime.

He pleaded for the night off, but was told, "You either work tonight, young man, or you don't work here at all."

After the curtain closed on the opera that night, he shared the news with his friends that he had quit his job. Moreover, he told them he was "off to Broadway" and thinking about "a career on the stage."

John, Sr. first became a tenor in the chorus with the Schumann-Heink Opera company. Shortly after followed roles in *The Lilac Domino, Sari, The Rose Maid, Going Up, The Chocolate Soldier* and at least one Broadway musical, *Love's Lottery* in 1904. Long tours with the

4

Metropolitan, Gallo English, and DeWolf Hopper opera companies produced reviews confirming that John Duffey, Sr., was as well known in New Orleans and Vancouver, and applauded as much in San Francisco as in New York.

By 1902, John Sr. returned to D.C. to play the Saengerbund Concert at The National Theatre. Writing in the July 1926 *High Hat* ["Long Island's Lively Review"] reviewer Thilman Orr said: "Mr. Duffey has indeed sung the country over in many and varied roles, his voice ever increasing in range and quality. To hear him at the zenith of his career in his perfect characterization of the Earl Tolloler in *Iolanthe* is a treat. His acting, diction, dancing, comedy sense are all the equal of the melody of his voice, and that ladies and gentlemen, is praise indeed."

John Duffey Sr. was a member of The Lambs Club, America's oldest organization for actors, songwriters, and others involved in the theatre. The Players Club, The Lambs Club and The Friars Club were three separate organizations at that time. When asked what's the difference between the clubs, playwright George S. Kaufman quipped, "The Players are gentlemen trying to be actors, the Lambs are actors trying to be gentlemen, and the Friars are neither trying to be both."

John Sr.'s first wife, Margaret Smith, was from San Francisco. As a young girl she came to New York to be a concert singer and for a short time was a member of the Augustin Daly theatrical company where she met and married the light opera tenor and actor. The Duffeys were divorced in 1920, with a daughter, Allen, and a son, Jefferson, known to John Jr. as "Jeff."

On March 6, 1930, Margaret Duffey, 45, was burned to death in a fire. She had been in Arizona visiting her daughter, Allen Deppe, for two months. *The New York*

*Times* reported the cause of Margaret's death: "She is said to have escaped her daughter's burning house and returned evidently to save $10,000 worth of diamonds."

Duffey Sr. told the *Times*, "It was quite possible she had returned for her diamonds. She possessed considerable jewelry."

Duffey, Sr. and Jr. © G. Allred

In the 1930s, with his New York years behind him, John Sr. returned to Washington. In his early 50s, and still involved in music, an ad in the December 2, 1938, *Evening Star* revealed the singer had taken on new roles.

A Woodward & Lothrop full page ad included: "You are invited to hear a 15-minute program of songs presented by the Potomac Electric Company glee club, under the direction of Mr. John Humbird Duffey."

He participated in many of these glee club events around town and also served as choir director of Washington's Fifth Baptist Church.

*My father sang opera for 25 years. In 1913 he cut six sides for Columbia records. Dad was 54 years old when I was born and had long left the Met company when he moved back to Washington. I have the records by my father, but they are very old and thick 78rpm's and are warped so badly. Plus, they play backward to the way records play today. I got to hear one of them at a recording studio, Capitol Transcriptions, on 11th Street. where The Country Gentleman recorded. They had a machine there that played the old-timey records. One record was all I ever heard him singing. Unfortunately, it wasn't a solo, but rather a duet with a woman.*

The woman was Ernestine Schumann-Heink famous contralto at the turn of the century and star of the Schumann-Heink Opera.

John continued: *"My father was teaching as a boys' choir director at Fifth Baptist Church down in Southwest D.C. That's where he met my mother Florence, in the church there. He later worked for Grayline Tours."*

The 1940 Census Bureau lists John, Sr. then 61, having a day job at the Census Bureau. He also gave private voice lessons in his home to students.

Florence was divorced from a man named Herbert Reamy when she married John Sr. Florence was a petite, quiet woman who worked in the dress department of downtown D.C.'s Garfinckel's department store. She served many wealthy customers including Shirley Temple Black. As a child actress Shirley Temple was the number one box office movie star in 1934, the year John was born. Black would call and ask Florence to gather orders for her. John Jr. was their only child. His favorite cologne was *English Leather* and his mom would buy it for him from Garfinckel's.

If the Great Depression and subsequent war years were hard on the Duffey family, then John was cavalier in discussing his upbringing in 1984: *"My parents told me we lived on 14th Street right off Chapin Street when I was born. I do have a recollection of living on Rock Creek Ford Road near Military Road. We were never able to buy a home, and always rented and made out as best we could. I don't know why we moved so often—every time the rent was due, I guess,"* John joked. *"But at one point I counted up to 13 different places in the Washington area that we lived."*

The last house where John resided during high school and a few years beyond was on Verne Street, just off River Road in Bethesda, Maryland.

John remembers when the Metropolitan Opera was broadcast on the radio every Saturday at 2 pm. *"My father would sit me down beside the radio and say, 'Now listen. This music is good.' I was a little kid barely speaking English. I didn't know what was going on because the operas were in a foreign language. He knew because he had played the parts in the opera. Perhaps if I could've seen them live it would have made a difference to me."*

John's father disapproved of Duffey's popular musical tastes but when asked if his father gave him any musical encouragement, John answered: *"Not really encouragement. He once asked me, 'Why don't you put that mandolin down and go out and get a job?' But he could tell that I had a bit of musical interest as a little kid because I used to go around the house humming, singing, and squalling (sic)."*

*"But he once told me, 'you have a diaphragm down there so make that thing work and push the singing out your throat. If you're going to sing, you might as well do it right.' He showed me some breathing I could try to help me, and that taught me the feel of getting it out from my gut."*

John listened to Frank Sinatra on the Saturday night radio show, *Hit Parade*, during World War Two, and was struck by hearing the girls swooning over Frankie. John's favorite singer throughout his life was Dean Martin, a member of Sinatra's swinging, hard-partying Rat Pack. John's 1973 recording of Martin's "A Small Exception of Me" on The Seldom Scene's *Act Two* album is an example of John's affinity with "Old Dino."

## Five-string Banjo

*"One day I happened to be cruising the dial. I was about 13 [1947] when I heard the sound of a banjo. A five-string banjo. I thought, 'Boy that's a neat sound.' And I started listening to that station. In those days they called it 'hillbilly music.'*

*"It was Bill Monroe and His Blue Grass Boys that really turned me on—music that caught my ear. And Flatt & Scruggs, Hank Williams, and Carl Smith. The music I'm involved with now.*

*"Other than just the sound of the banjo that appealed and fascinated me, I began to appreciate the fact that there was a lot of talent there. And once I saw an act that I'd been listening to on records, and then I went to see them live—gee, everything was right there. It sounded just like it did on the record. That's impressive."*

Soon after, he became a fan of deejay Cactus Matt's program on Arlington, Virginia radio station WEAM. Matt's show featured old timey hillbilly music with a little of the music that would come to be known as "bluegrass." The label "bluegrass" did not come into use until 1957.

Cactus Matt had started as a news reporter on station WOL in 1945 using his real name, Matthew Warren, and began his WEAM country music radio show in 1949.

Other influential radio personalities John cited were Fiddlin' Curly Smith and Don Owens on station WGAY, and later WARL. Both had begun in radio as part of a performing trio with Owens on bass and another player, Charlie Fetzer on resonator guitar. Don was also a "Bayou Boy" in local mandolin player, Buzz Busby's D.C. bluegrass band.

Don Owens would play a pivotal role in promoting bluegrass in the Washington area when he moved to station WARL. The late John Fahey, another Washingtonian guitarist growing up the same time as Duffey—who once worked at a gas station in Takoma Park just over the D.C. Maryland line—told the following story about Owens in his 2000 book, *How Bluegrass Music Destroyed My Life:*

"After Owens arrived, WARL DJ Mike Hunnicutt put on an obviously black [artist's] record, played it for about 45 seconds, then took it off and abruptly said, 'No. We don't play that kind of music on this radio station.'

"Why the hell did he do that? Hunnicutt didn't know anything about country music. All he knew about was popular music. I know all this because my father was a friend of Hunnicutt and helped him out a lot. Mike had a big problem with alcohol. A big Jones. He was a great talker. But he knew nothing about music. Nothing.

"So, Don Owens started making the radio song selections. We heard music chosen by Don Owens. He started playing more and more bluegrass and other acoustic, country music. In fact, he started each show with a Bill Monroe record. He played Molly O'Day a lot. Grandpa Jones, Carl Story, Jimmy Murphy, Wilma Lee and Stoney Cooper, Flatt & Scruggs, Jim Eanes and people like that."

Owens went on to a National broadcasting career and he was inducted into the Country Music DJ Hall of

Fame in 1989. Like Fahey, John Duffey was listening to Don Owens's morning show.

Curly Smith took over after Don left this morning show: Duffey commented, *"A little later on when I got into music and started to learn to play something myself, I met these people. In fact, Curly Smith used to play with us on Saturday nights at the Beltsville, Maryland Fire House dances. Actually, I didn't learn to play anything until I was 17 years old."*

Duffey Hurls Wright To Two-Hit, 8-2 Victory

John Duffey allowed only two hits and struck out 13 as he pitched W. B. Wright Real Estate to an 8-2 victory over the Arlington Rebels in the YMCA 17-years-and-under baseball league yesterday on the North Ellipse.

© G. Allred

John began school at Westbrook Elementary—still there today at the intersection of Allan Terrace and

Baltimore Ave—and Leland Junior High in Bethesda, Maryland. Leland offered duckpin bowling in John's physical education classes at the nearby Chevy Chase Ice Palace. John began his lifelong devotion to this sport then.

About high school, John said, *"I started at Wilson High School because we were living in the District, but then we moved back to Bethesda. I stayed at Wilson until they found out I moved and wanted the tuition, so I transferred to Bethesda-Chevy Chase around February of my sophomore year."*

John excelled at baseball at BCC and pitched a "two-hitter" in his senior year. He also became good friends with Dick Lightfoot, a fellow team pitcher who passed away shortly after high school of a suspected suicide. John's childhood friend, Bill Blackburn remembers John as "very broken up" when Dick died.

Hearing the banjo on the radio was a pivotal point for John. When asked if there was a great first experience hearing live music, he said:

*I can't remember the first band or person of note that I saw. I can remember some shows I saw early on. I did see Flatt & Scruggs on the Wilson Line at one of Connie B. Gay's shows. And the first time I saw Bill Monroe was also on that Wilson Line thing. In fact, Elvis played it.*

**Down on Elvis**

The Wilson Line boat cruises traveled from the D.C. Southwest dock on the Potomac River for two afternoon trips to George Washington's Mount Vernon estate, and one evening trip with a music show to the Marshall Hall Amusement Park.

Elvis Presley and his Blue Moon Boys, as they were billed, were booked on Friday March 23, 1956 to launch the new season of the '56 *Country Music Moonlight*

*Cruise* concerts, but the four-deck, 200 ft. *S.S. Mount Vernon* blew a valve that the crew couldn't repair by show time. Some of the hundred folks waiting in line on the Maine Avenue dock asked for their $2.00 admission back. But the show went on—for an unexpected three hours.

Opening for Elvis was local D.C. player and TV star, Jimmy Dean. Dean, a native Texan, started playing D.C. bars when he was stationed at Bolling Air Force Base in the D.C. neighborhood of Anacostia. Jimmy Dean worked the clubs and earned a hosting spot on Gay's radio show, *Town and Country Time* where he helped local musicians Patsy Cline and Roy Clark get their start. The radio show moved to local TV Channel 7 and became *The Jimmy Dean Show.* Elvis dropped by before his 1956 Wilson Line concert to provide Dean with a slightly nervous TV interview.

The 21-year-old Elvis had just released "Heartbreak Hotel" two months earlier—his first million-dollar record. His back-up studio band included Chet Atkins on guitar and Floyd Cramer on piano. This record was No. 1 on the Country and Western charts when Elvis boarded the old ship that night, accompanied by his classic trio of Scotty Moore, Bill Black, and D.J. Fontana.

Writer Peter Golkin creatively chronicled the evening in a *Washington City Paper* article (2/15/2007). Peter cleverly ended his story with "The show, unlike the boat, rocked."

When asked if he saw the Elvis boat show, Duffey said, *"No, I didn't see Elvis on the Wilson Line, but Elvis didn't hit [impress] me. I know many people love the '50s music. I can appreciate some of that music now, but at that time I hated it. I know when that happened: It was when I went to my neighborhood jukebox to play the 'Pike County Breakdown,' and my bluegrass song had been*

13

*replaced by Presley's 'Blue Suede Shoes.' It bugged me because it was taking music that I liked off the jukebox and, really off the radio."*

However, Presley recorded a robust version of Bill Monroe's "Blue Moon of Kentucky" for the "b" side of his first single and sang that tune instead of his hit song, "That's All Right" for the millions of listeners on his debut at WSM's Grand Ole Opry.

It was Connie B. Gay who brought Elvis Presley to the Wilson Line for Presley's first and only Washington D.C. appearance on March 23, 1956 [although Elvis did play nearby Landover, Maryland's Capital Centre twice in 1976 and '77]. Connie demonstrated country music's respectability by selling out Constitution Hall for 27 straight Saturday nights in 1948 with his country music shows, a record that still stands. Some called the place "Connie's barn."

About Connie, John declared, *"I don't give Connie B. Gay much credit for bringing bluegrass to Washington. If it wasn't commercial from Nashville, he usually wasn't interested even though he started Jimmy Dean off. He discovered him over at the Harmony Club bar by Union Station. I played the Harmony once. They had a bandstand and it was a typical bar, but they had a heavy mesh wire in front from floor to ceiling and around the sides, and a caged door. The first time I saw this I asked the bartender 'What the hell is this for?'*

*"The bartender said, 'Well, we don't want the band to get hit by flying debris.' Yeah, that's for real. And that's where Jimmy Dean got his start. Personally, I'm not a country music fan. I stopped listening to it when Hank Williams died."*

John watched Roy Clark—later of *Hee Haw* TV fame —playing banjo on Dean's local TV show. Clark, a year older than Duffey, hailed from Meherrin, Virginia and lived as a teenager in Southeast D.C. while his father worked at the Washington Navy Yard.

"*So, on the wild side, I decided to learn how to play five-string banjo,*" John revealed, "*It took me about a month to figure out that I couldn't do it. I couldn't catch on. And there were no instruction books and nobody that I knew could teach me. I just couldn't get anything out of it.*"

## First Guitar

"*There was a little kid that lived around the corner from me who had an old Kay acoustic guitar and he could play it. He taught me about nine chords and let me borrow his guitar to take home. I'd run home from school and beat that guitar until I had to go to bed. It took me about a week to learn the chords and how to change from one to another.*"

John's interest in the guitar motivated his mother, Florence to buy him a Harmony "Orchestra" model guitar that cost 19 dollars. It didn't last very long as it got so warped that John couldn't play it.

John was now hooked on music and determined to upgrade his instrument. Fortunately, he knew how to achieve his goal.

# Chapter 2: Reasons for Being

In high school, John had a *Washington Post* newspaper route. He remembered: *"I served about 500 newspapers before school. It was a good thing that many were in an apartment complex, which made it easier. The route managers would drop them off at specific places, so I'd go to a pile and take them up and then move on to the next pile. I imagine if I asked some kid today to serve 500 papers, they'd say 'there ain't no way man.'"*

Coincidentally, Roy Clark had an afternoon *Evening Star* paper route around the same time John was delivering the morning *Washington Post* papers to his neighbors.

John's saved paper route money allowed him to buy a Martin model 00 guitar to replace his warped Harmony. He couldn't afford the D model he preferred at the cost of $125, but his $70 did the trick for the Martin 00.

*"My Martin made all the difference in the world and really got me interested in the music because I could play it and it sounded good, and it didn't come apart in a month."*

In 1951, John was a junior at Bethesda-Chevy Chase high school. He'd catch the school bus at 7:30 am on River Road a few blocks from his house. The school didn't start until nine, so he always arrived early.

*"It was the last stop with miles to go and boy, that was a hike if you missed the bus. They opened the school cafeteria for us kids to hang out before school began so I start taking my guitar. Some kids began to gather around me and then 'lord' I find out there are about a dozen kids that could play guitar and one kid, Sterling Ellsworth, had*

*a bass. So, we started these morning guitar sessions in the school cafeteria."*

It's Dr. Sterling Ellsworth these days, an acclaimed clinical psychologist living in Eugene, Oregon. When we reached him in 2018 to contribute to this book, the 85-year-old Dr. Ellsworth noted this was the first time anyone had ever asked him about playing music with John Duffey.

## Rainbow Mountain Boys

Dr. Ellsworth told us: "I was a senior, playing bass in the school orchestra. I had an old German bass fiddle but was getting tired of playing with a bow. I met John and we started in on learning bluegrass songs along with Bobby Slack on mandolin, and another student from Wilson High School named David Swann on banjo, with me plucking the bass. We called ourselves the 'Rainbow Mountain Boys.' I lived a few blocks from school, so John, David and I would go to my house for lunch, and practice with Bobby joining up after school."

When asked what kind of kid was Duffey, Ellsworth answered, "John was very shy. Shy people are not comfortable in social situations where impromptu communication is required. So, John concentrated on music and singing, which is set and predictable. He didn't do sports or have any girlfriends that I knew about. And I never met his folks. He was just a very nice kid dedicated to learning the music. Music was our fun. We practiced every day and got pretty good. John could play, sing and yodel very well. Finally, we entered a ten-school [Montgomery County, MD] talent contest."

"John sang and yodeled on a song called 'Chime Bells Are Ringing.' When we got to the end of the song Duffey extended the high note for as long as he could while Bobby played mandolin lines.

COLORFUL QUARTET: Latest to join the parade of teen-age talent on the Student Assembly show are the "Rainbow Mountain Boys." They are (left to right) John Duffy, Bobby Slack and Sterling Ellsworth of Bethesda-Chevy Chase, and Dave Swann of Wilson. The program is heard every Saturday evening at 6:45 on WASH-FM and 7:15 on WWDC.

"The Rainbow Mountain Boys". 1951. (l to R) John Duffey, Bobby Slack, Sterling Ellsworth, and Dave Swann.
© Sterling Ellsworth Collection

"When John finally ran out of breath, he ended the song. The audiences cheered. And we won the School Assembly talent contest and received a one-hundred-dollar war bond as the top prize." These talent shows were carried on two radio stations, WWDC and WASH on Saturday evenings. This was Duffey's first time on radio.

Sterling left for college in Chicago after high school to become a doctor, departing before the prized war bond arrived. When he returned to D.C. for Christmas break, he found out John had spent his share of the prize money.

"We didn't think you were coming back," John explained matter-of-factly.

With Sterling in college, Duffey continued to play music after school at the house of another friend, Frank "Sonny" Johnson, who mentioned one day that his father used to play mandolin years ago and it might be up in his attic.

*"Sonny went and found it, and sure enough it was playable. So, I asked him, 'Gee, I wonder if I could borrow this, take it home, and see if I can learn to play it?' And that's what I did.*

*"I listened to Bill Monroe and other mandolin players on the radio. Monroe was the only one playing anything that was hard to do but I had to practice in the basement because I'd get a lot of 'just shut that racket up,' from my father."*

One anecdote John offered about teaching himself the mandolin goes like this: *"I listened to the lead vocal on the Monroe records when I was first trying to learn. On one song, 'When You Are Lonely,' I heard his mandolin going on in the background and I thought he was singing, too. That's really something I thought. You can sing and pick notes at the same time.'*

*"So, I used to stand in front of a mirror so I could see my hands and try to do play while I sang. Not just chords. Play notes behind myself. And I learned how to do it.*

*"I didn't know anything about recording then, I was dumb. Later I discovered that it wasn't Bill Monroe singing at all. It was Lester Flatt. And Bill was there just having a grand time picking his mandolin."*

John's story has a kicker: Around 1976, he was playing a "Bluegrass Canada," festival workshop in Carlisle, Ontario. Bill Monroe was there. John walked up to him:

*"I said to Bill: 'I'm going to show you something you taught me, and I don't even think you can do it.' I was standing there in front of him and started singing and playing all kinds of licks at the same time."*

"The Piedmont Valley Boys." (l to r) Bill Blackburn, John Duffey, Frank "Sonny" Johnson, and David Swann © Bill Blackburn

This was before John and Bill had perfected their routine of insulting each other, so Bill's response was probably subdued and respectful.

Bluegrass player and music writer Jack Tottle once commented on variances between John and Bill's mandolin techniques. Jack wrote, "Some mandolin players like John Duffey and Jesse McReynolds rest the third and/or fourth fingers on the mandolin. Others, including Bill Monroe and Frank Wakefield do not. Resting the fingers may give slightly better control on intricate passages, but it also may interfere with tone." (*Bluegrass Mandolin*, Jack Tottle, Oak Publications, 1975).

## Next bands

The geologic Piedmont runs from New Jersey to north Alabama with a broad swath cutting across the state of Maryland. It is the hilly area between the Appalachian Mountains and the Coastal Plain. The word piedmont means foot of the mountain, or foothills.

John, in senior year now and now on guitar and mandolin, started his second bluegrass band, "The Piedmont Valley Boys." It was Sonny Johnson who suggested the name.

*"Durned if somehow or other our Piedmont Valley Boys got on one local radio station, WDON and played on Saturday at noon to 12:30. We had no business being on the radio. This was around 1952. I'm sure it was terrible. Then we played occasionally on another station, WINX in Rockville, Maryland."*

John worked at a printing store and later drove a surgical supply truck after high school. Meanwhile, his focus on music deepened.

Another neighborhood friend, Bill Emerson, born January 22, 1938, described meeting John:

"I lived on Goldsboro Road, about two miles from John's house. The first time I saw him was in the parking lot of the Bethesda Hot Shoppes drive-in restaurant on Wisconsin Avenue. He'd back his car up there and get his mandolin out and sit on the hood and play. Showing off. I was 16 and he was a few years older."

Bill Emerson had bought a banjo around this time but had no clue on how to play it. He put the banjo across the bars of his bicycle and rode to John's house. John greeted him with, "Come on in and I'll show you what I know."

"John taught me how to put the finger picks on and gave a basic, sketchy idea on how to tackle the thing and really got me started with the banjo," said Bill. John also taught Bill to sing baritone vocals, and really the musical theory of harmony singing.

John and Bill
© Bill Blackburn

**Bill Blackburn**
*Around 1953, I discovered that a high school friend, Bill Blackburn had learned the banjo. Bill was the first person I met who could play with finger picks on, just rolling and playing the way it was supposed to be played. And he kept at it and got to be fairly proficient."*

"John and I met in first grade in elementary school in Bethesda and maybe even before that," Bill Blackburn reminisced in 2018 by telephone from his home in Dewey, Arizona. "I knew John's parents. His father was older and smoked a pipe. The house always smelled good. John's dad was great at woodworking. His mother was very low-key and nice.

"In 7th grade, John and I started singing in the Leland Junior High Choir. He was not known for having a tenor voice at that time. I believe it was much later when John had decided to play the mandolin that he asked his father to help him improve his voice. Mandolin players were expected to have high tenor voices back then.

"In Leland Junior High School, we started listening to DJ Don Owens on WARL playing music by Hank Williams, Ernest Tubb, and the like. We'd go to the Hollywood Music record store on 7th street in downtown D.C. and buy 78rpm records.

"At first, it was just a listening thing, but John met student musicians, Sterling Ellsworth, Dave Swann, and Bobby Slack and began his first band. I also knew another banjo player, Graham King in the area and John played with him a little.

"It was after I saw John with these kids that I went down to a pawnshop and bought a banjo for $10 dollars. I went home and called John to tell him I got a banjo. He replied, '*Sapling.*'

"Sapling" was joking like 'You big dummy! Why'd you do that?" I didn't know a thing about the banjo, but we were off and running. It took me a couple of years to play reasonably well. With Bobby Slack and Dave Swann, we got good enough to play in public. Once at Wilson High we had to tell some teachers what we planned to play. John told them 'Roll In My Sweet Baby's Arms.' They thought that was a horrible thing and wouldn't let us play that," remembered Bill with a laugh.

"We'd perform at the Veteran's Hospital in the nearby Forest Glen Annex to Walter Reed Army Hospital.

"John was playing guitar, some mandolin at this time, and tenor singing. Sometimes it was just John and me playing. We started to settle into our band with Sonny Johnson on guitar and vocals, and me on banjo. Sonny and I became fraternity brothers at American University, and the band's name reverted to the Rainbow Mountain Boys.

"Next there was a succession of bands we went through. From 1953 through 1956. John would find bands and call me to come play with them, and I'd do the same for him. About four bands. Most of our involvement with these bands was very short.

One of these bands was the Whitetop Mountain Boys with the Blevins Brothers, Otis and Jack, who later became the Red Hill Ramblers. Blevins is an old name in Virginia. The first Blevins settled near Whitetop Mountain in the 1770s. Whitetop Mountain is the highest point in Virginia you can drive to.

It was the band with the Blevins Brothers where John and Bill played a contest in Warrenton, VA, and then started attending shows where Bill Monroe, Flatt & Scruggs, and other big acts would appear.

"John would try and talk with them every chance he got," Blackburn said. "It was easier to talk with the musicians back then at these shows. John and I got in a good discussion once with Earl Scruggs at Sunset Park in Pennsylvania. I had a friend, Callie Veach, who was a musician, banjo collector and instrument repairman down in D.C., who wanted Earl to have this Paramount banjo that Callie owned. Earl said, 'Thanks, anyway but this old thing is good enough for my rough hands,' nodding to his pre-World War Two Gibson banjo."

When asked what John Duffey was like as a kid, Blackburn explained, "Well, I always thought he was kind of shy, but he had an extrovert side. Once in second grade we were both walking home and passed by a house being built on a corner. John climbed up high on the beams and began to show off. I would have nothing to do with that kind of behavior.

"That side of him came out later in the music. He was shy except when he was on stage. There, he was totally different and told lots of stories. I heard some nasty ones, too. Some weren't funny and he'd often blurt out things that didn't even make sense. He did this emcee stuff on his own."

## Baseball, Bowling, and Drag Racing

Back in junior high, Bill Blackburn and John learned to bowl, frequenting the lanes at the Ice Palace on Connecticut Avenue in Chevy Chase.

A glitzy Art-deco strip center opened in 1938 that included the Ice Palace which housed the city's lone ice skating rink on top with 41 bowling lanes, a pool hall and ping pong tables underneath, all surrounded by an A&P grocery store, Peoples Drug store, and Washington's first Best & Co. clothing store. These shopping centers began springing up on the outbound lanes of the main D.C. roadways, conveniently located so that commuters could pull off easily to shop on their way home.

The Ice Palace melted away in 1950 when WMAL-TV (Channel 7), owned by the *Evening Star Broadcasting Company*, leased the spacious second floor for its new television studios.

Bill confirmed that John was a pretty good bowler, but also added that, "bowling seemed to bring out the worst of John's temper. John went nuts if he did something wrong. I once watched him kick the ball rack so hard he lifted it out of the floor. He was excused from the premises." Tom Gray bowled with John when they were in The Country Gentlemen. Tom commented that,

"John had good form, like a ballet dancer. But I thought he need not roll the ball so fast."

Bill said both he and John smoked *Old Gold* cigarettes—"the cigarette for independent people"—with John saving the coupons to redeem for gifts. John also had a serious girlfriend after high school, and he liked to work on cars and race them.

On racing Blackburn remembers, "John would drive his Oldsmobile down to the Old Dominion Speedway in Manassas, Virginia on Saturdays and run his car in the races. I'd go with him as his 'pit crew,' even though I didn't know anything about cars. But that way I could get in where the drivers were."

John won trophies for some of his races including a Class E race in June, 1955. The Class E designation was for heavy stock cars. *The Evening Star* mentioned his name in a news story on winners but incorrectly listed his car as a "Studebaker."

John told a reporter in 1974: "Nowadays the cars have gotten so complicated with all the pollution controls I can't keep up with them."

Blackburn recalls, "And between races, we'd get the instruments out. I understand from Bill Emerson that he and his brother were down there once. Bill has said that I was the first one he ever saw play banjo live."

In talking about Bill Blackburn, John said:

*Bill introduced me to a fellow from Frederick, Maryland named Lucky Chatman. He invited me to play with him, so I'd ride 50 miles up to Frederick, Maryland and play mandolin with Lucky and his Ozark Mountain Boys. We began doing carnivals for $10 to $15 each. We even landed a Saturday afternoon radio show on WFMD. I think I played with Lucky for about a year and a half."*

Lewis "Lucky" Chatman came from Frederick, Maryland, was married to his wife, Imogene, and had a daughter. In 1951 he was working from Front Royal, Virginia and appearing on radio station WFTR with his band.

By 1956, Bill Blackburn and John Duffey were playing with Lucky. Bill remembers, "Lucky would bring his four-year-old daughter up on stage with him to tell some risqué jokes. The Saturday radio show was all very exciting," Bill states, but adds modestly, "There really wasn't that much competition in those days."

The Ozark Mountain Boys (l to R) Bill Blackburn (banjo), Carroll Harbaugh, (bass), Lucky Chatman (guitar), John (mandolin), and Bill Poffinberger (fiddle).© Bill Blackburn

Bill remembers a car ride with John and Lucky; "We were driving back from a radio show in Frederick and began talking about band names. We agreed we didn't really like being anybody's 'boys.' After all, we were virile young men. We talked about other names, and one was The Country Gentlemen."

John's first recording with Lucky was "I've Waited So Long," written by Chatman and released on the Maryland Label in July of 1956. On the flip side was an instrumental, "Blue Grass" composed by Duffey. Lucky's last name was misspelled as "Chapman" on the record.

This debut record was made in the basement of Bill's parents' house in Bethesda. The band wasn't happy with the sound and they re-cut "Blue Grass" in Joe Bussard's basement recording set-up in 1959 for Joe's Fonotone label.

Joe Bussard was born in Frederick, Maryland in 1936. When he was 12, he discovered Jimmie Rodgers and learned about bluegrass music. Today he is a famed record collector and DJ, and subject of a film documentary, *Desperate Man Blues: Discovering the Roots of American Music* (2003). John made two more recordings with Lucky Chatman and The Ozark Mountain Boys: "Swing Low Sweet Chariot," and "Put My Little Shoes Away." (Bluegrass label, 1958)

Bill with John, playing his first mandolin in
1955, a Kalamazoo © Bill Blackburn
Archives/William Petrini.

During a competition hosted by Rockville radio
station WINX, while John was playing with Lucky, he
met a Western High School bass player in a band called
the Rocky Ridge Ramblers comprised of fellow students
Monte Monteith on guitar, Jerry Stuart on mandolin,
Bob Lindter on banjo and Ron Roswell on fiddle. The
bass player was a fifteen-year-old Tom Gray.

Beginning in late 1956, John played Dobro on a few
of country singer Luke Gordon's recording sessions with
Buzz Busby on mandolin and Scotty Stoneman on
fiddle. Dobro is an American brand of resonator guitar
currently owned by the Gibson Guitar Corporation.

Luke, whose real name was Ruffice Gordon Brown,
came to D.C. via Kentucky. He and his wife owned a TV
repair shop in Falls Church, Virginia. Luke is best
remembered for his signature song, "Dark Hollow."
These recording sessions were sometimes held at
independent producer Ben Adelman's D.C. recording
studio at 323 Cedar St., N.W. where the Takoma Park
Metro station now stands. While recording at Ben

Adelman's studio, you had to stop while railroad trains rolled by on the nearby tracks.

# Chapter 3: Accidental Gentlemen

*Bill Emerson was playing banjo with a D.C. band called Buzz Busby and His Bayou Boys. On July 4, 1957 Bill called to tell me that Buzz and some of the band were in a terrible car crash.*

JD

© Courtesy *Bluegrass
Unlimited* Magazine. Cover story
by Rhonda Strickland

**M**andolinist Bernarr Graham Busbice, known as Buzz Busby, was celebrating his Independence Day holiday by bar-hopping in North Beach, Maryland with fellow

Bayou Boys, Vance Truell [bass] and Eddie Adcock [guitar]. Their car hit a telephone pole going 70mph almost killing them. Their friend, Sonny Presley—no kin to Elvis—was driving the car with Buzz, riding shotgun. Eddie was sleeping in the backseat next to Vance. Eddie woke up briefly the minute after the crash and told Sonny he was driving too fast. He then went unconscious and woke two days later in the hospital. Buzz fared the worst. Considered dead when he reached the hospital, he was resuscitated and lingered in a coma for 36 hours.

Born near Eros, Louisiana on September 6, 1933, Buzz became a self-proclaimed 'Bill Monroe fanatic' as a teen and developed a brilliant high tenor voice and high energy mandolin style.

After his 1951 high school graduation where he was class valedictorian, the FBI recruited Buzz to work in their finger printing division so he moved to Carmody Hills, Maryland, just over the D.C. line. He soon befriended Scotty Stoneman, the fiddling son of Ernest "Pop" Stoneman, whose musical family lived in the same community. Scotty and Buzz became hard-drinking musical pals. For an overview of the spectacular Stoneman Family see Ivan M. Tribe's, *The Stoneman's An Appalachian Family and the Music That Shaped Their Lives* (University of Illinois Press, 1993).

Scotty introduced Buzz to "Cowboy" Jack Clement, a flamboyant, free-spirited musician and Marine who would go on to discover Jerry Lee Lewis, produce records for Johnny Cash, Charlie Rich, and Roy Orbison, write hit songs, make films and produce U2's 1987 *Rattle and Hum* album. The Country Music Hall of Fame inducted him in 2013.

Jack, Scotty, and Buzz teamed up and played the rougher bars in D.C. For a time, Roy Clark added his banjo to Scotty's fiddle, Jack's guitar and Dobro, and Buzz's voice and fast right-hand mandolin tremolo. Buzz would claim to everyone throughout his life that his trio was the first to play true bluegrass in the Washington, D.C. area. True. His single "Lost" was recorded and released in 1956 on the Jiffy label while Buzz, with Charlie Waller on guitar, were back playing on the Louisiana Hayride. The other side of that single was "Just Me and the Jukebox." Two years later, Buzz released "Lonesome Wind" on the Starday label backed with a re-recording of "Lost." The 1956 Jiffy version of "Lost" is an important example of early bluegrass.

When Buzz discovered his band earnings were greater than his FBI salary, he became a full-time musician. Local radio gave Buzz opportunities, and he'd sometimes work with Mac Wiseman who Buzz knew from the *Louisiana Hayride*. The late Wiseman had played with both Bill Monroe and Flatt & Scruggs before his very long and successful solo career. Mac's 1955 recording of "The Ballad of Davy Crockett" became a beloved national hit song.

In the summer of 1954, Busby and his band entered the National Country Music Championship in Warrenton, Virginia and won first place in the contest. Their success attracted the attention of local WRC TV producers so Buzz, along with John Hall on fiddle, Don Stover on banjo, and Lee Cole on bass were hired for the afternoon *Hayloft Hoedown*, the first bluegrass TV show in D.C.

Over the next year, Buzz's popularity soared, and money seemed limitless. Unfortunately, so did Buzz's ability to consume alcohol and amphetamines. Don Stover and Pete Pike would leave the group and be replaced by Bill Emerson, Charlie Waller, and Eddie Adcock.

## After The Crash

John continued: *"With three Bayou Boys in the hospital, Emerson was trying to hold on to a regular bar gig they had at the Admiral Grill in Bailey's Crossroads, Virginia. Bill wanted to know if I would fill-in and help him out."*

"Do you know Charlie Waller from Baltimore?" Bill asked John.

*"No, I don't know Charlie,"* answered John.

John met Charlie that night to play the Admiral Grill. The initial plan was to be the substitute Bayou Boys band while Buzz and Eddie recuperated. However, Waller's beautiful low tenor voice paired perfectly with John's assertive, high harmonies.

*"After two weeks Charlie and I thought, 'well, gee, we're good together.' Charlie had been playing with Earl Taylor in Baltimore. Maybe we should just stick together and see if we might do something,"* John concluded.

It was Duffey who suggested the band name, selected from names he had thought up with Bill Blackburn and Lucky Chatman.

*"We're not going to be Mountain Boys. We'll be Gentlemen. The Country Gentlemen. We kept trying to get a bass player and one named Larry Leahy showed up for a week and then we never saw him again."*

The word went out that The Country Gentlemen might be "stealing" Buzz's band, but the car crash debilitated Buzz for over a year. The sad truth is that Buzz never recovered from the crash. The brilliance of Buzz Busby's musical talent began its decline after the accident. Vance Truell, his bass player, returned to his North Carolina home and played with various bands, while Eddie Adcock worked day jobs and played banjo for Mac Wiseman, Smokey Graves, Bill Monroe, and other musicians.

John continued the Gents' story: *"We played the Admiral Grill for a short time, but it was such a rowdy bar. Another bar, The Crossroads, was around the corner and Charlie and I walked over one night and talked the owner one night and talked the owner into hiring us. The bar had a small space for a stage."*

In the 1984 interview John mentioned the Gents' first bass player *as "Larry Leahy who showed up for a week and then we never saw him again."* John then named Jim Cox as their first regular bass player. This second assertion is incorrect.

According to Tom Gray, "the Gents hired Tom Morgan as bassist, not as a fill-in, but as a full member who stayed with them for over a year and recorded several singles for the Starday label. The Gents did not record any albums during Emerson's time or Kuykendall's time. They were all 45rpm singles. The first Country Gentlemen album came out in 1960 with John, Charlie, Eddie Adcock, and Jim Cox. Jim Cox was actually the third bass player of the Gents, following Tom Morgan and Roy Self."

"There weren't that many places we could play bluegrass then," Bill Emerson emphasized in 2018, "as the club scene wasn't what it became. The Crossroads bar was also known as Bill's House of Beef, and we played a few other 'hole-in-the-wall' bars. John was more of a traditionalist then. He was into Bill Monroe, the Stanley Brothers, and music like that."

Today, there is an Acura dealership where the Admiral Grill once stood. Emerson joked that he hoped they'd give him a car but "none are forthcoming."

Duffey continued: *"While we were fooling around at the Crossroads bar, we got a radio job at WARL, five days a week, at 7:30 in the morning. It was only supposed to be a 15-minute music show.*

*"But that's when commercials came into radio. Would you believe that our 15-minute show took an hour? It was the damndest thing you ever heard. We'd play one song, and, by God, they'd play 20 minutes straight of commercials. I couldn't believe that this station could stay in business doing all these commercials.*

*"And it was terrible, and we, like idiots, were there doing this live.*

*"Finally, we just didn't show up one morning. We thought it was ridiculous and just dropped it. Then back in the bar we heard friends tell us they liked hearing us on the radio, but the commercials were awful. It was making us look bad.*

*"It might have been Tom 'Cat' Reeder, but someone let us tape a week's worth of shows in one evening at [radio station] WDON. We got smart."*

Based in the Washington, D.C. area and starting in the mid-1950s, Reeder was one of the most popular DJs in the Nation's Capital at station WDON in Wheaton, Maryland, also WKCW in Warrenton, Virginia, and he became a celebrated radio personality in the U.S. In 2001, Reeder joined WAMU to host their *Bluegrass Overnight* program, as well as his own *Tom "Cat" Reeder Show*. Tom "Cat" Reeder passed away in 2012.

The Gents began playing four nights a week at the Crossroads earning $36 dollars per night, split among the members. They also had a "pitch pot" where customers could throw tips. At this time, John moved from his parents' house into an Arlington, Virginia apartment by himself, and also dropped the Junior from his last name.

Asked about rehearsing, Bill Emerson explained, "Our rehearsals were at the places we played live. We were beginners and had no idea on how to act professional or make records. All of that would come later. Nobody thought John would develop into the visionary that he became. His creativity rose to the surface, and his ideas of what he wanted the band to be were beginning to come into play around the time I left The Country Gentlemen after two years."

Increasingly John's dominant iconoclastic personality began to blossom. Charlie started letting John take over part of the emcee work.

Many factors fueled The Country Gentlemen's success. One important element was their innovative song selection. They embraced folk, pop, vintage country and other diverse kinds of music as candidates for bluegrass conversion. John took credit for this during the 1984 interview:

*"I'm very spontaneous. I don't particularly plan anything. I never have. I either do or say what comes off the top of my head as long as it doesn't screw the rest of the band. They say I'm so great because I was the one who figured out that you can't go around just copying Bill Monroe or somebody else. You've got to figure out something else to do which I did instrumentally, and I finally got a style of my own. When we started, I thought the worst thing about the music was that it was stale. There was this catalog of two hundred songs that every group picked from and that's all they did.*

*"Here comes a new group. What do they record? 'Mother's Not Dead, She's Only Sleeping' for the 140th time. I said look we can get new material, other forms of music, and we can solicit material. It's hard to really tell somebody what we're looking for. It's contemporary, especially lyrics. Now, I'm into really pretty songs. My bag is harmony trios and so forth. I listen to a piece of music for the parts in it.*

*"And great lyrics like Kristofferson's 'Casey's Last Ride.' That song damn near makes you cry. [*"Casey's

Last Ride," was Charlie Waller's all-time favorite Gents recording.]

*"Another is Bob Dylan's 'It's All Over Now, Baby Blue,' which I never [completely] understood. I still sing it. I found out that Bob Dylan and Joan Baez kept house together for about a year and then it began to make sense. Some of the lines I still do not understand what he meant by them. But I still love it."*

Overall, Bill Emerson learned much from John. "He'd had a head start on me with music," Bill said. "Charlie had been a solo singer. I didn't know much about singing and John was generous. He taught me how to sing harmony."

Looking back, Bill enjoyed his two years as a member of The Country Gentlemen. "The group started getting a following around town, and we got a record contract. Our first record was something John engineered as a 'pay for your own record' deal on our own Dixie label with, 'Church Back Home' written by John, and a tune that Carter Stanley gave us called 'Going to the Races.'"

Carter later wrote a second version of this song and called it "Going to Paint the Town," which the Stanley Brothers recorded at their first Starday session in the latter half of 1958. (More about Ralph Stanley in Chapter 10)

Bill continues, "Then we got a phone call from Ben Adelman. Starday Records in Nashville contacted Ben asking if he knew of any groups who wanted to break into the business that could make and sell records.

"Ben was what you called a 'rack jobber' who would make budget records to sell in racks at local stores. He had a few guys who worked for him who would go around to the stores, distribute the records and collect the money. I was one of them for a while. Ben put out a lot of stuff that I recorded for him on labels like *Prestige* and *Coronet,* labels that nobody had ever heard of, for cheap music to sell in the racks."

One story Bill offered from the fledgling days of The Country Gentlemen: "John heard about a bar in Newark, New Jersey that hired bands and paid well. We drove there, checked into a motel and found this rather high class bar, where Lefty Frizzell was playing."

Lefty was then a very successful, well-known, country and honky-tonk player, with two hit songs, "If You've Got the Money (I've Got the Time)" and a sad song he wrote to his wife, "I Love You a Thousand Ways" while serving prison time for having sex with an underage fan.

"The hotel was not interested in us with Lefty performing. After a short conversation with the manager, we tucked our tails between our legs and headed back to Washington in John's '49 Oldsmobile," Bill recalled.

## Bill's Exit

What exactly happened to make Bill Emerson leave The Country Gentlemen after two years? Bill explained: "It was more or less a personality conflict between John and me. We were equal partners. Somebody had to be top dog. There were disagreements that escalated and festered. It was a long time ago. The best I can tell you is that John and I disagreed on a lot of things. Sometimes it was the material. Or what clothes we wore, although he wasn't wearing bowling shirts and pajama pants back then. That would have been a real sticking point with me. I was more of a traditionalist like Bill Monroe or Red Smiley.

"People either loved or hated John back then. A lot of people wanted to beat him up because they thought he was too arrogant. But he wasn't truly arrogant. Deep down he was a shy guy. But he was also a showman.

And depending on what day it was you never knew which John would show up."

Eventually tired of their personality conflict Bill told John and Charlie that he was leaving the band. Bill admits, "They exclaimed 'great.'"

After Bill Emerson left, the Gents used Pete Roberts and Porter Church for a short time on banjo. Pete Roberts, aka Pete Kuykendall, was one of a committee that founded the *Bluegrass Unlimited* newsletter and later magazine. He became General Manager in 1970, and Editor in 1972 (More about Kuykendall in Chapter Eight.)

Kenny Haddock played Dobro on some Gents' recordings including "Two Little Boys." On a few early recordings, Duffey overdubbed Dobro himself after he'd laid down the mandolin track. For a few months in 1961, Earl Taylor's Stoney Mountain Boys' banjo player, Walter Hensley played with The Country Gentlemen.

Bill in the Country Current.
© B. Emerson

"The Gents hired Eddie Adcock after Pete Kuykendall left. This was about the smartest thing they could have done," Bill Emerson declared. It was Gents' bass player, Jim Cox, who suggested Adcock after a chance meeting at a Alexandria, Virginia gas station.

Emerson played as a side-man in bands with Bill Harrell, Red Allen, and

Jimmy Martin. In 1967, he formed Emerson and Waldron, recording on Dick Freeland's *Rebel Records*. By 1970, he was back in The Country Gentlemen.

"John left the Gents in 1969, replaced by Jimmy Gaudreau. I returned on banjo when Eddie also left in 1970. I was right back at the Shamrock, which had the same owners and was the same deal."

In 1972 Bill Emerson was shot by an unknown person in a passing car outside Bethesda, Maryland's Red Fox Inn. The bullet passed through Bill's right arm. After a full recovery, Bill joined the Navy in 1973, performing for the next 20 years in the Country Current bluegrass ensemble with the U.S. Navy Band. He retired in 1993.

"Music is all I ever wanted to do," said Bill. "I never got rich, but I had a good time."

## Hall of Famer

Bill Emerson was inducted into the International Bluegrass Music Association Hall of Fame on September 26, 2019.

When he received the first edition of this book Bill said, "*John Duffey's Bluegrass Life* touches my heart. Sometimes I lay in bed at night and think of him. I still can't figure him out. We fought, but he was my friend. John Duffey is so much of who I am."

## The Shamrock

Duffey recalled: "*After playing at the Crossroads, Roger Woodward, owner of the Shamrock bar asked us to audition. We were hired and I knew we had hit the big time. We started out playing the Shamrock one night a week on Tuesday and the crowd started getting pretty good. Then they added Thursdays every week. So, it turned out that the Gentlemen's stint with the exception of about a year, lasted about ten years. They were still there when I left."*

The Country Gentlemen began to build their D.C. following at the Shamrock in the heart of Georgetown. Founded in 1952, a green glow from the neon sign bathed the Shamrock's entrance to the noisy, smoky bar at 3295 M St., NW. The stage was to the left of the doorway as patrons walked in; straight ahead was a long bar against the wall. A giant "We Have Cold Duck" sign was hung over the stage around 1966.

The Shamrock building itself was constructed in the 1850s and was only a short walk from John's birthplace, the Columbia Hospital for Women. Brothers Mickey and Roger Woodward owned the Shamrock. They were country musicians, playing pedal steel and lead guitar respectively. In fact, they performed regularly with the budding country music star, Roy Clark in 1960 calling themselves the "Shamrock Trio." People who knew the place well all agreed that two things were true about the Shamrock: It was run down to begin with, and that never changed.

After the Shamrock closed in 1972, Winston's Bar occupied the location. Tom Gray relates that, "the building that housed the Shamrock was torn down. I went looking for the building a couple of years ago, and it was gone." At that address today is the upscale Club Monaco.

The Country Gentlemen felt fortunate to have two weeknight gigs, which freed the band to take weekend jobs. Initially, Roger paid them about $40 dollars a man for each night minus any bar tabs. In a few years, they were earning 100 dollars a gig, their wages boosted by the contributions of satisfied customers to the pitch pot.

Of this time John emphasized: *"I thought to myself, damn, we're playing here for a living in the big city and* *we're getting audiences. There's no reason why this music needs to stay out in the woods. I mean we didn't get rich by any means but rather than driving to Columbus, Ohio for $150, we could eventually make $400 a week at the Shamrock. That's a big increase there and that helped. I knew that we had hit the big time when we started at the Shamrock."*

During this time the Gentlemen would also check out the folk acts at the nearby Cellar Door, a small magnificent nightclub that featured national music acts. One of John's favorite Cellar Door acts was Ian & Sylvia. When Ian & Sylvia played the Cellar Door, they'd walk down the street to the Shamrock to take in a Country Gentlemen set. A great friendship developed between the Gents and Ian & Sylvia, especially Duffey's bond with Ian Tyson.

John was impressed by their "Four Strong Winds" and wrote a song, "The Traveler," which he hoped would be as popular. John also liked their "Spanish Is a Loving Tongue." It became "The Border Incident" on the Gentlemen's *Traveler* album, with John listed as author. The truth is, the lyrics date to 1907 when cowboy poet Charles Badger Clark wrote "The Border Affair."

A sample listing of songs the Gents were playing at 1961 gigs includes:

| | |
|---|---|
| A Good Woman's Love | Honkey Tonk Rag |
| My Aching Heart | Jesse James |
| Blue Moon of Kentucky | Jimmy Brown, The Newsboy |
| Dream of The Miner's Child | Little Maggie |
| Darling Alalee | Long Black Veil |
| Drifting Too Far From Shore | Paul and Silas |
| Poor Ellen Smith | Roanoke |
| Foggy Mountain Chimes | Roving Gambler |
| Save It! Save It! | New Freedom Bell |
| Have Thine Own Way | Love Letters in the Sand |

Nine Pound Hammer
Panhandle Country
Sunny Side of Life
Before I Met You
Gosh, I Miss You All the Time
Under The Double Eagle
The Little Sparrow
The Story of Charlie Lawson

Tomorrow's My Wedding Day
Ain't Gonna Work Tomorrow
Turkey Knob
Two Little Boys
Two Lonely Hearts
Weeping Willow

In addition to the Shamrock, the Gents began playing bars in Laurel, Maryland, and Falls Church, Virginia. Eddie's banjo licks and John's mandolin leads became increasingly imaginative. A turning point for John's musical development came on The Gents' 1961 instrumental "Sunrise", copyrighted by John Duffey. It was based on Les Paul's "The World Is Waiting For The Sunrise," with different chord changes.

*"I never touched on the melody just to see what would happen. I guess I started something,"* John noted.

# Chapter 4: Charlie Waller

Charlie Waller. Gettysburg Bluegrass Festival,
2003 © Cindy Howe

Charles Otis "Charlie" Waller was born on January 19, 1935, in Joinerville, Texas. Duffey would call him a "true cotton picker" because when his family moved to Lake Charles, Louisiana, Charlie picked cotton.

In 1945, he came with his mother to Washington, where she ran a boardinghouse. Charlie didn't like bluegrass music much when he first heard it. He was inspired by Canadian country singer Hank Snow, and although he did appreciate some Flatt & Scruggs songs, he never thought he'd ever be playing bluegrass.

He got a guitar, but it took him a long time getting started because he didn't know how to tune it, or he couldn't find anybody to tune it for him. He ended up using a tuning fork throughout his career, even after electronic tuners became available.

As he began to self-teach himself, his friends would stop by his house. He'd pick up the guitar, and they'd say, "Oh, no, we're never gonna get out of here now!"

Later as he improved, Charlie remembers, "it was just the opposite; they all wanted me to pick some." By the age of 13, he was playing professionally in Washington, D.C. hillbilly bars.

One day while singing on the porch, a postman stopped when he heard young Charlie singing, telling Charlie he liked what he heard. He said, "I used to play that kind of music with my brother. Perhaps you've heard of us. We were the Blue Sky Boys." The Blue Sky Boys were the most popular of the brother duet groups, recording from 1936 to 1951 for the RCA Victor record label. Charlie's visitor was Bill Bolick, who began to work for the U.S. Post Office when the Blue Sky Boys retired.

Obsessed with music, Charlie quit school in the eighth grade and worked at a gas station and body shop while playing music at night.

In 1955, at 20-years-old, he returned to Louisiana as a guitarist with Buzz Busby's Bayou Boys. Charlie would proudly tell interviewers. "With Buzz, we played on the *Louisiana Hayride* with all the fellas that became big stars back then: Elvis Presley, George Jones, Jimmy Newman, The Browns..."

In a 1973 interview in *Pickin' Magazine*, Waller explained to writer Doug Tuchman his bluegrass epiphany: "It was the song 'Maybe You Will Change Your Mind' by Reno & Smiley circa 1955. I had to stop the car. I couldn't drive; it tore me up. Then I got turned on by Ralph Stanley. I just got goosebumps all over because of what Ralph was doing. That door opened, man, and that's when I really started digging bluegrass."

Charlie adopted bluegrass rather than chase Nashville for success because he felt that bluegrass was more like the Eddie Arnold and Roy Acuff type "country" music he loved. With the electrification and so forth, country music was moving away from what he liked.

Charlie came back to the D.C. area in 1956 to play with Earl Taylor in Baltimore. Taylor, a Virginian who settled in Rockville, Maryland met seventeen-year-old Waller and invited him to be in his band, The Stoney Mountain Boys.

Earl Taylor found his success playing in a more traditional mode—often called "hard-driving Baltimore bluegrass"—and would go on to appear on music historian Mike Seeger's 1959 ground-breaking anthology, *Mountain Music Bluegrass Style* (Folkways Records FA-2318.) Seeger would also become the Country Gent's first record producer. Charlie Waller left Earl Taylor to join Buzz Busby's band, later in 1956. Fortunately for Charlie, he had left Buzz's band in mid-1957, before that terrible auto crash.

Before Busby could leave the hospital following the car accident, Charlie told Buzz that he wasn't returning to the Bayou Boys. In a few years, Charlie's name was inlaid in mother of pearl on the neck of his 1937 Martin D-28 acoustic guitar and both his beautiful voice and reliant guitar accompaniment would become treasured. "Charlie Waller was a rock, the foundation of the whole

Country Gentlemen, just a great lead singer, and people wanted to hear him sing. He was the one who kept it constant," said Bill Emerson.

*"I loved Charlie, and I still do,"* John admitted. When asked if Duffey ever asked Charlie for something 'artistically different' in the Gents, John said:

*"No, not artistically. There were a lot of problems with Charlie. His greatest problem is that he's so stubborn. He'd get things in his mind that he didn't want to do and wasn't going to do. A lot of times it was a bad choice on his part."*

An example of one bad choice that Duffey shared was once playing with the Gents on Martha's Vineyard, and their opening act was Jerry Corbitt, a young folk singer from Tilton, Georgia.

*"We were playing a club called the Moon-Cusser Coffee House,* ["Moon Cusser" refers to the early pirates in the area who cussed the moon because they couldn't sneak up on their victims in the dark] *and I listened to Jerry's set. One song he did was "Last Thing On My Mind." I had never heard it.*

*"Boy, that's a neat song," I told Jerry.*

*"A friend of mine named Tom Paxton wrote it," said Jerry.*

*"Would you mind passing along the words?"*

*"Sure. Tom hasn't recorded it yet. Go ahead and cut it. Tom would love that," answered Jerry.*

*"Unfortunately, Charlie had a different reaction when he heard the song.*

*"I ain't singing no fucking folk song," Charlie said. He didn't care whether I sang it or not, he wanted nothing to do with it. So, we lost out on first recording a song that became a big hit for Tom Paxton and several others."*

Charlie Waller. 2003. © Cindy Howe

As of 2019 "Last Thing On My Mind" has been recorded by dozens of artists, including Johnny Cash, Dolly Parton, Glen Campbell, Phil Everly, Porter Wagoner, The Carter Family, The Dillards, Gene Clark, Rick Danko, Neil Diamond, Judy Collins, Peter Paul and Mary, Willie Nelson, Chesapeake, and Flatt & Scruggs. The Seldom Scene performed it in live shows in 1972 as well.

Corbitt would go on to form The Youngbloods, with Jesse Colin Young

Jesse remembers, "I think the first gig that I played as a folk singer was at The Cellar Door. Right down the street was the Shamrock tavern and then the Little Tavern hamburger joint. We'd go to the Shamrock to see The Country Gentlemen and then to the Little Tavern and listen to the Beatles on the jukebox. This was around 1965."

When asked how did he persuade Charlie to do the other "folk" songs like Dylan's "Girl from the North Country?" John replied, *"The only way you could ever get Charlie to do anything was finagling around to make him think it was his idea."*

On selecting material, Charlie explained, "It has to pass on me. If it is something I realize isn't me, or I couldn't sing, then I'd have to say 'no' on it. But most of The Country Gentlemen's stuff, traditional or not, doesn't have to do with who's in the group." [1973 *Pickin' magazine* interview]

Another Waller comment on the Gent's early folk song, "Copper Kettle:" "Originally this was a waltz, but I didn't like the tempo. I put it to the tempo of "Movin' On" by Hank Snow, and asked Duffey what he thought. He liked it," said Waller. "Ages and Ages Ago," was an old Gene Autry tune that Charlie very much liked and presented to the band. [WAMU radio interview with Jerry Gray].

One difference that John imposed on Charlie was how they harmonized. Charlie thought the ideal vocal blend was when you look at three people singing together, and you can't tell who is singing what part. But with Duffey's loud, domineering and uniquely identifiable tenor voice you always knew when and what he was singing. When John quit the group, the Duffey harmony domination was a characteristic that didn't continue in later iterations of Charlie's Gentlemen. Classic Country Gent's bass player, Tom Gray confirmed this assertion.

The Gents were invited to join the Grand Ole Opry in the mid-sixties. Membership would require the band playing the Opry at least 20 times a year. "No," Duffey sneered. Tom Gray adds, "From the beginning of the Gents, and continuing into his years with The Seldom

Scene, John harbored a resentment of the Nashville music industry and its control of country music. The Gents got no respect from Nashville. He said, 'they must think we're aliens from outer space.' Duffey was proud that The Country Gentlemen and later The Seldom Scene would thrive despite being out-of-favor with the Nashville industry."

Rick Allred played mandolin in the late 1970's with the Gents. When asked about Charlie, Rick maintained that, "Charlie stood by his beliefs. When I was with him, we played many festivals with the Osborne Brothers. Bobby Osborne told him, 'I can get you membership in the Grand Ole Opry.' Charlie didn't want to do it."

Rick adds, "John Duffey would help Charlie in the early days with lyrics because Charlie admitted, 'if a pretty woman walked into the bar, he would forget everything.' And as far as drinking, Charlie wasn't a guzzler but rather he sipped all day. It was constant from the time he awoke until he went to sleep. Charlie always treated me very well. He thought that the people who played with him should know when they weren't playing well, so he never said anything negative. He was a good guy."

Others did the managing for the post-Duffey Country Gentlemen tours. When Charlie was once told he'd be gone a month on tour, he showed up to board the bus and joked, "I didn't know which shirt to bring so I brought them both." Charlie had a dry sense of humor. He insisted that, "It's hard to be the straight man when you're as funny as I am."

## Junkyard Prank

Once on a long drive to a bluegrass festival, John became amused that Charlie had slept for the whole trip and was still asleep when the Gents reached their motel. Adjacent to the motel was a junkyard. So, John took Charlie's guitar and left it on the motel porch and then, with Charlie snoring, pulled the car into the junkyard gates, and left him there. Charlie eventually woke up alone, with the band watching from afar and laughing. Charlie walked to the motel office and asked, "Did three son-of-a-bitches check in here?"

When asked what he'd be doing if he wasn't in the music business, Charlie would answer, "be a hobo." adding, "In '68 when Duffey didn't want to travel, the Gents recorded but did very little playing. I lived in my car."

In a 1980 interview with *Washington Post* writer Angus Young, John talked about his own voice:

"It's apparently a medical fact that as you get older your voice goes down a little bit. The high notes start to dwindle. Age I guess, and the effects of body abuse.

"Frankly, though, I think my voice has more quality now than it did when I was screaming four octaves. After I could stand to hear myself sing, I'd listen to a recording and I'd think to myself, 'Sounds like you're reading it off paper.' I realized there were ways of getting into a note, besides just blasting it out. This may sound conceited, but I think phrasing really separates the men from the boys. I like it when it sounds like I just swallowed a fifth of whiskey."

Again, John admired Dean Martin, who always sounded like he'd had more than his share of whiskey.

## Charlie on Singing

In 1974 Charlie talked with author and bluegrass player, Peter Wernick for his book, *Bluegrass Songbook*. [Hal Leonard]. Pete, the first President of the International Bluegrass Music Association, is also known as "Dr. Banjo. He was a founding member of the Hot Rize bluegrass band, formed in 1978 and still playing as of 2020. The following quotes are either from Pete's book or unpublished excerpts from his interview with Charlie.

The "Classic" Country Gentlemen in the studio 1989 (l to r)
Charlie, John, Tom and Eddie. © Penny Parsons

Charlie told Pete: "I don't know how to explain it really, but music is feeling. And it is so often lost in the fast pace of groups trying to be so technically perfect about trying to pick just like somebody else, or get note for note, or trying to concentrate so hard on the picking. But a song has to be sung, even as a trio or anyway with feeling. That's why you can listen to these older records and they'll do something to you.

"Some people hold back when they sing. But they don't hold back when they're yelling at their kids. I don't copy anyone. I sound like me. I did in the beginning, but I realized that there's no point in trying to be somebody else. So, you go on and look for your own sound. Everybody sounds a little bit like somebody else because they start out that way. But if they have the right idea, they try to sound close to themselves and not somebody else. George Jones sounds like George Jones, but even he was influenced by earlier artists.

"I hope the old traditional sound never leaves. That's the reason we have people trying to preserve it. But if I could sing a Bill Monroe song or a Ralph Stanley song better than I could with what we do [in The Country Gentlemen], then maybe I'd be doing it. I can sing those songs, but I think people ought to do what they can do best."

*Q*: I'm trying to pin down what might be different about bluegrass singing. Is it louder for example?
*A*: That would depend on the individual. You can sing a high note both loud and soft and it would still be bluegrass. The word, "bluegrass" comes from Bill Monroe's band, but we really play Country Gentlemen music. Some of what we do is in the style of what Bill Monroe does, but also a lot isn't.

It used to be years ago that if you played bluegrass music you couldn't get a job in a club. It was the high nasal singing. And people didn't want to hear that. They wanted either country music or rock and roll. But now bluegrass has a foothold. The kids have discovered it.

It's not like "country" music that's all about beer and sad songs. Although there's nothing wrong about sad songs. People like to cry. But the country songs are all 'my baby left me. Think I'll get a six pack. You take the table and I'll take the chairs. And we will stay unhappy for the rest of our lives.' I can't stand those kind of songs.

*Q:* What influences really got you? You had mentioned Hank Snow?

*A:* Yes, Hank Snow and Roy Acuff. I suppose everybody has witnessed something they really liked to hear. A sound with good words that make chill bumps go up (sic). For me it can have a beautiful melody—something that you like to hear—or beautiful chords and good words. Sometimes it can have bad words but a good, fast moving thing that you like to hear. But I appreciate both. And it is getting so that I appreciate intelligent words a whole lot more than I used to. I [might have] liked something years ago that I wouldn't care for now. But everyone wants to better themselves.

*Q:* How did you actually learn to sing?

*A:* (Pauses). I'm originally from Louisiana and we went to church where everybody sang. That was the first. I listened to the radio. I got a harmonica and when I wasn't playing it, I was walking down the road singing.

*Q:* Then singing became a part of your life?

*A:* Very much so. I lost jobs over of it.

*Q:* Really?

*A:* Yea, I worked at gas stations and I'd go home for lunch and get to playing the guitar and forget all about the time. I used to carry my guitar to school and play it in the playground. I've skipped school to play music. I left school after the 10th grade. I dreamed about being professional. It's been a hell of a big part of my life all the way until now and making a living with it.

*Q:* Was music something you wanted to do, or something you had to do?
*A:* Well, I guess both. I wanted to so bad that I had to.

*Q:* When you started to take yourself seriously as a musician, and wanted people to listen to you, did you work on your singing in some way?
*A:* When I was seventeen, I had an old '37 Plymouth. Every night after I finished my date with my girlfriend, I'd park and sit in the car for two hours with my guitar [working on my singing]. I had work in the morning as an apprentice in a car and body shop.

*Q:* How did you work on your music? Was it just playing it over and over?
*A:* I played and listened and [discovered] what turned me on. I thought if somebody really believes in something then others might like it, too.

*Q:* Do you ever practice today? Doing exercises for your voice?
*A:* Not like I should...You can get tired of anything, and I don't want to ruin the feeling of playing the music. I don't want music to be my whole life. It isn't.

*Q:* Do you listen to the words when you sing?
*A:* That has been a problem. I sing the songs so often that it sometimes becomes automatic. If I stop and think about the lyrics too much then I mess up.

*Q:* Do you ever paint a picture in your head when you sing.

*A:* Yes, and that helps keep the feeling of the music. You have good days and bad days, but you know when you've done it right. [These days] it's mostly the audience that turns me on. If I'm playing for someone who is really digging what I'm doing then I can play so much better and get something out of it then when I'm playing for someone who says, 'OK. Entertain *me.*"

*Q:* What advice would you give to other people who might want to sing?

*A:* (long pause). I might not be the best person to ask about that. I just came to music naturally, singing as a kid. I never took lessons. I suppose people can learn by taking lessons, but I could never teach someone because I wouldn't know what to tell them.

*Q:* If someone came up to you and asked how they might learn to sing better, then what would you say?

*A:* The only thing I can think of is 'don't hold back.' A lot of people with a pretty voice are afraid to sing out. They are not afraid when they are yelling at their kids. But that's what you have to do with singing. It has to come out powerfully.

*Q:* Many people imitate The Country Gentlemen harmonies. When you are developing your sound or teaching a new person [in the group] what do you tell them to do?

*A:* With a trio you need three people with the right blend. Someone with a strong lead. This lead should sound good even if there is no one else singing. Then add to it a high tenor voice. Which would be all right just there as a duet. Then add a third baritone voice which gives a much fuller sound. I don't sing baritone and I've always had plenty of baritones in my group. Right now, Bill Yates has taken over as baritone singer these days. The tenor lead comes to me naturally, but baritone doesn't.

*Q:* It is usually a weird line.
*A:* It's a very pretty part. Eddie Adcock I think was probably one of the finest baritone singers.

*Q:* He made the lines into something that made sense.
*A:* Yes, with those little raises at the end. And the tenor has to have the blend, and sing high and make the notes. We had a very good trio when Jimmy Gaudreau was with us. The only thing that was funny about that combination was that I'm from Louisiana and Jimmy is from Rhode Island. He'd sing 'I'd look all around the *cah,* but Mary wasn't there' [from "Bringing Mary Home"]. We used to tease him about that.

When Doyle Lawson came with us, many people said that his voice blended better because he had a southern voice. I've heard people from New York City who never sound like they're from New York. For southern country singers I would often rather hear them sing than talk. It's like the difference between an English accent and a Cockney accent: One is pretty, and one isn't.

*Q:* In The Country Gentlemen harmonies, is it important that all voices be heard equally?
*A:* Yes, I think in a trio you should be able to see three people singing and sing and not tell who is singing what. Technically I think that is the perfect blend. In the beginning Duffey was always the much louder singer. Although we had a good blend and it made it. People liked it and accepted it. But always you could hear Duffey above everyone else. He had such a powerful

voice he had to stand back in the studio. Of course, they could have turned him down.

If anyone should be loudest it should be the lead singer technically because that is the tune.

*Q*: When you practice do you work hard on phrasing?
*A:* In my position, I just sing it and they get with me. I was never good for anybody telling me how to sing words.

## Len Holsclaw

As manager of the post-Duffey Country Gents from 1971 to 2004 when Charlie passed away, Len knew Charlie very well. Holsclaw was born in Staunton, Virginia on November 2, 1933. "It was a cold day, in a poor country on the poor side of town," he said. He attended high school in Manassas, Virginia, and served in the military for two years before he became an Arlington County, Virginia police officer. The following Holsclaw memories come from a 2004 interview by co-author, G.T. Keplinger.

Len asserted that, "Charlie Waller had a voice on par with all the great singers who ever sang. He could have sung anything he wanted to, and it was his own fault when he didn't. He had one of the great voices in any kind of music. It stayed with him until the day he died. Charlie sang the best version of 'The Fields Have Turned Brown' by Carter Stanley."

Tom Gray confirmed that, "Carter at Watermelon Park and other festivals would always go out front to hear Charlie and the Gents sing that one." Note: Once at Watermelon Park, when the Stanley Brothers played after the Gents, Carter Stanley got in a dig and a compliment at the same time. He said, "Those Country Gentlemen are doing a good job of singing our songs.

Now here's one they forgot to do, but I'm sure they could do a good job of it." At the time, the Gents hadn't yet learned the etiquette that you should not go out on stage before an act and play their songs.

Growing up, Holsclaw loved all the music he heard on the radio and saw in high school auditoriums. From hillbilly to pop and from Earl Scruggs to jazz drummer, Gene Krupa, "It was all good."

"I first saw The Country Gentlemen on a wagon bed truck in Warrenton, Virginia when they opened up a shopping center there. Duffey, of course, was irreverent, and they played a lot of pop music in their own fashion, but when Waller and Duffey sang together it was magic. They just knocked me out as a fan, and then we became friends. They were not your typical black suit, white shirt, brown shoe, no-teeth, hayseed bands. I never even considered them a bluegrass band. They were great musicians."

As for John, Len said, "Duffey was not the greatest mandolin player in the world, but he could make you think that he was when he performed." Len was the perpetrator of a rumor that coaxed Duffey out of musical retirement in 1971. (More about that cleverness in Chapter 13.)

Len maintained, "With Adcock, who had no peer, Duffey and Charlie just clicked. They had a great trio, and a great show. They'd sass the crowd. They were fun.

"By comparison, when Bill Monroe's band smiled, it was almost out of character. When they'd play a gospel song, the band would take their hats off. Crowds understood the relevance and appreciated the reverence.

"But anyone could go see the Gentlemen at the Shamrock for a dollar cover charge. They were accessible. John wore bowling shirts. The band was sophisticated and didn't play down to their audiences. The Gentlemen changed the bluegrass paradigm."

On August Aug. 18, 2004, Charlie had completed a new album—his 50th with The Country Gentlemen—and was to head out on a tour the day he died at age 69 of a heart attack in his Gordonsville, Virginia home. He had told his bus driver, Kenny Wurzberger that he felt a pain in his liver a month before. An autopsy would show he was in the early stages of liver cancer when he died.

Charlie's heart attack struck him as he was working in his garden. He then went into the house, and died. It was in that same vegetable garden that Charlie's mother passed away years earlier. Isn't that spooky? His son, Randy Waller said, "Grandma called Daddy home."

Randy had become a featured player in the Gents by the time his dad died. Fulfilling Charlie's wish, Randy assembled a new group of talented musicians and carried on the group's esteemed name for many years.

Twenty-two days before his death, Charlie gave his final local D.C. performance at the Birchmere on July 26 after nearly 50 years of performing. *Washington Post* writer, Richard Harrington, who was very helpful with this book, reviewed Waller's show stating, "his smooth, powerful tenor was as unmistakable as ever, his enunciation natural and easy, with every syllable clear and beautiful. Waller's voice was strong, deep and distinctive, without the nasal quality of his predecessors. And beautiful. Some have suggested that had Waller chosen country music over bluegrass, he'd now be talked about in the same breath as George Jones."

"It is still a subject of wonder when bluegrass fans and pickers talk of Charlie," said Tom Gray. "Although his body was failing in his later years, his voice always sounded great, up until the very end."

Charlie's *Washington Post* obituary by staff writer, Matt Schudel, ended as follows: "Mr. Waller's first marriage, to Mona Waller, ended in divorce. His second wife, Kathy Waller, died in the 1960s.

"Survivors include his wife of 25 years, Sachiko Waller of Gordonsville; a son from an early relationship, Randy Waller of Falls Church; a daughter from his first marriage, Dori Lane of Cape Coral, Fla.; a son from his second marriage, Danny Graves of Avon, Colo.; and a daughter from his third marriage, Mina Waller of Gallatin, Tenn.; five grandchildren; and two great-grandchildren.

"Of the hundreds of songs Mr. Waller performed, one of his favorites was a John Duffey composition called "A Letter to Tom." Symbolic of a musician's lonely, memory-filled life, it concludes with these words:

> *But when our time shall come, dear Tom*
> *And we are called to go*
> *I hope they'll lay us where we played*
> *Just fifteen years ago. "*

When Charlie learned of John Duffey's death in 1996, he sighed, "No, he can't do that! I'm not finished singing with him."

# Chapter 5: Blame It on Tom's Baby Sitter

Tom Gray, 2018. © S. Moore

**T**he legendary leading bluegrass bass player of his generation, Tom Gray, was born in Chicago in 1941 and raised in the Palisades section of Washington, D.C. from the age of seven. His father moved to Washington to work for the National Highway Users Conference trade association.

"D.C. was a good place to become familiar with bluegrass music. It is where I first heard it live," Tom said in 2018 for this book. "My parents were jazz fans. Mom also liked classical music, but she blames me liking bluegrass on my babysitter when we lived in Chicago."

Mattie Bowers, a young woman homesick for Tennessee would take care of toddler Tom and his two brothers. Mattie would come over every Saturday night to listen to the Grand Ole Opry on the radio and sit Tom on her lap. It was 1945 when Bill Monroe was the hottest act on the Grand Ole Opry. "I think there was a subconscious thing put into my brain that this was neat stuff," Tom said

Later in elementary school, a classmate performed a folk song on an accordion at a school assembly. ["Oh Susanna," he thinks]. Tom was fascinated. "She was a girl my age making all these notes and music come out of that box. I went home and asked Dad for an accordion."

Tom's father agreed and arranged for him to have lessons. Tom finished the 12-week course in two weeks and was ready for more music.

"I started playing piano for Sunday school kids. After several years you could put the hymnal in front of me, and I could play all the songs by sight while the choir sang. This kept me active in playing music."

When Tom was 14, he heard bluegrass music again. "My mind exploded, and this music is what I wanted to play," he said. Although his first bluegrass instruments were guitar followed by mandolin, it was the stand-up bass that stood out for Tom. He was influenced by the walking bass lines of George and John Shuffler on the

FEATURING THE COUNTRY GENTLEMEN, SELDOM SCENE, AND WASHINGTON, D.C.

Stanley Brothers' recordings of the early 1950s. Tom was also inspired by Washington jazz bassist Keter Betts, who played with Charlie Byrd and Ella Fitzgerald.

Tom Gray was too young to see live bluegrass regularly in the D.C. bars, but he'd occasionally watch Buzz Busby's 1954-1955 TV show on WRC TV. "Buzz was filled with energy and had the bluegrass high tenor voice and also the fastest tremolo on the mandolin than anybody," Tom said. Tremolo refers to the fast picking of one, two, or even three notes in an alternating picking motion. John's lead on The Seldom Scene's, "Wait a Minute" is an example of mandolin tremolo.

When asked if Buzz was the best mandolin player he ever knew, Tom said, "Although a very subjective question, he wasn't, and neither was John. There are so many great ones. The list should include Bill Monroe, Jethro Burns, Jesse McReynolds, Chris Thile, and Frank Solivan."

Tom Gray first met John Duffey in 1956 when they entered a contest in Rockville, Maryland sponsored by radio station, WINX AM 1600. Tom was in a high school bluegrass band called the Rocky Ridge Ramblers. John was with Lucky Chatman's band.

"John always had that air about him where he felt he was better than everybody else. He was always arrogant," said Tom with a laugh. "That was John's self-defense mechanism from the very beginning. But beneath that, he was a shy person, sometimes afraid to speak with people."

Tom made friends with Duffey, Charlie Waller, and other local bluegrass musicians at the weekly lawn parties that WARL would host during summers.

By high school, Tom became a regular fan at The Country Gentlemen's shows at the Crossroads Restaurant in Baileys Crossroads, Virginia bonding with

Charlie, John, Pete Kuykendall on banjo and Tom Morgan on bass. He'd sit in for songs and even recorded with them on a Starday session on May 13, 1959. "I was a smart aleck kid trying to learn every lick I could and showing off. I'm sure I overplayed," Tom admits.

In 1960, John and Charlie invited nineteen-year-old Tom to join the group replacing Jim Cox formally. This foursome, Waller, Duffey, Adcock, and Gray are considered the Classic Country Gentlemen band.

The Gents were regularly playing the Shamrock bar in Georgetown on Tuesdays and Thursdays and the Shamrock Room [no relation] on weekends in the West End Shopping Center in Falls Church, Virginia and a "very depressing place" called the Tremont Inn, also in Falls Church.

The Tremont Inn is where a drunk stumbled on stage and fell on Tom Gray's bass fiddle laying on its side. It fell backward on Charlie's guitar and Duffey's mandolin—snapping the necks of both instruments. The drunk then stared at the band and slurred: "Someone wants to make something of this?"

From across the room, Eddie Adcock sprinted over a table, grabbed the inebriant by the neck until the drunk offered to pay them for repairs. "It was fortunate that Duffey was a luthier who saved the guy some money by fixing the instruments himself," Tom remembers.

Tom described the group at this time as an excellent bar band playing cover songs of traditional bluegrass artists. "The guys called me 'young Tom' since I was younger than them and looked more like 16 than my real age, 20."

As Duffey would often liken a music gig to a sports game—"*Sometime you win big but not every show is a winner*"—the Classic Country Gentlemen would be a very winning team for four years. John was also a generous musician at times helping other players. John would freely offer advice.

When asked his overall opinion of John's musicianship, Tom carefully answered: "John Duffey would come alive when he was playing for an audience. He wanted some feedback from the people out front. If he could do something to impress people then he would do so. Sometimes what he chose to play would fall flat on its face like a train wreck."

What would he do then?

Tom answered, "Oh he would flash his eyes, and sometimes just make noise with his instrument and move on. Finishing up a break that he had started but couldn't come up with enough ideas to complete it. A lot us who play music have been in the same position. John was very human that way." John would give the advice: "If you make a mistake, play it again."

"But as much as he might slough it off instrumentally, he was always perfect vocally. Perfect pitch. He knew how to blend voices. And to change the notes of a melody to make the song sound better."

What was playing at the Shamrock like? Tom explained, "I'm sure the sound system was crude. It was four people standing on the stage with one microphone, and that's all. One mic to pick up all the instruments and the voices. But the choreography around that microphone made for an entertaining show; the audiences could hear everyone. The guitarist [Charlie] would be standing so that the mic was on his right. If he wanted to play a lick he could lean over, and he was close enough to sing his parts. The bass player would stand behind the guitarist. So, we were the rhythm section on stage left. The lead instruments, on stage right, would come in to play their breaks and always exit in a clockwise circle. You finish your lead sidestep to the right so the next person can come in behind you. With my bass I just leaned in and played a bass solo or sang and avoided the rotation. I stayed behind the guitarist. That's what Bill Monroe, Flatt & Scruggs and other bands did with the clockwise rotation in those days.

## The First Limousine

Tom was the only single bandmate, still living at home with his parents when he became a Gent. His National Geographic job meant he had more income than the others, so Tom was persuaded to buy a band vehicle—an old Limousine used for sight-seeing by the Grayline company where John's father worked.

"It cost about $800," Tom recalls, "and the deal was that John and Charlie were going to repay me." John reimbursed Tom, but Charlie never did. Eddie also asked to buy a banjo that Tom owned and gave him his toolbox as collateral. A week later he asked Tom for the toolbox back so he could earn mechanic money to repay the banjo loan, which he never did."

Tom dismisses all this now, insisting that none of them owe him anything as, "my life has been enriched by being bandmates with them." As of 2020, Tom is still playing gigs with Eddie Adcock and wife, Martha and also Valerie Smith and Liberty Pike, and others. The picture at the top of this chapter was taken at bluegrass fan, Brian Murphy's pickin' party.

## Bill Clifton

*"I first recorded in Nashville with Bill Clifton. Bill was a person of some stature in the business at that time."*

Born in the Baltimore suburb of Lutherville, Maryland in 1931, musician and folklorist, William August Marburg played an essential role in the promotion of bluegrass. He took the name "Bill Clifton" when he became a musician —vocals, guitar, piano, and autoharp—so not to concern his affluent family who disapproved of his music pursuits. A more traditional musician in his performances, Clifton was a strong supporter of Bill Monroe-style bluegrass. In 1953, he published an influential songbook, *150 Old-Time Folk, and Gospel Songs.*

Bill was impressed with John's abilities and John was an admirer of Clifton, as were the other Country Gentlemen. Bill was a guest player during Country Gentlemen sets often at the Shamrock along with Russ Hooper [Dobro] and Mike Seeger [banjo].

After the first Nashville sessions, John did another three recording sessions with Clifton in D.C. Through the suggestion of John, Bill Clifton hired Tom before he first joined the Gents to back his regular banjo player, Johnny Clark. They, with Duffey, played a three-band mini festival at a ballpark in Salem, Virginia outside Roanoke. Since Clark was Bill's tenor singer, John sang baritone on the recordings. He did with Bill as well at this show.

"That was a really big event," Tom Gray states. "There were three bands, Bill Clifton, Grandpa Jones with his wife, Ramona, and Jim Eanes and his Shenandoah Valley Boys. Each band did two sets."

In 1961-62, the Gents played several shows as Bill's back-up band. Duffey enjoyed good-natured jokes at Bill's expense like adding empty beer cans and a whiskey bottle on the floor of the rear passenger seat where Clifton rode so when he got out, the cans and bottle might follow, or telling other people that Bill was actually the leader of the Kingston Trio.

Tom said, "As we traveled together, in our limousine, we pulled those pranks on Bill. He was such a refined gentleman; he was easy to embarrass."

On July 4, 1961, Bill organized an outdoor "Bluegrass Day" concert at Oak Leaf Park in Luray, Virginia, featuring the Stanley Brothers, Bill Clifton & The Dixie Mountain Boys, Bill Monroe & The Blue Grass Boys, Jim and Jesse, Mac Wiseman, and The Country Gentlemen. This concert is considered to be the very first bluegrass festival in the world.

In 1962, a young banjo player working at the Johns Hopkins Applied Physics lab in Laurel, Maryland went to a party at Bill Clifton's house. The Country Gentlemen arrived to play two sets. The banjo player had never seen them before and remembers them as, "not the friendliest people," so he didn't talk to them at the party. His name was Ben Eldridge and little did he know then that his future would be magnificently connected to Duffey.

Bill Clifton moved to England in 1963 and introduced bluegrass to audiences in Great Britain and Europe. Eventually, he also introduced bluegrass and American folk music in Australia, Asia, and Africa.

On return trips to the states in the early 1970s, including the first festival The Seldom Scene played in— The Indian Springs Bluegrass Festival near Hagerstown, Maryland run by *Bluegrass Unlimited* magazine. Clifton used the Scene as his backup band. He also sat in with them at the Red Fox Inn.

Bill's box set of 8 CDs, *Around The World To Poor Valley* was issued by Bear Family Records in 2001. The booklet included in that set contains much information and photos with Duffey, Mike Seeger and others.

As of 2020, Bill and his wife Tineke are enjoying life in Virginia.

## Map Freak

Before the Gents, Tom Gray had been playing bluegrass three nights a week with Buzz Busby and Pete Pike at the Dock Restaurant in Lexington Park, Maryland outside the Patuxent Naval Air Station gates, a two-hour drive from Tom's house. Buzz and Pete were mainly doing every George Jones song they knew on this gig, with Buzz on electric guitar more than mandolin.

Meanwhile Tom attended George Washington University studying geography and cartography. "I had always been a map freak," Tom said. Although he would nap in the car going and coming from the Dock, playing music meant he couldn't keep his grades up in the literature and other courses that required much reading, so he dropped out of college in his fourth semester. "It was music or college, and music won," admits Tom.

"I applied at the National Geographic and got hired for an entry position for very low pay. My job was gluing the names [of cities, rivers, etc.] on maps. Somebody else compiled the names. Someone else drew the maps. And I really got into my job. I enjoyed arranging the names so that there would be no doubt in anyone's mind what each name refers to. I kept this entry level job for three years because I honestly enjoyed it."

Tom was in the Country Gents the last two of those years, and often played music until 2 am and then off to work by 8:30 in the morning. He decided to just play music and quit his day job.

While still working at National Geographic, Tom married Sally nee Govers (1940-2010). They had their first child, Lane. Sally worked as an editor at *Bluegrass Unlimited* magazine in the late 1960s.

Sally and Tom with their six-month-old son took a long drive throughout the country from Virginia to Alaska down to Mexico and back. While driving, Tom decided he'd visit his friends at National Geographic when he returned to reclaim his job. They hired him back with a raise. Tom went on to become an expert cartographer with an expertise in rivers. "They also put me in charge of a division which was a mistake because managing people was never my thing," Tom said.

Soon after, John Duffey gave his very first mandolin, to Tom's young son, Lane.

## Quitting the Gents

By 1964, Tom said he knew he'd have to leave The Country Gentlemen. The long hours in the band and on the road with the low pay of a full-time musician was taking a toll. In addition, he had heard the left-wing protest songs growing in popularity in the folk music market where the Gents often played and was not impressed with their political arguments. Gray and Duffey argued during the studio recording session of "A Cold Wind A' Blowin," a protest song co-written by John and Ann Hill about negative conditions a' brewing in America with lyrics like, "the hatred in their eyes I cannot understand."

Tom recalled, "I told John we should not be playing this song and that I did not want to do it. We were booked for shows in Canada and I didn't want to go outside America singing songs about why America is so rotten."

John strongly disagreed, saying, "This is the most commercial kind of thing we can do, and you're either going to have to play this song or get out of the band."

At that moment Tom decided to leave. "John could be harsh, and the statement about quitting the band over that song had been made and I had to stick by it. We had our disagreement there and I walked out of the studio with my bass fiddle to the car and bawled like a baby. I thought being in this band was the greatest thing in my life and here I am throwing it away."

John Duffey overdubbed the bass on the recording of that song himself, but he didn't let that be known on the record jacket. The credit went to "Big" Ed Ferris, Gray's replacement, an outstanding, cheerful bassist from Maryland who has backed such talents as Don Reno and Bill Harrell. Ferris (July 12, 1934 – June 24, 1993) would cite Jake Tullock, bassist for Flatt & Scruggs as his greatest musical influence.

Writer Lou Ellen Wilkie wrote in *Bluegrass Jamboree* in 2018: "Ed was known for his ability to keep a steady beat earning him nicknames such as "Metronome" and "Boom Boom." Through his regular studio work with *Rebel Records,* Ferris became one of the most recorded bluegrass bassist of all time."

Gray continued to play locally around the Washington, D.C., region in the mid and late 1960s with Buzz Busby, Leon Morris, Red Allen, Emerson and Waldron, and Benny and Vallie Cain, who he had first seen on 8th Street S.E. near the Marine barracks as a teenager.

In 1999, Tom reflected on the legacy of The Country Gentlemen in an interview with co-author G.T. Keplinger, "I was with The Country Gentlemen four years. That was from 1960 to 1964. It was a very exciting time. You know, I'm the luckiest guy in the world. I just happened to be in the right place at the right time in so many instances and this was one with The Country Gentlemen. Here I was only nineteen years old and, these guys who really were the most advanced thing in bluegrass at the time asked me to join.

"We played several nights a week at local clubs and then we started playing concerts at colleges. The folk music boom was starting then. And it was a good thing it did because at that time bluegrass was being excommunicated by the country music industry. You know, the country music industry was headed toward the Nashville sound a crossover sound and, things like banjos and fiddles, high singing didn't fit the mold. So, it was really being cut out of the only market it ever had so, fortunately the folk music boom came along at just the right time and all of these hillbillies became folk singers. You know, Flatt & Scruggs put out Hootenanny albums and so did the Stanley Brothers and so did The Country Gentlemen.

"At the time, we, regretted that we had used the name Country Gentlemen because our music wasn't country any more. A lot about the music certainly was very country but it didn't fit the mold of contemporary country any more. I think what John Duffey was trying to do with The Country Gentlemen he continued with more success with The Seldom Scene. That is, making bluegrass acceptable to the average person on the street in an urban or suburban area, as opposed to the previous generation of bluegrass players who were all country people. They were basically playing music of the country to people from the country. Well, there were a lot of city people who liked that music too. And John Duffey and I, and Bill Emerson, and others like us who grew up around the Washington area were very much the symbol of that. So, I think what John did with The Country Gentlemen is to sing songs that were a bit more contemporary and he would sing with a clear voice and enunciate so you can understand the words much better than people had done fifteen years earlier."

In late 1971, Tom rejoined his friend Duffey in John's second band, The Seldom Scene (See Chapter 13). In 1996, Tom became the first bassist to be inducted into the International Bluegrass Music

Association's Hall of Fame (IBMA) as a member of The Country Gentlemen, also the first bluegrass band inducted as an entity. He was inducted a second time when The original Seldom Scene became Hall of Fame members in 2014.

# Chapter 6: Eddie and Martha Adcock

© Eddie and Martha Adcock

*Eddie Adcock is more versatile and can do more things with a banjo than anyone. Musically, Eddie could land in a pile of shit and come out smelling good. He could always come up with something. That really helped the band when Eddie came with us because he was half loony anyway as well as a tremendous player...Eddie and I would throw lines at each other all night long. Sometimes it was corny and sometimes it was funny. And some of the early ideas like playing "Cripple Creek" at a slow speed were kind of collected between Eddie and myself.*

JD

Eddie Adcock was born in Scottsville, Virginia in 1938 about three hours south of D.C. As a teenager, he once sold a calf he raised to buy a banjo and was doing gigs with his older brother, Bill shortly afterward.

"My brother brought instruments home, and I'd try them. Thank you, Bill, for giving me a life of poverty," joked Eddie.

Bill and Eddie sang in nearby Charlottesville, Virginia churches and radio stations. Eddie left home when he was fourteen years old and began a semi-professional boxing career in addition to music. He later began racing and achieved 34 back-to-back wins with his car, "Mr. Banjo."

Eddie joined his first band, the James River Playboys, from 1948 to 1953, followed by Smokey Graves and His Blue Star Boys, 1954 to 1955, Mac Wiseman and the Country Boys, 1956, Bill Harrell and the Country Boys, 1956, and then Busby's group until the 1957 car accident. Before joining the "classic" Country Gentlemen in 1959, he worked for Bill Monroe for a year.

It was 1948 when Earl Scruggs resigned from Bill Monroe's Blue Grass Boys, citing the group's "exhaustive touring schedule." Bill tapped Don Reno, then Rudy Lyle, Ralph Stanley, Sonny Osborne and many others to fill his band's banjo spot.

When it was his turn, Eddie brought a new banjo style to Monroe's band—different from Earl Scruggs—chiefly because Eddie had started into music as a guitarist. Much of his technique was self-invented but included the popular Merle Travis thumb-rhythm, finger-picking guitar style as well as pedal-steel effects, string-bending, and improvisation that would extend to rock, jazz and even gospel territory. In 1996, the International Bluegrass Hall of Fame inducted Eddie with the Country Gents honoring him as "one of the truly original banjo stylists in bluegrass history."

Sixty years after his stint with Monroe, during a small gathering of pickers at the 2018 Joe Val Bluegrass Festival in Framingham, Massachusetts. Eddie was asked why he couldn't make a living playing banjo for the great Bill Monroe. Eddie answered, "Bill had four apartments for the four women he was screwing, and he had to pay for all of them. Those payments were more important than paying his musicians. The first night I worked with the Gents I made the same amount of money that I had made in a week with Monroe."

"It's been a big turnover in the way of the banjo pickers," Monroe would say in interviews when the topic of his parade of banjo players arose. Bill would also say that Eddie was the best baritone singer of all the Blue Grass Boys. High praise.

Eddie's wife and longtime musical partner, Martha added that this was at the time Elvis was surging in popularity. Many bluegrass groups disbanded as the demand for bluegrass music diminished. "Bill Monroe stuck it out," Martha said

Charlie Waller would say, "Eddie had such an unusual banjo style with a lot of feeling that we asked him if he'd join up with us. It worked out very well for a long time."

## Eddie's 2002 Interview

In a 2002 videotaped interview by co-author, G.T. Keplinger, Adcock talked about his career beginning with John Duffey:

"There ain't gonna be but one John Duffey. That's a cold, hard fact. He was 'one of a kind.' He didn't care what others were doing. He had no pre-conceived notions that got in the way of his creativity. He did what he did, and that's what he contributed to bluegrass. After that, all the mandolin players in the world could become as good as they could get and if they got up on stage with John, he could blow them away. And he wouldn't even have to play the mandolin. He could just blow them away, period. Just holding the mandolin and giving it a swat."

"We were a Yankee band. Whenever anyone asked where we were from, we'd say 'From the rolling hills of Washington, D.C.'" recalls Eddie. "The Country Gentlemen were more or less Osborne Brothers clones when I first went with them in '58. I had just left Bill Monroe and previously worked with Mac Wiseman. When they asked me to join them, I told them I would not do Osborne Brothers material. I was also really soured on music because I hadn't made any money with Bill Monroe."

Both Martha and Eddie believe that The Country Gentlemen rescued bluegrass from "sure death." Eddie said, "It was going to be absorbed by the country music and discarded. The Country Gentlemen breathed life into bluegrass because they didn't particularly care about following the code of traditional bluegrass. Even though we respected that tradition, we saw it as a dying thing. So, we started playing music that would appeal to the college crowd and that younger generation. That worked for us pretty quickly. By 1961 we were playing ten college dates a year and it grew from there."

Eddie agreed that the Gents were very mindful of their young, urban audiences. "We were playing at clubs like the Cellar Door, which booked either sophisticated acts or soulful acts. And we pulled those off."

"The music critics didn't like us. They wanted us to be more like Pete Seeger or the Kingston Trio," Eddie thinks. The Gents would poke fun at the Kingston Trio.

"They would hire us to perform at private parties in D.C.," Eddie revealed. "The Kingston Trio band members would love it when we made fun of them singing 'Tom Dooley.' They got off on it because they knew they weren't the greatest pickers."

The Carnegie Hall show gave them a shot at New York City. Eddie remembers, "From there we played, the Village Vanguard, the Village Gate, Gerde's Folk City—the major clubs at that time for Hootenanny type stuff."

When the Gents weren't on the road, Eddie would work Tuesdays and Thursdays at the Shamrock with them, and then play electric guitar with a country band on the other nights of the week. "Country music had such a presence on M Street Georgetown clubs then. The Gents packed the Shamrock on their nights, and bluegrass drew bigger crowds. I would know since I was in both bands."

Eddie said that the Grand Ole Opry was interested in inviting the Gents to join around the time "Bringing Mary Home" was a hit record if they could promise to play about twice a month in Nashville but the band didn't want to commit to that schedule.

Eddie was surprised when Duffey returned to music later with The Seldom Scene. "John took everything he learned from the Gents to The Seldom Scene."

Praising Eddie Adcock, John McEuen, of The Nitty Gritty Dirt Band told Nancy Cardwell in the May 2009 *Banjo Newsletter* magazine, "I have always been inspired by Eddie Adcock's forceful, yet not forced banjo playing and his pursuit of developing his art. ...Out of the box? In his box, more likely—that's what drew me to Eddie. He hit it hard like Don Reno, had chord sense like Bill Keith and played Scruggs-like rolls in a different way—with a drive of his own. 'Pallet on the Floor?' 'Heartaches?' Single strings tied into rolls? I grew to love that Adcock sound...grew to like it in about three minutes after I first heard him. I think it was 'Handsome Molly' and I still do."

## Eddie's Essay

In 2018 Eddie Adcock contributed the following essay for this book. His only request was to print it exactly as he wrote it.

I suppose there's really nobody around who knew John Duffey the way I did at a certain time and worked in a band with him at that time for about ten years. So, I don't feel like I have to glamorize him or the band, if people want to know about how things really were. They'll form their own opinions. By the way, I've always told Martha lots of things I remember about my life and music times, and she thought it was interesting enough to write a book, so she's been working on that for years.

The way John and I happened to eventually work together was because Bill Emerson had called Charlie Waller and John Duffey the day after Buzz Busby and I, and a couple of others from Buzz's band, were in a terrible car wreck one night after a show. Bill and I had been working with Buzz, and the wreck hurt three of us in the band so bad that it put us in the hospital, Bill had to call people to replace us for some upcoming shows that were booked, since he was the only one who hadn't gone with us and gotten hurt in that wreck that happened in the early morning hours of the Fourth of July, 1957. Since the rest of us were so messed up for quite a while—especially Buzz—that put-together bunch kept playing together, and soon they were calling themselves The Country Gentlemen.

People came and went in the band, including Bill Emerson; and after about a year and a half, in the early spring of 1959, John and Charlie came to my house and tried to get me to come to work with them. I'd come back from working with Bill Monroe—and starving out there—and because of the hard times bluegrass was going through in those Elvis days, I was freelancing and staying out of full-time bands. So, I said "no" to them because they didn't have any kind of track record, and I'd already played in the big leagues with Mac Wiseman and Monroe.

So, they tried and tried all night long to persuade me. And even though I loved Charlie's great rhythm guitar playing and really liked his singing, and thought John had a very strong voice, to me John's mandolin playing was just "regulation", not special. And at that point I just didn't want to commit to a total unknown band thing anyway. But when we finally sang some together, it only took a few bars for me to know our vocal trio was magic. With those three unique, excellent voices, we definitely had something to go with. And so, I agreed to be a member, as long as it was on a full partnership basis. By the way, we eventually developed musical ESP, and we could switch parts and change arrangements right on stage in the middle of a song, without notice, without a word, without even looking at each other. We just felt it. It proved to me that ESP existed, before I knew what it was, or had even heard of it.

But back when we started working together, John was a nobody who wanted to be somebody, but he didn't know how. He was really audience-shy at first, and did not know what to say to people on or off stage. So, he would just go blah-blah and say something rude.

[When asked to confirm Eddie's assertion, Tom Gray responded, "Eddie exaggerates this a bit, but it is true that Eddie and Charlie did handle much of the emcee work in the early days."]

Also, his teeth were terrible, which made him self-conscious. But he had a strong voice, and when he got more confidence, his solo singing got stronger. He was a little unsure at first. He was so insecure that he played and sang sideways, with his back mostly to the audience.

I had come from a background of playing and being entertaining any way you could, because when I was a young teenager I'd worked with Smokey Graves, who had a great country and bluegrass band called the Blue Star Boys that played shows and radio programs and dances up and down the East Coast. That was my first truly professional, full-time music job, and that's where I learned almost everything I needed to know to have a career in music. So, it was set in my mind to play and sing in my own way—be creative—and that I'd better be as entertaining as I could too, even if I had to be a clown and tell corny old jokes sometimes. Onstage with the Gentlemen I mostly made smart remarks and showed off with outrageous stunts—walking on stage rails, pretending to fall, jumping way down off the stage and stuff like that.

And so, John caught on to all that: I mean, the entertainment factor, and then playing in a unique way too and having his own style. He would try to mimic my jazzy banjo stuff and freewheeling attitude, and after one of my breaks he'd just play any weird notes he could come up with, any way he could play them. People liked it, though.

The band came into its own, and you probably know about what all it did and what it meant to bluegrass. Actually, we saved bluegrass music from certain death due to the new rock and roll and Elvis Presley's popularity. Everything else was folding. We revitalized bluegrass, gave it a whole new shot, expanded audiences, and put it on the map in a new way.

John never used to like to travel, though. It didn't suit him—he liked his routines in life. And by the latc 1960s, it got to where he'd rather stay around D.C. and go bowling. He was a pretty good bowler but not really the professional quality he'd like to have been. Nancy, his wife, was better at it, and he didn't like that.

But anyway, it got to where he didn't really want to go play music out of town on the weekends because of his bowling, and that's what caused real trouble. I told him, "We've got to do something, or you've got to get off the pot." So that was that. We'd had a good run and left a good thing behind, but I was ready to go too, and soon I left for California to make newer, fresh music. I'm proud of what we did, and I know the impact it had, so that makes me happy.

**Eddie's Surgery**

In October 2008, Eddie's hand-tremors began to impair his performing career. Doctors used deep brain stimulation (DBS) surgery at Vanderbilt University Medical Center to treat Eddie. A local anesthetic was used during this innovative surgery so that Eddie could remain conscious and be able to play banjo during the procedure to check the effectiveness of the treatment in progress. This ground-breaking surgery was a first to be performed on a musician to restore professional-level playing ability; and the resulting television, newspaper, radio and Internet publicity was explosive, amazing the entire world.

"I am blessed to have regained my banjo playing through this surgery," said Eddie after the surgery. "It's the most wonderful thing that ever happened in my life."

## Martha Hearon Adcock

On April 23, 2018, Martha Adcock, Eddie's wife and musical partner since 1973, graciously answered the following interview questions for this book.

Q: How did you meet Eddie?
A: I moved from South Carolina to Nashville, Tennessee, in the Spring of 1973, basically on what I thought of as the strengths of my singing and songwriting and having my own ideas and approach. A great deal of new, exciting music was happening there as a country-folk-songwriter-rock style was being born at the time, and I saw Nashville as the place for me to be. I knew I would grow there. And some music friends of mine from back home—Walter Hyatt, Champ Hood, and David Ball, collectively known as Uncle Walt's Band—had already made the serious jump I wanted to make.

Also, there was the happy coincidence of an invitation to a job working as an instrument craftsman in Nashville. Having recently worked for a time in Charlotte, North Carolina, at luthier C.E. Ward's shop doing pearl cutting and inlay, on word-of-mouth recommendation I was invited by Randy Wood to come to work for him doing that at the Old Time Picking Parlor on Second Avenue North in Nashville.

The Picking Parlor was easily the most happening place in town, where musicians gathered to socialize and jam, buy themselves a vintage instrument or have theirs repaired, or have a new one custom-made. It was located in a row of old brick buildings on a downtown street not far above the Cumberland River, and the adjacent connected building was turned into a nightclub to serve the folks of the burgeoning new-music scene. In my first weeks at the Picking Parlor I met, got to know, hung out with, and jammed with a breathtaking array of stars, high-profile journeymen, and soon-to-be stars, from Roy Acuff to John Hartford, Vassar Clements, Leon Russell, Vic Jordan, Norman Blake, Mac Wiseman, and Marty Stuart, plus a hundred more. It was heady stuff for me and confirmed my decision to move to that town. There the emphasis was on music as something inventive, real, and necessarily excellent. And the picker who made the biggest impact on me was Eddie Adcock. One sentence in that night's short journal entry reads simply, "Eddie Adcock came in and knocked me out."

Q: What do you admire most about his musical talents?
A: Even though I'm from a musical family and had been exposed to a lot of great live and recorded music early in my lifetime, from classical to R&B, Eddie was the best musician I ever heard, bar none: the most creative and able talent I had ever witnessed. It seemed he could play anything in any style, and play anything for as long as he wanted to and never run out of ideas, constantly challenging himself in unbelievable musical flights. He intimately knew every single centimeter of a fingerboard. He could convey tremendous emotion, too, in his playing. He just seemed to have a direct line to Music Itself, but he always referred to it as 'fishing in the river of notes.' Whatever musical idea entered his head could just come right out of his fingers instantly.

Q: What would be your top three favorite Country Gentlemen recordings and why?
A: That's harder to answer than you'd think it would be, because for me it's really difficult to choose. First, let me just say that of the total recordings that constitute bluegrass music, The Country Gentlemen's recordings are my favorite. They had an amazing magic sound, and their irrepressible spirit comes through.

"Matterhorn" is one of my favorite songs. It is the way Eddie's Epiphone banjo sounds capo'ed up in D, like a golden hammer hitting a silver anvil. And, of course, it's the vocal trio; and it's the song: the music—the melody and chord progression—and the lyrics telling such an affecting story. Sometimes at home when I'm running through some songs and really thinking of them, that song moves me a lot, even chokes me up.

I love all of Eddie's instrumentals, and "Nightwalk" is a real standout to me because it's so different, being in a minor key and with a lot of punch and syncopation. We recorded it on our *Many A Mile* CD. "This Morning At Nine", a great hammer-down set-ending song, is on that CD too, which was all basically some of our favorite Gents songs. And we put Eddie's beautiful, sentimental, autobiographical "Uncle Joe" on our *TwoGrass* CD. And I love Eddie's song "Let's"—that one went on *TwoGrass* also; it has great lyrics, and the way it flies along is so exhilarating. Then Eddie's song "The Sentence" is a true story in that it came to him in a dream, and that's the way the song is written too. He had an epiphany about the awfulness of capital punishment—an unusual lyrical subject—and the song has a lot of impact, just smacks you in the face.

Q: When did you meet John Duffey and what were your initial impressions of him?
A: Actually, I really don't remember the very first time I met John Duffey! It likely would have been either at a club in D.C., like the Red Fox, or at a bluegrass festival on the East Coast, probably not long after Eddie and I met. When Eddie and I met we instantly became a couple, and in short order I had left off working at the Old Time Picking Parlor in Nashville and begun traveling with Eddie and his band, II Generation, running the

sound board for them at concerts for a few months until I joined the band. Though he had moved the band to Nashville at the behest of booking agent Don Light, Eddie often gravitated back to the D.C. area, his old stomping grounds.

Well, so John was his own thing, quite the unique individual, and I'm sure that's the first impression I had about him when we met, whenever and wherever that was.

Q: Did you become good friends with John Duffey?
A: John and I automatically had a good, comfortable relationship, given the length and strength of his and Eddie's own relationship; and I was prepared to like and respect him because of Eddie and because of what they had accomplished together. Their own relationship hadn't been perfect, as I was to hear over the years, but Eddie always maintained that John was 'an old sweetie-pie,' which he certainly could be. John was known to many as a very stand-offish or even rude person, but he couldn't seem to help that; and the only time I was ever on the receiving end of an oddly 'off' comment from him, it seemed to be sort of an accident, as if he wanted to say something but didn't know what to say or how to say it. He was often a little flirtatious with me, but only in a complimentary way, and only in the presence of others.

Q: Various articles and interviews refer to the "outrageous antics" of Duffey and Eddie in their stage appearances with the Gents. What would be specific examples?
A: Eddie has always told me he brought into the Gents his 'entertain-or-die' philosophy, and that after a while the spirit infected the rest of the band. Eddie said that within a year's time, "John picked up on it after listening

to the applause I'd get not only for solos but for the silly things I'd say and do off the top of my head. Like, I'd say I needed to tune my banjo, and I'd pull my little booking calendar out of my back pocket and pretend to thumb through it. Then I'd look at a page, tune one string, turn another page and look at that and tune another string, and so on. The audience would just roar. Or I'd step right off a tall stage, maybe even six feet, pretending to fall, and John and the rest of the guys would react to that. The first time I ever pulled it, they had no warning, and their reaction was genuinely horrified."

Eddie continues, "We started doing "Cripple Creek", really fast, just to have another rapid instrumental to throw in on the show, since we'd do five sets a night sometimes. And one day onstage I just decided for kicks to play it really slow, and then I sang it distorted like a slowed-down record, and then kicked it back off real fast. It worked great for the crowd. When we started doing it onstage as a regular bit, the trio would sing it real slow and act it out too, moving in slow motion. People loved it.

This really got John in on doing stuff, because the audience loved us being funny, and that became part of our reputation. The Country Gentlemen kept it as a routine even after I'd been gone from the band for years, and over the years other bands have copied it too."

There was an uptick in Charlie's onstage presence as well, as he, "started being a little more active too, smiling more and doing his leg-dip." He would occasionally make a droll comment, although, "there wasn't nearly enough of that from him, because we knew how funny he could be offstage. He had some great one-liners. But he said he couldn't feel them right when he was onstage."

Eddie states, "When John had opened up, so to speak, we'd enjoy doing comic stuff together, as well as making smart remarks, of course. Like, I'd be doing 'Mocking Banjo' and acting crazy, and at one point John or somebody would pretend to try to stop me from getting into the mic to play the chorus where I'd really take off and rip it up, so he, or sometimes Tom would just pick me up off the floor, and I'd curl my feet up under me and kick a little bit. Charlie would order him to put me down, and John would drop me on my rear end, and I would bounce a couple of times and get up rubbing my butt. You wouldn't see it, but having my feet under me cushioned the fall.

"Also, on 'Mocking Banjo', the whole thing became a shtick. I usually played the first part and John played the copy part, but sometimes I'd start to go into another break and push John away, saying it was still my turn. Then I'd pretend to slip, and I'd fall toward John at the mic. My left elbow would catch in the crook of his right elbow and stop me from falling, and people would gasp because they thought there was going to be a big crash. But then I'd right myself and take my break.

"Offstage one day John kidded me, saying he was gonna let me miss hooking onto his arm, and then I'd really fall and bust my tail on the floor, and the banjo too. So, I said, 'Go ahead', I'll catch your belt with the crook of my fingers on the way down and pull your pants off!

"Then John got into doing his gay shtick. Now and then he would answer a funny comment from me in a gay-sounding voice, and it just went from there. Some people were offended, most not. We recorded 'Big Bruce' which went well, and we even began to develop a small gay following for a while, until one of the owners of the Shamrock, where we played every week, insisted out of his own prejudice and fear of 'turning the Shamrock into a gay bar' that we quit doing the song there.

"Another thing John liked to do now and then was to let out a really loud growling yell right into the mic during a song, and it would scare the audience to death. Then they'd laugh out of pure shock."

Q: Will you describe some of the anniversary shows you and Eddie have participated in?

A: (Martha continues) It's too bad we weren't in the Washington D.C. area for the Scene's 15th anniversary show at the Kennedy Center. Our new band Talk Of The Town, was pretty hot and out on the road touring most of the time, and we had just driven back from the West Coast. And on November 10, 1986 —I looked up the date of the show's recording—we had just gotten home to Nashville and were resting up.

We had actually, however, recently played the Kennedy Center just prior to that, on August 13 of 1986, as part of the big Legends of Bluegrass tour which featured Bill Monroe, Ralph Stanley, Mac Wiseman, and Jim & Jesse. Talk Of The Town backed up Mac as well as playing our own show.

As for anniversaries, on July 4, 1982, we had been part of a huge Country Gentlemen 25th Anniversary reunion concert at Wolf Trap in northern Virginia, featuring as many former Gents as could get there, and who played in several different configurations. It was a major event; and it was well-covered by the press, since the Gents had always been the darlings of the D.C. crowd.

But the Gents' 50th Anniversary celebration concert in 2007, held at Watermelon Park near Berryville, Virginia, was likely the largest event of all; there was a tremendous turnout with old friends, fans and all kinds of folks long connected to the band coming out of the woodwork to be there for that. In the enormous crowd circulating the festival grounds I met a number of people whom Eddie had told me about for so many years that they had attained near-mythic status to me! Everyone missed Duffey, though, and all lamented his too-early passing.

Q: What are your all-time favorite musical experiences in your career?

A: Looking back on forty-five years-full of a memorable musical life—and that's only my time with Eddie in mostly bluegrass—it's impossible to select specific events, so I'll go with situations or spaces of time: My most consciousness-raising and spirited musical time was with our band II Generation, because it was very heady to do something new and unlooked-for and wonderful. There was stratospheric musical talent in there, with Eddie who could play anything he thought of—and he thought of a lot of things!—and who had that beautiful, powerful baritone voice... amazing Gene Johnson on tenor vocals and unlimited mandolin... heart-of-the-beat Johnny Castle on electric bass, who could dance at the same time so that we called him bionic... and Jeff Wisor, who wasn't afraid to reach for the heights on fiddle, and always got up there. It was truly synergy, and it was the band I had dreamed of, naturally synthesizing its own form of bluegrass-rock-folk-country-jazz-blues, And, by the way, going back as far as The Country Gentlemen, Eddie is the true "Father of Newgrass" music. The word "newgrass" was a natural extension of "bluegrass", and it spontaneously popped into his mind as a personal musical descriptor back when Sam Bush was still just a pup. While The Country Gentlemen really broke through the fence of what

92

bluegrass had been, II Generation blew the fence apart completely and took us all to entirely new pastures.

Another important component of my musical life has been, simply, the people. And of them all, bluegrass musicians and fans everywhere are literally my family, the best family anyone could want, the best group of people you can find. They mean so much to me. I really learned to love people because of them.

And the places I've been fortunate to go have had tremendous impact on me... getting to know intimately this whole gorgeously varied country... touring the world and getting paid to do it. It's been amazing. Who would have thought you could get homesick for faraway places? Sometimes, though, you're traveling so fast that you might pass by the road going up to, say, the Grand Canyon a couple dozen times before you have a chance to stop there."

Martha and Eddie, 2019 © S. Moore

# Chapter 7: The Gents' Break Through

In 1933, First Lady Eleanor Roosevelt attended a "Folk music festival" held at White Top Mountain in Virginia. President Roosevelt also posed with a hillbilly string band at Warm Springs, Georgia. One year later, they began hosting concerts by hillbilly musicians at the White House.

Music historian Bill C. Malone estimates over 300 music clubs and bars catering to government and military personnel emerged in the D.C. area during the subsequent war years. Many featured hillbilly music where musicians, as Roy Clark noted, "would fight their way in, play a little music, and fight their way out." Mike Seeger, like John Duffey, was too young to frequent these bars, but both were fascinated by the music and listened to it on D.C. radio in their teen years.

Mike was the son of musicologist Charles Seeger and half-brother of folk music icon, Pete Seeger who had joined the military in 1943. Charles moved his family from New York City to Washington D.C. suburb, Chevy Chase, Maryland to work as a technical advisor to the Music Unit of the Special Skills Division of FDR's Farm Security Administration. Mike and his sister, Peggy attended Bethesda-Chevy Chase high school. Peggy was John Duffey's classmate.

Mike had helped Alan Lomax catalog his field recordings of rural American blues singers for the Smithsonian—the same catalog that Duffey would frequently peruse in search of "new" material for the Country Gents. Mike's keen interest in early folk and country music inspired him to learn claw hammer banjo, guitar, and autoharp. He became close friends with Richard "Dick" Spottswood.

Today Spottswood is an iconic record collector and legendary radio broadcaster. He received the Lifetime Achievement Award from the Association of Recorded Sound Collections in 2003, and the Distinguished Achievement Award from the International Bluegrass Music Association in 2009. His current radio show, "The Dick Spottswood Show" is streamed on the *Bluegrass Country* Internet website, as well as local FM HD2 radio in the Washington area.

Mike Seeger later founded the New Lost City Ramblers folk group. Bob Dylan, autobiography *Chronicles* (Simon & Schuster, 2004) noted that Mike Seeger was, "Unprecedented. As for being a folk musician, he was the supreme archetype."

By the time Mike was sitting in with The Country Gentlemen playing autoharp at the Shamrock, he was also working at the Capitol Transcriptions studio, mainly taping political speeches and events, including then Soviet Premier Nikita Khrushchev's 1959 visit to D.C. At this time, Seeger also produced a ground-breaking anthology, *Mountain Music Bluegrass Style* for Folkways records.

Folkways, a New York City label founded in 1948, was an early promoter of Woody Guthrie, Pete Seeger, Huddie "Lead Belly" Ledbetter [usually written as 'Leadbelly," Lead Belly is how he wrote his name and how it appears on his tombstone] and the new American folk music revivalists. When Mike began looking to record some modern bluegrass performers, The County Gentlemen were the most innovative, and Mike knew and respected them. Duffey and band gladly accepted his offer to produce their 1960 album, *Country Songs: Old and New* recorded at the Capitol Transcriptions studio. *Country Songs: Old and New* was indeed the Gents' first album. The Starday recordings before that time were all 45rpm singles. The Starday LPs were released later.

Pete Kuykendall helped choose the material for this album. Among the old songs were "Poor Ellen Smith," a 19th-century murder ballad, and "Jesse James," another folk song first recorded by Bentley Ball in 1919 [and subsequently by many others, including Woody Guthrie, Pete Seeger, Van Morrison Johnny Cash, and Bruce Springsteen]. "The Little Sparrow," and "Weeping Willow," were other traditional ballads included on the album.

Before recording was invented, traditional ballads like these were printed on inexpensive paper called broadsides dating back to the 16th century. Topics of broadside ballads included love, religion, drinking songs, legends, and budding journalism. Printed broadside ballads helped perpetuate the oral tradition of these folk songs.

Newer songs on the Gents album, like "The Story of Charlie Lawson," represented an early 20th-century hillbilly tune. "Tomorrow's My Wedding Day," aka "I Ain't Gonna Work Tomorrow," was an example of straight ahead "tradition of bluegrass". And one song, "Long Black Veil," was a 1959 hit song for Grand Ole Opry star, Lefty Frizzell. Many '60s folksingers like The Kingston Trio covered it, and it has become a bluegrass and country music standard. Joan Baez picked the Gents version to record.

Tom Gray elaborates, "Actually, the Kingston Trio, wanting to learn "Long Black Veil," invited The Country Gentlemen to jam with them privately. We (John, Charlie, Eddie, and Tom) jammed with the Kingston Trio in a conference room of the Jefferson Hotel in D.C. John said, "They want to pick our brains."

Two original instrumentals, "Turkey Knob," by Eddie Adcock, and "Honky Tonk Rag," by John Duffey were included, as was "The Double Eagle," aka "Under The Double Eagle," a 1902 march written by composer Josef Wagner. This march was a favorite of another Washingtonian, John Phillip Sousa, the "March King." On the Gents version, Charlie Waller flat picks the lead riffs on guitar.

John, Charlie, and Jim Cox
© Jim Cox, Jr.

"Smooth, folk-like bluegrass," "stunning harmonies," "crisp banjo" and "smart mandolin" were typical accolades in *Country Songs: Old and New* album reviews. Listeners discovered two extraordinary lead vocalists in Charlie Waller and John Duffey, with Eddie Adcock's beautiful baritone. Jim Cox played bass. It didn't hurt album sales that it followed a long essay in Esquire magazine by Alan Lomax on bluegrass. *Country Songs: Old and New* was the first album to connect to the Greenwich Village folk revivalists to set in motion a new progressive bluegrass movement, of which the Gents were the innovators.

They quickly returned to the studio to record their next LP, *Folksongs and Bluegrass* and would record a live album *On The Road* before leaving the Folkways label for Rebel Records. In 1987, The Smithsonian Institute acquired Folkways to become *Smithsonian Folkways*. Three years later they re-issued *Country Songs: Old and New* in a 30th-anniversary edition. *The Washington Post* wrote: "This is a crucial album in bluegrass history, introducing Charlie Waller, John Duffey, Eddie Adcock, and Tom Gray with their superb instrumentals and innovative melding of the high lonesome sound of the Stanley Brothers and the close trio harmony of the Osborne Brothers."

Bill C. Malone concludes in his Seeger biography, *Music From The True Vine* [University of North Carolina Press, 2011]: "Mike never lost interest in bluegrass, and over the years he performed and recorded extensively with such musicians as Bill Clifton, Don Reno, Red Rector, Don Stover, Ralph Stanley, The Country Gentlemen, Hazel and Alice, and other entertainers in that genre. He was beginning to feel, however, that bluegrass had become predictable and unchallenging, and that Scruggs-style banjo playing, for all its technical brilliance, lacked the diversity and soulfulness of the old-time styles. Therefore, despite his immersion in the bluegrass scene, Mike's heart remained wedded to the old-time sounds and styles that he first heard when he was a child."

## Neil Rosenberg

In May 1961, Neil Rosenberg, then a student musician, helped the Gents get their first college gig as the featured group at a concert in the Oberlin College auditorium. The crowd gave them an enthusiastic welcome, and John Duffey quickly saw a market opportunity for The Country Gentlemen doing college gigs and aggressively pursued leads for bookings. Dr. Rosenberg is now Professor Emeritus of Folklore at Memorial University and author of many scholarly books on bluegrass.

Four months later the Gents were invited to join Pete Seeger and other acts including Hedy West, Alan Mills, Jean Carignan, Bessie Jones, Odetta, and "Rambin" Jack Elliott at a *Hootenanny at Carnegie Hall* in 1961. Tom Gray recalls Odetta on the program: "As a matter of fact, you can see her close-cropped Afro head sitting onstage behind the Gents on the cover photo of the *Bluegrass at Carnegie Hall* album. That photo was taken by George McCeney."

*New York Times* reviewer, Robert Shelton, reviewed the Gents at this show as, "A five-man bluegrass band from Fairfax, Virginia, The Country Gentlemen, had clean vocal harmonies, and the mandolin playing of John Duffey was outstanding, but the over-all ensemble effect was lackluster. Bluegrass has not sprouted often in Carnegie Hall, so the use of a more seasoned group might have made a better case for the exciting, stringband style."

Shelton is credited with writing one of the first reviews of an unknown Bob Dylan. Despite singling out

John Duffey as "outstanding" in the *New York Times*, Duffey was angry that Shelton called the band's performance 'lackluster,' yet he acknowledged that, *"All of a sudden, I started to become somebody,"* when he read Shelton's review.

In his *Bluegrass Memoir* (University of Illinois Press, 2018) Dr. Rosenberg cites a letter John wrote to him after the show. "We played Carnegie Hall last night and sold well to the people but not to the critics. The people at Folkways [records] said we were just 'too slick for them.' They still want this music in the raw. From the looks of the other performers (Pete Seeger included), we made a big mistake in dressing and shaving."

**Dick Cerri**
Broadcaster Richard Anthony "Dick" Cerri had a profound effect in promoting folk and bluegrass radio in the D.C. area. A Utica, New York native, he became involved in music with his high school choir and became a radio announcer on Utica station, WBIX-AM. He came to Washington, D.C. in 1960 to work at station WAVA, formerly WARL, just as it was moving from country music to all news.

"The station owner wanted to keep some of the old listeners, so he started a *Music Americana* program," said Cerri in a 2006 interview with co-author, G.T. Keplinger. He told G.T. that he mainly took the nighttime program so he'd have time to look for a real job during the day.

"I knew a few music acts like The Kingston Trio and the Brothers Four, so I had a little fun with them in the studio. But then the phone calls started coming in," said Cerri.

"When are you going to start playing folk music?" the listeners wanted to know.

Cerri learned from a record distributor that the folk music his listeners were requesting was more haunting and beautiful Joan Baez and not so much, the smooth harmonies and light-weight material of the Brothers Four.

After research and many discussions, Cerri soon demonstrated a respected expertise through his *Music Americana* broadcast. It would become a seven night a week, five-hour folk music radio program. With folksinger Tom Paxton, Dick founded the World Folk Music Association in 1982 to support and connect folk music fans and artists.

In 1986 he told *The Washington Post*, "I don't have a degree in musicology or years of study on a musical instrument. To me, those are the experts. I'm a little embarrassed by that label. I have never looked at this music as scholarship. I guess my mind remembers a lot of things about the people I met and the music I played. I consider myself a professional spectator."

Early on in his Washington career, he met and befriended The Country Gentlemen, booked them at an Ocean City, Maryland club and began managing them. He arranged their first tour of Canada. "I got messages and letters from John Duffey complaining everyday about something concerning that Canada tour," Cerri said with a smile.

"Bluegrass musicians are often the most talented musicians around and when you find a band like The Country Gentlemen that sounded so good, you could bring anybody to see them and they'd become a fan that night. I later became friends with Mike Auldridge and he invited me to come see The Seldom Scene at the Red Fox. When I got there, I couldn't get in. It was packed. Fortunately, Duffey saw me in the door and yelled from stage, 'Let that man in.'"

"After that I used to go out of my way to bring friends who had told me they didn't like bluegrass music to see them. My friends were always won over."

"It was a little like hitting the donkey over the head with a two-by-four. To get his attention. The Seldom Scene got your attention. And you wanted more."

"I had a fellow from the National Symphony Orchestra drop by my studio once. He played the oboe.

"He said, 'You know, that bluegrass music you play is very similar to classical music.'

"I said, 'Sit down and tell me.' The oboe player proceeded to point out similarities like harmonies, drive, timing, techniques, etc. It was very gratifying to listen to how he came to really appreciate bluegrass," Cerri admitted.

In 1974, John Duffey told *Bluegrass Unlimited* writer, Pat Mahoney: "I listened to Dick Cerri play on one of his 'side by sides' on the radio the other day. He played 'Heaven' which Flatt & Scruggs did. Then he played our [Seldom Scene] recording of it. We were listening to the background. Both records have Dobro. On the Flatt & Scruggs version—and with no offense to anybody—you had a lot of 'hot licks,' that's the easiest way I can think to describe it in a song that really doesn't call for hot licks. And in Mike Auldridge's background you know there was the right thing at the right time."

Dick Cerri died October 3, 2013 at Holy Cross Hospital in Silver Spring. He was 77. The cause was congestive heart failure, said his daughter, Debbi Cerri.

**George McCeney**
Born in Baltimore in 1939, and raised in Laurel, Maryland, George McCeney was a teacher, bluegrass musician, and co-founder of *Bluegrass Unlimited*

magazine. For years George wrote music reviews for the magazine, and his support for The Country Gentlemen was enthusiastic and unwavering.

He also served on the Board of Directors of the International Bluegrass Music Museum and was a longtime supporter of the IBMA's Leadership Bluegrass program.

In 2004, co-author, G.T. talked with George about his beloved bluegrass and one favorite performer, John Duffey. The discussion began with the first time George saw a professional bluegrass show.

"I was 13 in the '50s and noticed a poster on our national guard armory in Laurel that Mac Wiseman was doing a New Year's Eve show. It was expensive. $15 a ticket which was big money. My friend and I saved enough to buy two tickets and arrived at 8 pm for the show. People were sitting at big white tables and it was probably BYOB, but we didn't care about that. We were there to see the show.

"Mac came out on stage and opened his set with 'Going Like Wildfire.' I'll never forget it. Unfortunately, when Mac finished the last lick of the song some guy stood up and made an awful comment to a woman and cracked a beer bottle over the head of the guy she was with. A huge fight erupted. A maelstrom. My friend and I headed for the door because there were beer bottles flying. It was a short show for me."

"When I first saw The Country Gentlemen at the Crossroads bar in the late '50s, their audience was suburban but certainly not a white-collar crowd. This was not the kind of music your parents brought home on LP's. And it wasn't popular with kids. It was music written by, made by, and appreciated by adults. And I think The Country Gentlemen would have become famous anywhere they started, and not just because they were in Washington, D.C."

On many nights George would stop by John Duffey's house after the Crossroads gigs and spend time talking with him. "John was like me in that we were both curious about things. The more I think about John Duffey, the more remarkable he becomes as a creative force. Some people don't like his sound. I loved it. But nobody can deny his level of creativity. He'd go out one way and if it worked, then great he would go with it. If it didn't work then he'd step back and try something else. Of all the musicians from the Washington area, you'd have to say that John Duffey was the most creative and the most dynamic. He had the energy. Each of The Country Gentlemen (John, Charlie, Eddie, and Tom) were innovators. They became an enormously influential band. The legacy they created. They laid out a tremendous groove that other musicians were getting. When they were forming the band, they were so fortunate to have found John. What would have happened to bluegrass music if John hadn't been around?"

George once attended a banjo convention near Hagerstown, Maryland. One event was Pete Seeger, Béla Fleck, Bill Emerson, Pete Kuykendall, Tommy Neal, and Roni Stoneman on stage for a symposium called "The Good Old Days" with the topic, "What was it like to play the Baltimore-Washington area in the '50s and early '60s?"

"These places were really not clubs," George said with a laugh, "They were bars. I personally knew everyone on stage except Roni Stoneman, but of course knew of her from the *Hee Haw* TV show. When each of them had talked about the bars and their experiences playing in the area I stood up and gave them an extended 'thank you' for all the years they had played for us. Roni Stoneman pointed at me and said 'I know you. You came into the Famous Bar in 1963 wearing a suit. You were the only person that night who was listening to us.'"

"I thought it remarkable that she would remember that. And how wonderful and generous these musicians were."

George passed away in August, 2018 at the age of 79.

# Chapter 8: Sam, Rick, Pete, and John

Ginger and Rick Allred. 2018 © S. Moore

**G**inger and Rick Allred live in Mount Airy, North Carolina. In March, 2018 they generously provided their memories, family documentation, and photographs for this book.

Ginger Marie "Sam" Allred is John Duffey's biological daughter, born May 23, 1959 in Washington, D.C. to John and Marion Cain Duffey. Since "Sam" is her bluegrass family nickname, we refer to her as Sam in this profile.

She acquired the nickname while her mom was pregnant. As John was leaving for a show he would say,

"Are you and Sam coming?" The name came from a switchboard operator on a popular TV detective show, *Richard Diamond, Private Detective.* Viewers only saw the operator's hands and legs but could hear her voice. It turns out that "Sam" was actress Mary Tyler Moore in her first regular TV role.

Later, her Mom found out that Ginger was also the name of one of John's old girlfriends, so she began to call her Sam, too.

Sam began her story with her mom's youngest brother, Uncle "Sonny" (Norris B. Cain, Jr.). Sam recalls, "He was a big bluegrass fan and took my mother, Marion to the Crossroads bar to see The Country Gentlemen in 1958. This is where she met John. As sometimes happens, I began before the wedding bells. John and Mom married but separated when I was about four years old."

One of Sam's few memories of her life with John when she was little came about when her Mom persuaded her to put ice on John's back while he was sleeping. "It was a joke. I was a toddler and John woke up screaming," said Sam. "As most musicians do, he'd stay out and play at night and sleep into the day. My Mom wanted him to get up and set me out to get him awake the quickest way. Of course, it came with a few bad words at the sudden awakening!"

Sam's life took a twist at the age of 5 when John and Marion divorced. Pete Kuykendall was a close friend of John's who was also a member of The Country Gentlemen during the early years of the group. Later Pete recorded the Gentlemen in his home studio. When he would visit John's home, he called Marion by a nickname, "Moron" and that irritated her. However, it must not have been too bad as he was the second person she dated after John had left the marriage.

107

John had developed a relationship with Nancy Mitchell, who he met at the club and enjoyed ballroom dancing together. They later married and stayed together until John's death. Marion briefly dated Nancy's husband Jimmy after John and Nancy left their spouses for each other. Pete stepped into Marion's life and took on the duty of raising Sam after marrying Marion on October 5, 1964.

John's mother Florence I. Duffey and his father, John Humbird Duffey, Sr. were the only grandparents Sam was able to spend much time with. Her mother's parents both died during her younger years. Florence called her Ginger and she remained close to her paternal grandparents until their deaths. "Granddaddy", as she called John, Sr., was a quiet man, due to his severe hearing loss and by Sam's teen years, had many health problems. He affectionately gave her the nickname, "Tiddlywinks" for the game they frequently played together on her summer visits.

Sam's prominent memories of her grandfather were him being sick often and she noted he had two or three heart attacks, and other health problems. He was in his late seventies when she was born. However, his mind remained sharp until his passing at age 94. She thought that John may have had, "some sort of falling out" with his father but isn't sure. She noted that he dropped the "Junior" from his name when he was older. Sam noted, "I never saw John talking with Granddaddy much. My Mom told me that when John started playing and singing bluegrass music, Granddaddy told him, 'If you're going to sing that mess, you better do it right and not sing through your nose.' Granddaddy had been a professional opera singer and I'm not sure he liked traditional bluegrass very much based on that comment."

"John was the center of my Grandma's world and she deliberately doted on her only child. I remember she would tell me that when he came over for breakfast, she'd fix him several eggs and bacon." Sam adds. "After Mom and John divorced, my Grandma wasn't about to let me go. I was a big part of her world, too. I'd stay with her a week each summer and visit at Christmas."

When Sam got her driver's license she would visit more frequently. After she moved to North Carolina Sam's Grandma called her almost every night. "I would get a little aggravated. This was before cordless phones and I'd be stretching the phone in the kitchen trying to cook. She'd call then because she knew I'd be home then from work. I still miss her and wish I could get those calls again," said Sam.

Four-year-old Sam with her mom, Marion.
© G. Allred

At 10 years old, Sam was given an A-50 mandolin by her father Pete Kuykendall when she showed interest in learning how to play an instrument. While at an Ohio bluegrass festival show with Pete and Marion, she met up with John. He was filling in for for Jimmy Gaudreau in The Country Gentlemen. Jimmy was fulfilling his annual commitment to the National Guard. Sam was hoping John would show her some mandolin licks. He was always nice to her but always a little distant.

By the time John was in The Seldom Scene, his mother was living in an apartment in Bethesda, Maryland. Sam was old enough to go to the nearby Red Fox Inn. John would sometimes come by and take her to the Scene's shows during her summer visits with her Grandma.

After John, Sr. passed away, Florence moved to Arlington, Virginia, living in an apartment closer to John. During visits with Grandma, Sam would later drive to see him at the Birchmere.

Sam recalls that she once had an opportunity when she was 14 years old to go on a beach trip with John and Nancy and some others.

"It was Ocean City, Maryland in July. Nancy's daughter Darcy, and I went along with them on a beach trip. We thought it may have been dual purpose because we would babysit Mike and Elise Auldridge's young daughter and their dog when they went out to eat, as well as enjoy the beach and amusement park. Mike and his family were in an adjoining room, but John had control of the thermostat for both rooms. "I heard John plotting a practical joke, telling Nancy, 'We're going to freeze them out.' He turned the air conditioning all the way down which controlled the temperature in Mike and Elise's room too."

"A couple of hours later Mike came over wearing a coat, knocking on the door. John answered to hear Mike say, 'What are you trying to do to us?' There was almost frost on Mike's windows. It *was* funny." John frequently expressed his entertainer's talent through practical jokes.

Another favorite prank was when the musician, Bill Clifton was over to John's house one Thanksgiving. Bill had told John that he liked the turkey skin the best. One year later, Bill was back at home in England, and on tour. John took all the skin off the Thanksgiving turkey, stuffed it in a manila envelope with a, "Because you like the turkey skin the best" note to Bill, and mailed it to England. When Bill returned from touring, he had a message from the post office asking him to pick up the envelope quickly, "because it smells."

July 1973 in John's parents' apartment
© G. Allred

Sam confirmed that, "John was an animal lover, especially dogs. He had a Pekinese and a Saint Bernard named Cuddles. His last Saint Bernard was Rumbles. When Rumbles died, John told me it was his last pet because it upset him so much when they died. The next time I visited him at his house he showed me how he had trained a squirrel to come to his sliding back door and tap on the door. John would let him in and feed him peanuts. The squirrel would eat a few peanuts and then go back out. John had a pet skunk at one time, descented of course, but it kept biting Nancy on the ankles."

Despite the pet-loving and practical jokes, Sam admitted she was a little bit intimidated by her biological father. "He could be ominous at times," admits Sam, "and I was always struggling with our relationship internally. I would have liked knowing him better. I always got along very well with Nancy," she said. "She was the one who called me and told me when my Grandma died."

John, Sam, and Nancy at The Bluegrass Classic Bahamas
Getaway, Freeport, Bahamas in April 1991.© G. Allred

Sam's husband Rick Allred was nineteen years old
when he joined Charlie Waller's 1979 Country
Gentlemen replacing Doyle Lawson. The Gentlemen were
playing at the Birchmere on Wednesdays, and The
Seldom Scene were there on Thursdays. Rick would go
to see them often

"For me, John was always easier to talk with when
he had that liquid courage," Rick observed. Sam agrees:
"John on stage wasn't the same person as John at
home. You never saw him performing without a cup
because I think really, he was a very shy person and his
'totty's', as he referred to them, were necessary for him
to be John the entertainer on stage."

Rick recalls, "He once told me that I could play better mandolin than him, but he could sell it. He made me understand that no matter how many clean notes I play it didn't attract that audience member watching if I was simply standing there."

Rick admires how John knew, "when to play and when not to play, should it be soft or hard, etc. And his voice made the Scene."

"His voice was his main instrument," said Sam. "His mandolin style was unique and when he was in the Gents he was 'on it.'"

## First Couple Visit

Rick describes the first time he and Sam went to John's house as a couple. John had been talkative with Rick at clubs and festivals but now acted very differently in his own home.

"I'm sitting in his living room in a recliner and he's in his recliner. I notice he has six recliners in his living room. No couch. He's not saying anything and I'm pretty shy and not much of a talker too. I mention he has a nice pool table, and he says go ahead and play if you want. Then he says nothing else. I'm thinking 'who is this guy?'"

Sam and Nancy did all the talking for a while and then John broke his silence by telling Rick that Gibson had made a mandolin for him. Rick asked,

"How it is?"

John answers, "It's a piece of crap. You want it? Go ahead, and you can take it with you and play it." John played an Gibson F-12 that he loved, but was commenting on this particular later model that was made for him. Rick declined to accept the mandolin, and that was the only mention of music that night even though both men were mandolin players. "I think deep down he wanted me to take it home and break it in for him," Rick said with a smile.

"Off the stage, John never wanted to talk about music. He wanted to be a normal person," explained Sam.

During the evening Rick noticed the phone John had sitting on his desk. "He had this long list of names and phone numbers of promoters with each one annotated with a comment, like 'works out well,' 'don't bother,' and 'a-hole'," Rick said. Sam added, "It was his caller ID system before there was caller ID."

Sam said, "John, like most of us, had phobias. Apparently, he needed some dental work and dentists were not his favorite. He also had a well-known fear of flying."

In 1979, Sam's mom wrote her a letter while she was in college with some news. John had spent $2,300 on dental work, and he was going to fly to Nashville. "Miracles never cease," Marion joked.

When Marion died of breast cancer in 1984, John called Sam. "He told me he didn't do weddings or funerals but wanted me to know how sorry he was. I thought that was nice of him to call."

Sam's favorite songs that The Seldom Scene performed were, "Wait a Minute," "Old Train," and "Rider." The song, "Heaven," was her Grandma's favorite. She noted that John's tenor was an integral part of every song he performed. No one really tried to imitate him because the power and quality of his voice was so unique.

Peter Van Kuykendall married her mother, Marion, and after her sister, Sharon, was born in 1965, Pete and Marion made the decision to have Pete adopt Sam so they could be a family, "with all having the same last name".

Sam reminisced about her Dad, Pete. "I remember when the lady from social services came to interview me, she asked me, 'Do you want him to be your Dad?' I remember telling her, 'Yeah, because he takes me places!'"

Sam admitted that going through all of the letters and photos in preparation for this book interview had been therapeutic. In her teen years, Sam kept a diary. Once, after a typical teen fight with her Dad, she wrote: "'I wonder what my life would have been like if John had stayed with Mom?" She recalls, "I found out that Mom had been reading my diary. She left me a three-page letter. In it she reminded me of all the things Pete had done for me, and that John wanted to give me up for adoption. But since I was born three months premature, with no fingernails and looking blue, Mom was afraid I was so ugly that nobody would want me."

Sam threw the diary and letter away. "I knew I had to get rid of it. I learned a valuable lesson to not write down what you don't want someone to read," exclaimed Sam. It brought her emotions into perspective. "I feel like God had a hand on my life and it worked out the way he intended it to. He sent Pete into my Mom's life to be my Dad and he gave me a good life and a good family. There's an old saying that I embroidered on a plaque for him one time. 'Anyone can be a father, but it takes someone special to be a Dad.' John never really cared for children that much. Pete stepped in and raised another man's child as his own and did a good job at it, I think."

In talking about Pete, she said, "He loved bluegrass music and was always trying to get something started that would benefit the music and help it grow." Pete was born in Arlington and he attended the Capitol Radio and Electronics Institute after high school. He was also a radio disc jockey. After he married Marion, he took a job

116

as a broadcast technician at the public television station WETA in Washington, D.C.

In 1954, when Pete was a senior at Washington and Lee High School in Arlington, Virginia, Pete gave a "What I Want To Do When I Get Out Of High School" presentation. He brought in records, including the 1949 recording of Earl Scruggs's "Foggy Mountain Breakdown," demonstrating to his classmates how he planned to be a hillbilly music DJ.

"Sam" with her Dad, Pete Kuykendall
© G. Allred

One of his high school classmates, a star center on the basketball team and class president to boot, who had never spoken to Pete before, stuck around to talk about this music after Pete's presentation. That student went on to become the famous actor and producer; Warren Beatty. A piano player himself, Beatty later contacted Earl Scruggs to contribute to the soundtrack for his ground-breaking 1967 film, *Bonnie and Clyde*. That movie enormously helped Earl's music and bluegrass itself gain an international audience.

The name Kuykendall is Dutch. He took "Pete Roberts" as his Disc Jockey radio name because he didn't think people would understand or be able to say Kuykendall.

Pete was interested in protecting songwriters. To obtain a copyright, a portion of the music—usually the song's chorus—had to be transcribed into charted music. With his background in music from his piano teacher mother, he frequently performed this service for songwriters. Pete also saw an opportunity to become a music publisher and this is how his Wynwood Music publishing company got started.

"If there was a dollar to be made, Pete was a smart man and would find a way to make it," said Rick Allred. "His heart was in music and he was smart enough to know how to make money at what he loved."

"Dad started a bluegrass magazine in our basement," Sam said. "*Bluegrass Unlimited* started out as a newsletter published by a group of friends, including Pete, who loved bluegrass and wanted to see it promoted. Pete took the newsletter to the next level to magazine status. The rest is history." The newsletter started in 1966 as a mimeographed document about 12 pages in size and grew to the international magazine, *Bluegrass Unlimited*—a magazine devoted to the enhancement of bluegrass music and this became his full-time job.

In Pete's earlier years, during his first marriage to Ann Hill, his basement also housed a recording studio where he recorded many bluegrass performers like The Country Gentlemen, among several others. His publishing company included songwriters Mississippi John Hurt and Skip James. Pete became the co-owner of their publishing rights and those of other artists in the process of recording them.

And then lightning struck twice for Pete. In 1964, Pete helped Dick Spotswood produce "Prodigal Son," a song written and performed by Reverend Robert Wilkins, a then-seventy-two-year-old former blues singer turned minister. This song is included in the album *Reverend Wilkins—Memphis Gospel Singer* (Piedmont 13162). Pete owned Wilkin's publishing rights. The Rolling Stones recorded "Prodigal Son" on their 1968 album, *Beggar's Banquet.*

"It was there at that mountain house while we were picking blackberries, with Dad on one side of the bushes and Mom on the other side, when he told Mom he was going to quit his WETA-TV job and build the bluegrass newsletter into a magazine. Even though Mom loved bluegrass music, Pete's decision to quit his job went over like a lead balloon."

As the magazine took off, Pete scored another bonanza payday song when Eric Clapton's Cream band recorded, "I'm So Glad," another Wynwood Music Company song for which Pete co-owned the rights. Sam recalls, "Dad made a little money on that one and bought a house in West Virginia because Mom loved the mountains. He called this home Glad Acres."

One of his other ventures was starting his own record label, Glenmar Records. The "Glen" for his son from his first marriage and "Mar" for Sam as Marie is her middle name.

Pete wrote several songs, among them "I Am Weary, Let Me Rest," which appeared on the soundtrack of the Coen brothers' blockbuster movie, *O Brother, Where Art Thou* (2000), performed for the film by The Cox Family. Pete enjoyed success from that movie's popularity and its accompanying hit soundtrack.

Sam offered a story told to her by Jerry Stuart [a long-time friend, bluegrass musician, and also classmate at the electronics school] about another of Pete's earlier entrepreneurial schemes: "Dad went to a record store in West Virginia that had many old 78's all mixed up in the bins. He went to the store owner and offered to organize the records for him. The owner replied, 'But I can't pay you.' Pete said, 'That's OK, but if I find any duplicates can I have them?' The owner agreed. Pete organized them alphabetically and came back home with a trunk full of records. So, he made a newsletter list of records for sale to his friends. Some he indicated as 'only one [left]' even though he had duplicates. He'd wait a few months and send another list out. This is one way he paid for his engineering school tuition."

"Pete knew and remembered everything about bluegrass, said Sam. "He could tell you about Bill Monroe's first recording, where it was, what clothes Bill was wearing, etc. But he could never remember our birthdays," she said.

"Bluegrass was his life," declared Rick. Sam agrees. "When we were kids our vacations were going to the bluegrass festivals. We'd set up a stand to sell *Bluegrass Unlimited* magazines and take subscriptions. My brother, Billy, sister, Sharon, and I would sell the program editions to make a little spending money ourselves." Dad was always willing to pay fair wages to his employees, even if it was his own children. He was a hard worker. We didn't have an average childhood where parents come to ballgames or take annual beach vacations, but I don't regret anything. I got to go the music shows and meet the musicians and be a witness to bluegrass history. It also led me to my wonderful husband!"

Ginger notes in a final comment, "Pete and John remained friends until John passed away in 1996. Both were icons in bluegrass music, and both left a mark that made bluegrass better for their being a part of it." Both are gone now as Pete passed away on August 24, 2017.

# Chapter 9: Only a Few Friends

*I can count my true friends on one hand. A lot of people think I'm their friend, but they are acquaintances because you can't have many friends. Friends are the people you enjoy spending time with, and you don't have enough time to have many friends. Only a few.* JD

**T**helma Williams and her late husband, Wayne knew John and Nancy Duffey for 31 years. They first met John through bowling. She and Wayne bowled in the major mixed-doubles league at Play-More bowling center in Falls Church, Virginia. John and Nancy were in the minor's doubles because John had a lower average than Nancy. John loved duck-pin bowling and would spend hours practicing in the afternoon.

"Poor John," said Thelma, "He just didn't have the aptitude for getting the higher scores, but he still wanted to play in the better league, so we had to vote him into the majors. We would compete in the tournaments. John once commented he would trade music for Wayne's expertise in bowling. Initially, John and Nancy's scores weren't high enough to qualify to get in our top league, but we endorsed them for membership, and they were accepted. He tried so hard but never mastered bowling the way he wanted."

Thelma continued: "Wayne and I would go out with John and Nancy for dinner about three times a month and return to either of our homes for about five hours of socializing when he wasn't performing. We'd play pool and talk, but both Nancy and John were not big talkers.

If they had something to say then they would, but not small talk."

On John's 60th birthday, Thelma secretly arranged balloons with funny sayings like "over the hill" to be delivered to the Birchmere. John suspected it was Thelma, but she denied it.

"So, he painted a birthday greeting for my 60th birthday on a huge poster board and stuck it on her garage door. Wayne was in on this and turned the garage lights on at 2 am so John could attach it to the garage. His wife, Nancy, said he spent a week trying to find the giant poster board and painted it on his pool table.

"Sometimes we'd stay overnight. I've always had the habit of turning off lights when I left a room. One time I missed a light in our upstairs guest bedroom and John confronted me walking down the steps, asking, 'What do you think we are here? The 'frigging' Electric company?' Nancy then laughed telling me that John had been waiting years to pull that joke on me.

"I saw him many times show up onstage at festivals when others were playing. Sometimes with his mandolin and sometimes without. He was a cut-up. That's for sure.

"John was always friendly and accommodating to fans. However, at festivals, he wouldn't accept a beer from a fan. This happened to my brother-in-law, who told me he didn't think he liked John because of this. 'He acted really snooty about it.' I told him for one thing he doesn't drink beer, and if he accepted all the beers his fans offered, then he'd be stumbling around drunk.

"John put his career and social life on separate levels. He would never perform, talk about his music or play his records with his friends. However, when we were together, he would tell us when a new Seldom Scene album was coming out.

"John was a heavy smoker of 2 to 3 packs of Camels a day. After being told his voice would be affected if he didn't quit, he tried various ways including nicotine gum and hypnotism. The hypnotist told him there were only two kinds of people where this wouldn't work: those people who don't really want to stop smoking and those that are too dumb. He next took John's cigarettes from his shirt pocket, crushed the pack and threw it in the trash. John had a fit."

John's friend Shawn Nycz tells this story: Once at a club, John, Shawn, with Seldom Scene players, T. Michael Coleman and Lou Reid were reminiscing on when they all started smoking cigarettes. Their stories were typical until it was John's turn: "Well I don't want to try and top anyone, but I started when I was five years old," John explained. "I used to go with our maid to the Safeway grocery store and they had a machine there that would give you a couple of cigarettes in a wrapper for a nickel."

Thelma recalls that: "John loved shopping. He bought Nancy nearly all her clothes, and she hated that. He loved watching Johnny Carson on TV, and also tapes of older Carson shows. The Country Gentlemen were asked to play on Johnny's *Tonight Show,* and the band was anxious to do it. But then John found out the band would have to pay the network to appear. He was extremely upset about that and refused to appear. But that didn't stop him from liking Johnny's show.

"He was also a Trekkie and loved the *Star Trek* TV show and all the science fiction shows and technology that went with them. He was fascinated with the sound effects in those shows. He'd watch these on television and didn't go the movies in theatres often.

"For restaurants, he loved the *Outback Steak House* for his filet mignons and *Red Lobster* for the lobster tails and shrimp. We'd also go to the old *Tom Saris' New Orleans House* in Rosslyn, Virginia. He liked their chocolate milkshakes. We'd always split the bill regardless of what each of us ate or drank. John never expected any special treatment dining out because of his notoriety, and he tipped generously. Turkey was his idea of a heavenly meal, and he never knew why Nancy would only cook it once a year.

On John's temperament Thelma explains, "John was often considered aloof and not friendly by people who did not know him. But to those who were lucky enough to be considered his friends, there could never be anyone more loyal. I would never had made it through my husband's heart surgery if not for John and Georgetown hospital. He visited Wayne every day for months and kept my spirits up. He would take me to lunch or dinner at his house during the 12 hours a day I spent with Wayne.

"He and Wayne had a mutual admiration for each other's talents. Wayne admired his music, and John respected Wayne's aptitude for all aspects of home construction. Nancy would say, 'if one of them were female, then we wouldn't have husbands.'

"John enjoyed his instrument repair activity and asked Wayne if he would cut the wood strips for the sides of the first Duck mandolins he created. He made two Ducks: One for Akira and one for himself.

"As for his stolen mandolin, John told me that the guy who had it called John and said if he came down to the Childe Harold bar he'd give it to him. And as soon as John walked in the door, the man walked over and handed it to him. And that's the one he played for the rest of his career.

"After John died, the *Bluegrass Hall of Fame* wanted Nancy to donate John's mandolins, but Nancy said, 'I'm not giving anything to them.' Instead, she arranged for Akira Otsuka to acquire John's Gibson F-12 mandolin. The other Duck went to John's friend, Shawn Nycz."

(Note: In 2019, Thelma called this book's authors to express her appreciation for the project and delight in being included. Very sadly, she told us about an unexpected and severe illness. She passed away later that year. Thank you, Thelma, for your memories.)

## Shawn Nycz

In the early 1980s, Shawn began to see The Seldom Scene at the Birchmere, although he had been an avid fan of The Country Gentlemen since he was six years old. "My father played music, and I knew the Gents recordings and had met Duffey when I was a kid," said Shawn, now living in Nashville. "It was $6.00 to get into the Birchmere every Thursday night the Scene played, and you could get a pitcher of beer for $5.00." That's where the friendship began between the two. Shawn started to working for John as his driver and helper during the recording of the Scene's *Change of Scenery* album released in 1988. Today, Shawn is a piggyback truck driver. He transports new trucks from the factory to locations throughout Canada and the U.S.

Shawn calls John, "the most honest and loyal person that ever walked the face of this earth."

## The Pants

Shawn walked out of a Virginia motel room one morning wearing a pair of black and silver lightning bolt pants. "As I was walking, I felt somebody grabbing my pants and it was John."

"Do those pants have pockets?" asked John.

"Yeah," Shawn answered.

John inspected the pockets and said, "I like these pants."

When Duffey took the stage at the Birchmere the following Thursday, hc had purchased every pattern of Zubaz pants he could find. He'd add them to his bowling shirts and it soon got to a point that when Shawn wore his Zubaz pants to the Birchmere, people would say, "Ahh, you're wearing Duffey pants." That's when Shawn stopped wearing his.

Initially created for wrestlers and weight lifters, the slogan for the Zubaz company, was, "Dare To Be Different." John was wearing a pair at his funeral. A few years later at a tribute to John event in Kentucky, Shawn with then-current Scene members, Dudley Connell, Fred Travers and Ben Eldridge were talking with the crowd. Someone asked about John's "pajama pants," and Ben pointed to Shawn and said, "He's to blame for those pants."

Shawn was friends with Jimmy Gaudreau since the '70s. He'd travel with Jimmy and Tony Rice helping them at bluegrass festivals. "Jimmy and I were at a show with The Seldom Scene, and Jimmy told me, 'Those guys don't bring records along with them to sell. They are missing out on a big opportunity.' Shawn confirmed that "Unless it were a local show that his wife, Nancy attended, they'd never bring records or other merchandise to sell, so they lost out on some extra money.

"John's uncle was a lawyer in Miami. John told me that his uncle had offered to pay for him to attend college and become a lawyer. John told me many times that if he had it to do all over again, he would have taken his uncle's offer. 'I would have been an attorney in my uncle's firm,' John would say, 'There's no retirement in the music business.' John told *Bluegrass Unlimited* writer Jack Tottle that he wished he had taken his uncle up on his offer.

"The Show." John's portable suitcase bar
© Becky Johnson

## The Show

John referred to it as "The Show." It was a small suitcase carrying Canadian Club whiskey, Tropicana orange juice, sour whiskey mix, and glass shakers to mix his special libation, "Panther Piss, Aged 2 days." He referred to these drinks as his "attitude adjusters."

This suitcase sat backstage for every show from the 1970s up until his last performance in 1996. John's wife, Nancy gave "The Show" to Shawn when John died.

In his early years according to Shawn, John might have started with a whiskey sour around 1 pm at home, but he eventually cut out alcohol at home when health issues came into play, and his doctors persuaded him to slow down. "Even up to the end, John seemed to need an 'attitude adjuster' drink before he performed."

"Around the house or on the road when he wasn't performing, he began to drink club soda with Hershey's chocolate syrup and always 4 or 5 ice cubes. And it had to be Hershey's, no other brand."

Shawn, John and Ben Eldridge drove all around San Francisco one night looking for the Hershey brand. "Ben and I looked at each other and said, 'Are you kidding?' when John wouldn't settle for anything but Hershey's."

"John wasn't well in his last years," Shawn stated. Another close business friend reported, "He had doctor friends who would come see him at the shows and give him prescriptions. He'd take a tackle box full of pills with him on the road and to festivals. Duffey would never do drugs, and he hated people who did, but if a pill had a name on it, then it wasn't a drug to Duffey. And toward the end, he was taking pills to get up and get down and every which way. But he never thought he was doing drugs."

"Around 1994, John was undergoing a lot of stress and lost his voice, temporarily," Shawn said. T. Michael, the Scene's bass player was carrying some of John's tenor parts. John went to Dr. Starling who could find no structural problems with his voice.

A few months later, John and Shawn were at LAX airport. Shawn told him:

"John, you should just walk into the Birchmere and say you've had enough and take a year off."

"I have enough money to take a hell of a lot more than a year off," John replied.

Shawn and John at a Hollister, CA festival in 1991.
Shawn with his Duck, © S. Nycz

## Chez Duffey

Everyone contacted for this book who knew John well commented on his eating habits. Shawn describes some food memories: "John had small tables around his pool table. On every one was a salt shaker. Even his drink kit, 'The Show' would have a salt shaker. There were always at least four dozen eggs in his refrigerator. And fatback.

"If John wasn't hungry, he would eat four eggs for breakfast, toast with melted butter and slabs of fatback on top, all heavily salted until it glistened. We even watched him salt country ham. If he was hungry, it would be six eggs. This was his breakfast at home for forty years."

One theory on the excess salt is because John smoked so heavily. He needed the salt for flavor since his taste buds were shot. Ben Eldridge said that when they were traveling, John couldn't get his beloved fatback for breakfast, "so he'd order lots of bacon, and strip the lean meat off the bacon and share it with us, so all that would be left is the fat for him, which he loved. We called it 'field stripping.'"

John talked food in the 1984 interview at his home:

*Mike Auldridge and I have similar eating tastes. He and I both damned near starved to death in France until he came and knocked on the hotel door. He said, 'I found a McDonald's five blocks down the street.' I said wait until I get my pants on. So, we went down there, and I swear to God it looked like the Black Orchid to me. Everything tasted the same except the milkshakes, which were a little different, but not bad.*

*In France they had rented this whole restaurant to take us to the night we arrived. We had translators with us. We would point to the menu and ask, 'what is that?' And they would tell us. Okay. I ordered a steak and it came out looking like it just passed over the fire. I couldn't eat it so I asked, 'could you cook it a little more?' I really wanted it medium, so they got even. They sent it back burned up about the size of a pack of cigarettes. It seems like they can take anything good over there and damn near poison it with some sort of sauces or glop. I heard they do this because their beef isn't that good.*

*But when we went to Paris we stayed in the Holiday Inn and don't laugh because it was one of the most gorgeous hotels, I ever stayed in. It's right in the center of Paris in the Square where you can get to anywhere from there. The band said before we got there 'why did you put us up in the goddamn Holiday Inn?' but when we got there they said, 'Johnny did real good.' I'd talked to the girl over there who said I think you'll like this. It's pretty expensive. I said well we expected that. She said 'it's about $90 a night.' Well I said, 'what the fuck.' We may never get back to Paris again. The first night we went for* *dinner I ordered a steak fillet. It came out beautiful, gorgeous. Delicious.*

*It was funny because the next night Mike had a headache. He stayed in his room and ordered room service. He tells me the next day that he ordered the same thing I had. Mike told me the chef sent him his left shoe. He asked for scrambled eggs and evidently the eggs they sent Mike looked like it already had been eaten and thrown up.*

Ronnie Simpkins, Seldom Scene bass player with Duffey during John's last year chimed in on John's eating habits in a 2000 interview with G.T.: "John had a sweet tooth which I do as well. He would have his special chocolate drink. He invited me to his room before the last show we did in New Jersey before he died. We sat around and talked for a half an hour or so. Band members were always welcome to come to his room and just kind of unwind. We'd kind of gotten into a real good habit since I had a minivan with the bass and all. I would either meet John, pick him up or he'd drive to my house and we rode together quite a bit. That was always a fun experience running down the road with John."

## Duffey on France

*That France trip was to play a festival in Toulouse, about 600 miles south of Paris. This was our first trip to Europe. The response was magnificent. I think my wife counted six standing ovations. The only thing that bothered me was that I kind of like to rap with the audience. And there's a lot of people who speak English, but when it comes to jokes or short-liners, by the time it catches on it takes five minutes to pass through the audience. Oh boy, Jesus, keep your mouth shut and play. That's kinda what we had to do. We'd announce the name of the song and just let it go at that. Apparently, that made them happy.*

*Then we did some workshops and went to Paris and goofed off for several days.*

# Chapter 10: So, You Don't Like The Way We Do It (or Damn Your Tape Recorder) by John Duffey

In 1967, John wrote the following essay for the magazine, *Bluegrass Unlimited*. In it he shared his feelings about playing bluegrass music with The Country Gentlemen and other insights. We are grateful to John's daughter, Ginger "Sam" Allred, for her permission to include it here in its entirety.

For several cycles of the moon my ears and eyes have been blessed with verbal and printed forms of slander upon our group [The Country Gentlemen] and anyone else for that matter who does not use "Molly and Tenbrooks" or "Uncle Pen" as a strict guideline for their music.

First of all, let me enlighten you to the fact that there are different ways to play other than the style of Bill Monroe. Do not be misled by this statement—Bill is the finest in his style and no one can surpass him at it! However, anyone in the business knows that no success or fame can be achieved by copying note for note an already established artist.

Next, let us go into why groups leave the so-called beaten path. One reason is to try and establish their own "sound" but still retaining the designated and accepted instruments. Another reason is the record companies who are interested in selling their little discs of vinyl plastic. This now brings me to one of my pet peeves—That damn tape recorder!!!!! It seems that too many dyed in the wool bluegrass fans would rather tape it than spend a couple of bucks on a record. They don't seem to realize that what they have on tape doesn't help the artist one damn bit. I talked to some of the people who were taping at the Bluegrass Festival in Roanoke last year who were complaining about the music we play now as compared to five years ago. One of them had purchased one of our records (we have seven albums and twenty some singles at present) and the others confessed that they don't buy records they "borrow" someone else's and tape it." This same story is repeated over and over everywhere, and to this day I can't understand why. I am informed by electronics experts that a phonograph record under good care will last a hundred years, whereas a tape will deteriorate in twenty-five years. I recently talked with someone else who wanted to know when we would be playing in his area so he could tape us. He mentioned specific numbers he wanted—I suggested he buy the record, he replied, "I'm fascinated with the tape machine, I don't buy records."

Unfortunately, this taping mania seems to be confined to bluegrass. The proof of this being you don't see a mass of tape recorders at a concert by Frank Sinatra, The Beatles, or Ernest Tubb, but if there is a bluegrass band appearing it looks like the United Nations as far as microphones leading into tape machines. Why do you think Buck Owens for instance is always on the charts? People don't tape him; they buy his records! Record sales are the only thing the trade papers have to go by. This is one good reason why bluegrass will probably never be a tremendous commercial success. I can't figure out if bluegrass fans are unintentionally ignorant of the facts or if they are just a bunch of tightwads! Remember clods, in our dollar-minded society, if there is a demand, there will be a supply.

Now let me tell you why we (The Country Gentlemen) have tippy-toed into other realms of possibilities in our music. I think the preceding paragraph is some-what explanatory. If we can't sell our straight bluegrass to bluegrass fans, then we have got to sell something to somebody else. Believe me, if you don't sell records, the company doesn't want anything to do with you. In 1961 we began venturing into the booming "Folk Field." Why? It's very simple, we would name our price and the concert promoter or the coffee house owner would say, "Great, when can I get you?" We would name our price to a hillbilly park owner or country promoter and they would say, "We don't pay that kind of money for bluegrass, we can get the Nashville Sound for half the price and a bottle of Old Crow." Going into other fields involved some change in material in order to give our audience what they wanted to hear.

However, this alteration brought no change in our instruments or singing. It merely brought new material to the field. These slight deviations also made bluegrass music more palatable to many more people. I think I'm safe in saying that possibly other than Lester Flatt and Earl Scruggs, we have converted more people to bluegrass than any other group. The old saying "when in Rome, do as the Romans do" also applies in music. When you can make the snobs think you're one of them, pretty soon they are on your side. And they will take notice of what you are doing. This makes it easier for the next group who comes along. Before you scream commercialism, remember that everyone in the business whether it be opera or bluegrass is trying to make a living. You who scream the loudest have probably never tried to earn a living playing bluegrass music.

135

Let's take a look at the instrument which is always the #1 subject of controversy—the five-string banjo. To some of you, there seems to be only one way to play it, and that is "Scruggs Style." BOSH!! If you think a fast roll would sound good in the middle of "Bringing Mary Home," then your musical taste is in the part of your anatomy on which you sit! Necessity is the mother of invention, and when you need a banjo for other uses than breakdowns, then you need someone who has two hands instead of one. Eddie Adcock is more versatile and can do more things with a banjo than anyone within the realm of public notice. However, some people who have not outgrown childhood jealousies will beg to differ. Another point to be mentioned is if you can't do what the other guy is doing, then knock it—spread the word, tell the people it's bad, and if you happen to be the "big wheel" in your sewing circle you can probably convince some of your sheep that you are right. I also would like to give due credit to the banjo players who are very skilled in the Scruggs style. I have heard too many to mention but, in my opinion, the number one man in the category is Bill Emerson, who is unsurpassed for clean, straight, hard-drive playing. He has perhaps more drive than Scruggs himself. So, you see, right here is a typical example. The inventor of a product does not necessarily make the best one! Also, we should not forget Bill Keith, who came up with a superlative new sound for the banjo. I've heard people knock him also.

On behalf of other groups such as Flatt & Scruggs, Jim and Jesse and The Osborne Brothers who have received much criticism, they have the habit of having to eat just like you. They got a little tired of driving five hundred miles to make a hundred dollars and decided it was time for a change. I for one admire every dollar they've made, and I'm sure they cry all the way to the bank every time they hear a derogatory comment about their music. Apparently, there are enough good supporters on the other side of the fence to make it worthwhile.

In answer to a snide remark in a recent article about The Country Gentlemen being conspicuous by their absence, I am well aware of how cheaply some groups sell themselves. It is appalling to know that one can make a better living sweeping streets than some well-known groups make playing music. We have no intention of saving up to go on tour, and therefore if it is not worthwhile, I would rather stay home and glue guitars together. Doesn't that make sense? And just in case you plan to make a case of it, I am in a position to back up everything I say!

In summing it up, I'll give those of you who are just dying to say "he must be conceited" something to rave about. I've had lots of criticism about how I play my little mandolin. Well, it may be good or it may be bad, some like it and some don't, whatever style you want to call it doesn't matter, but remember, IT'S MINE! What have you contributed besides criticism, buddy boy?

In closing, one word of advice to bluegrass bands. Through the years it has been the policy for bluegrass musicians to stand upon the stage and look mad at the world or as if they died the day before. We have found that this is a bad policy. If you look like you are enjoying yourself and put a little "show" into your performance you'll be surprised at the amount of new faces you will attract.

EPILOGUE: To those of you who have never tried to make a living playing straight bluegrass music; get out and try, or keep your damn mouth shut!!

# Chapter 11: Dr. Stanley's Rant

"As a man, John Duffey could be as mean as a striped snake. He did all kinds of things that I thought were just plain wrong."

> Dr. Ralph Stanley in his biography,
> *My Life And Times.*

*"I appreciated the Stanley Brothers. They were one of the few groups I ever drove out of my way to see."*

> JD

Pretending to pee on Ralph Stanley's tour bus. © Thelma Williams Archives

The Stanley Brothers became stars in the first generation of bluegrass players. From McClure, Virginia—about six hours from D.C.—Ralph Stanley and his older brother, Carter became enthralled by Bill Monroe's music in 1946.

With Ralph on banjo and Carter on guitar, they were the first artists other than Bill Monroe to play the music Bill had created. The Stanley band was the Clinch Mountain Boys. Dr. Ralph, as he became known after receiving an honorary doctorate from the Lincoln Memorial University in Tennessee, earned a Grammy for Best Male Country Vocal Performance for singing "Oh Death" in the movie, *O Brother, Where Art Thou?* Although Ralph was best known for singing "Man of Constant Sorrow", it was the voice of Dan Tyminski channeled by George Clooney in the movie.

A teenaged Ricky Skaggs became a budding musical luminary when he joined an impressive 1971 version of Ralph Stanley's band The Clinch Mountain Boys and helped his boss recreate the early Stanley Brothers' classic harmonies.

Stanley's 2009 autobiography, *Man of Constant Sorrow: My Life and Times* (Gotham) co-authored by well-respected Washington freelance writer, Eddie Dean, reveals that Bob Dylan sent Ralph a congratulatory telegram on his 50th anniversary in the business with the last line, "You will live forever." Dr. Ralph knew it was his songs like "Man of Constant Sorrow," "Pretty Polly," "O Death" and other classics that would keep his spirit alive.

In his book, Ralph devotes a chapter to "Professionals and Amateurs," providing examples of musical behavior he has observed in both categories. His co-author, Dean explained that he was contracted to assist this "as told by the author" project and helped Stanley get his memories together.

Stanley brags about how he experimented with the old-timey music to find his unique mountain sound.

"Professionals care about the song," he wrote. His idea for instrumental breaks was "just play the notes that go with the song...no hot fancy licks that play all around the melody."

Then there was fashion. Ralph never took the stage without his suit coat and hat, pressed pants and cleanly shaved chin held high. He thought the younger players in their tee-shirts and long hair were sloppy.

He cites a practical joke his brother Carter played on Jimmy Martin right before a significant performance where Martin was trying to make a name for himself. Carter slipped him ex-lax.

"Somehow he made it through the set and then he knew he had to go, fast," Stanley recalls. "Right after he finished, he ran off the stage looking for a Port-a-John, but he couldn't find one close by. Last we saw him he was headed out into the woods pulling his britches off as he was running."

And after several pages of listing the various reasons he disliked "amateur" musicians, he writes the following:

"Now there's something that's worse than just being amateurish, and that's being dumb and stupid. This happened some and most times I would let it go and not pay no mind to it. Sometimes it would get under your skin and really get to you. There was one musician I want to call out on that: John Duffey."

Ralph starts his Duffey treatise by stating many positive things about John, whom he knew was a Stanley Brothers fan. No problems with Duffey as a musician since his tenor voice could not be beaten. He admired John as a businessman and agreed that The

Seldom Scene attracted new fans to bluegrass music and opened doors for some of the acts to get more gigs and money for their performances. "John also helped get more respect for bluegrass outside the country music world with the college fans and city people," he wrote.

And then come Ralph's negative assertions: For example, he says that John would travel for hundreds of miles to record Stanley Brothers shows in the late '50s and early '60s. "He'd be there with the tape recorder right by the stage, and that's was how he learned our songs that ended up on those early Country Gentlemen albums," wrote Ralph.

Tom Gray confirmed in 2018: "This is part true and false. John was indeed a big Stanley Brothers fan. He traveled to see their shows and befriended Carter Stanley early on. But Ralph has confused John with others who taped the Stanley's shows. What John learned came from seeing them live and buying their records."

Ralph next accuses John of repainting the letter "S" on Jimmy Martin's tour bus changing his band's name from "The Sunny Mountain Boys" to "The *Funny* Mountain Boys. Ralph states, "this was the worst prank he had ever seen." It appears he thinks this prank was far worse than slipping laxative to a performer hoping to make a good impression.

Again, Gray sets the record straight: "There's no way John could have done that. He certainly would have gotten a good laugh about the stunt, whoever did it."

The most serious example of Ralph's mean-spiritedness occurs when John allegedly asked Ralph if he could join him on the 1973 re-recording of one of Stanley's finest songs, "Lonesome River."

Ralph asserts that Duffey told him it was a real honor and he was nervous to do this song. Ralph wrote,

141

"I wanted to test him a little bit, to see if he had what it took to really do the old Stanley Brothers style the way it could be done. I just sort of nodded over to Roy Lee and we threw it up about two keys higher than we'd ever done it. Me and Roy Lee Centers were really pushing him, and Duffey couldn't quite make it to the high baritone he was supposed to. We got our parts fine but Duffey failed on this. We had to lower it down a notch for him so we could get through the song."

Tom Gray's rebuttal to this story is: "Neither John or Ralph asked the other. Here are the facts: The owner of Rebel records, Charles R. "Dick" Freeland, was producing an album for Ralph, and he was the one who asked John to come to the studio to sing and play on the 1973 recording of 'Lonesome River.' Dick Freeland was a great admirer of both John and Ralph, and suggested they sing together on that song. It had been recorded on an early 1950s Stanley Brothers recording on the Columbia label, in which Peewee Lambert sang a high baritone part over Ralph's tenor. Dick foresaw in his imagination how great it would sound to get Duffey's voice to sing that part some 20 years later. He was right. It was that recording session where Ralph tried to make John fail by moving it up three keys higher, from D to F. Ralph in his book made the claim that John's voice let him down. That was another case of Ralph's resentment of John."

When Stanley's book was reviewed in *Bluegrass Unlimited,* Tom Gray wrote the following editorial letter:

"To *Bluegrass Unlimited*

"In Murphy Henry's review of Ralph Stanley's book, *Man of Constant Sorrow,* she mentions that Ralph spent six pages attacking the late John Duffey. Indeed, Dr. Ralph heaps all kind of scorn, much of it lies. This makes me so sad because I still respect Dr. Stanley and his music, and found the book very enjoyable with the strong exception of his pages wasted criticizing John. Perhaps it was a case of sour grapes toward someone who had found success in this music business while Ralph was still struggling.

"Admittedly, John Duffey wasn't the easiest person to get along with, but I feel compelled to say a few words in his defense. I was a bandmate of John's for almost 20 years in both of the trend-setting bands of which John was a member, The Country Gentlemen and The Seldom Scene. Ralph shows his resentment of both bands, as he berates John. I also had the privilege to be a temporary member of the Stanley Brothers' band on three occasions, so I'm also familiar with Ralph Stanley.

"Actually, despite their differences in background, John and Ralph are alike in many ways. Both became self-made successful musical businessmen. Neither learned the business from any school, but from experience and a good sense of making the right choices at the right time, sometimes against the advice of others. They both made their mark as tenor singers, both valuing their singing above their instrumental work. They both saw themselves as entertainers who know how to sell what they do to an audience. Both created a sound of their own within this field we call bluegrass, not wanting to copy anyone else's style. On the one occasion when John sang on Ralph's recording, *Lonesome River* in 1973, the result was outstanding.

"Now let me get down to some of the statements Ralph made about John. He started right off by accusing John of being "dumb and stupid". Now, John was a really smart guy, as anyone who has negotiated contracts with him can testify. I always considered myself lucky to have John on my side when handling band business.

"In his book, Ralph goes on to accuse John of a prank of vandalizing Jimmy Martin's bus. Someone had re-painted "Sunny Mountain Boys" to make it say "Funny Mountain Boys". I know John was not capable of doing such a thing. For one thing he was not an artist who could have repainted the bus. For another, John was not a prankster, anyway. Not having been there, I asked around if anyone knew about that story. I did hear reports about the incident, blaming it on another person from another band. I'll not spread any rumors about who did it.

"Perhaps Ralph's rant is a case of professional jealousy. Let me illustrate. In 1976, we [The Seldom Scene] made our first appearance at the bluegrass festival at Wise, in the heart of Stanley country, in the mountains of southwestern Virginia. The audience was so excited to see us, we got a standing ovation when we first stepped out on stage, before we had played the first note. Ralph saw his people adoring John Duffey and the rest of the Scene, and felt threatened. These were his people who had gone crazy for the Stanley sound 25 years earlier, and now they were fans of those guys from the city. We played that festival for four years in a row, when Ralph made his stand to put an end to it. The Shriners Club, of which Ralph is a member, sponsored the festival. He called the Shriners around and gave them a piece of his mind. He said "those Seldom Scenes and those hippie bands "don't belong here, and they should not allow Glen Roberts [who had done the booking] to run another festival here. Sure enough, that 1979 festival was the last one held at Wise. Mr. Roberts moved his festivals to Elizabethton, Tenn. and continued to book the Scene there.

"Part of John Duffey's schtick was his smart aleck way of talking to an audience, trying to shock people, to get a reaction. I'm sure this did not endear him to sincere people like Ralph Stanley. That's really too bad. For I respect both Ralph AND John. Ralph mentions something John had said a few times onstage, mentioning "Ralph and the Rip-offs". Well, John was not meaning to insult Mr. Stanley at all, just making up a goofy-sounding name. There were other goofy names John gave to us, some in poor taste, I'll admit.

"Something that may or may not have any bearing on Ralph's resentment of John was an agreement back in the late 1950s between John Duffey and Carter Stanley. John, who had always liked the Stanley's music, had befriended Carter. John asked Carter if he had any songs, he'd written that John's new band, The Country Gentlemen, could record. Carter gave John *Going to the Races*. He allowed The Country Gentlemen to make the first recording of the song with Duffey singing the solo verses. It was the first recording the Gents ever made. I wonder if Ralph had wanted the song for the Stanley Brothers to record. I'm sure it would have been great. I'd like to hear what John would say about this if he were still alive today. Can you imagine?" Tom Gray.

Ralph's brother, Carter, passed away in 1966. Carter's daughter, Jeanie Stanley became a big fan of John Duffey after Tom Gray sent her a Seldom Scene cassette in the 1980s. Jeanie is a member and

145

contributor to the Facebook group, "John Duffey's Bluegrass Life," who provided essential support and information for this book.

Dr. Ralph Stanley toured until December 2014 before dying of skin canccr in 2016 at the age of 89.

# Chapter 12. The Gents Lose John

*"Money isn't everything. Maybe it should be, but it isn't. Everything is just being happy."*

JD

**J**ohn quit The Country Gentlemen on his 35th birthday, March 4, 1969. When asked why he left the group, he explained: *"Well, I had myself an instrument repair business up here and it was getting quite lucrative. It wasn't the fact that I would rather glue instruments together than go play, but goddamn it, I was tired of traveling these tremendous distances, you know? It was like we were saving up to go on tour.*

*"You're supposed to go on tour to make money and I couldn't get Charlie and Eddie to set a [gig] price regardless of what it would be. Say $500 or something. Whatever. And we wouldn't play for less than that.*

*"'I don't know, man. They [promoters] said $350, so let's pick up everything we can,' would be Charlie's attitude.*

*"We had already beat around the bars. We had paid our dues and I didn't think we really needed to do that. I began to realize that we don't have to play out on the roof of the men's room at the Drive-In Theatres, you know? There are better places that we can play, by God, and I wanted to. I think the main reason I decided to hang it up with the Gentlemen was that I said, look, we've got a product. I think we can create a demand. Can't we do something else? I mean even if we have to pump gas or cook hamburgers. Just don't go to everybody that calls and wants to give us $150 bucks to play the swamp in Florida.* (Note: John called Florida "God's waiting room.")

*"So, I just said, the hell with this. I'll just stay at home and glue my guitars together. I was out of the business, I guess, for almost three years."*

**B**y the time Duffey quit The Country Gentlemen, Charlie Waller had graduated from an old Cadillac limousine to a used 1952 Trailways bus to carry the band to their ubiquitous gigs. He added booze, a kitchen, plush carpeting, and hot and cold running water.

John hated it. When Rick Allred was in The Country Gents, John asked him, "How do you all stand traveling together in that tour bus five days a week? I couldn't stand that."

One early showbiz discouragement for Duffey came in 1965 when the Gents were invited to perform on Johnny Carson's *Tonight Show*. Their "Bringing Mary Home"—co-written by Duffey and often erroneously asserted to be inspired by a *Twilight Zone* TV episode— was then a hit song. An appearance on national TV was a grand opportunity, with the bonus that John Duffey loved Carson. He used to watch Johnny Carson religiously with a notepad handy for copying quips for later stage use.

"When Johnny would throw one off that he really liked he'd write it down and memorize it," said Ben Eldridge. Many of John's stage quips had the feel and cadence of Carson, especially Carson's Carnac The Magnificent character. Carnac was a "mystic from the East" who could psychically "divine" unknown joke answers to questions sealed in an envelope.

Duffey might channel Carnac when the audience groaned at a joke or got restless. For example, a lady in the audience once heckled John when he announced a song she didn't like. "Don't play that," she yelled.

John retaliated with, "May your gynecologist keep his rubber gloves in the freezer," right out of the Carnac jokebook.

The 1965 *Tonight Show* incident was reported by writer Robert Kyle in *Frets* magazine in1980: The band director controlled the musical acts that appeared on the Johnny Carson program. Before agreeing to audition the Gentlemen, he made it clear that he expected something in return for the national exposure he was in a position to give them. Rather than the band getting paid for the appearance, he suggested they slip their fee back into the pocket of the music director. The Gentleman realized that meant they would be playing for free, but they decided the exposure was worth it. However, as Duffey recalled there was more to the negotiation.

"The band guy said that would do for a start, but he wanted more money to put us on, but we said no, goddamn it, because in the first place we couldn't afford it. It was payola, a bribe—whatever you want to call it. We would have had to pay him to be on the show."

That experience was a rude awakening to the realities of big-time show business, and it left John embittered and resentful. "It became not what you knew but who you knew when he wanted us to pay to be on, and I thought we really had something to offer."

John and Eddie said no to the kick-back deal. Charlie still wanted to do the show. Ed Ferris wasn't a full partner in the Gents and didn't have a vote. Duffey made the call to decline the offer. He never regretted his decision, and the experience never diminished his appreciation for Johnny Carson. In his later years, he owned the video compilations of *The Best of Carson* and enjoyed watching them at home.

## Fear of Flying or Love for Bowling?

"It was John's aversion to travel which lead the rest of the band to suggest to him that he should leave the band," said Tom Gray. "They told John 'Shit or get off the pot!'" Band members at the time, who asked John to leave, were Charlie Waller, Eddie Adcock and Ed Ferris.

The Gents had an offer to tour Japan in 1969 and John didn't want to go. His close friend, Thelma Williams said, "Initially, he was afraid of flying when he was in The Country Gentlemen and even early in The Seldom Scene. When he did, he became very interested in all aspects of flying especially the planes' engines."

Tom Gray added: "For years, The Country Gentlemen and The Seldom Scene were held back from accepting any gig that would require flying. John Duffey was afraid of flying and would only accept jobs where he could drive. He turned down job offers from overseas."

"There was a very good reason for John's fear of flying," explained Tom Gray. "When John was 17 years old, his half-brother Jeff Duffey was taking flying lessons. Jeff invited John to come along and take a flight. The flight instructor took John up in a small plane and showed John how he steered the plane. 'It's pretty simple. To turn left, I move the stick to the left, to turn right I move the stick to the right.' John then accepted the instructor's offer to take the controls and steer the plane. John took hold of the stick and moved it far to one side. The plane rolled over upside down. John was very frightened. The instructor grabbed the control and righted the plane. Once John got back on the ground, he swore he'd never again go up in an airplane."

"Many people tried to get John to consider flying, but he refused. A scheme and an opportunity conspired to get John to finally give it a try. National Public Television hired The Seldom Scene to participate in a big bluegrass show to be filmed at the Grand Ole Opry in Nashville. Part of the band's pay was airfare to Nashville and back. At first, John assumed his wife Nancy would ride with him, driving to the gig as she always did. But band members got Nancy to use this opportunity to try to get John to agree to fly. She told John she had too much work to do on her day job. She wouldn't have the time to drive there and back, but if John is willing to try flying, she'd go with him on an airplane.

"It worked! John said he'd try it. My wife Sally Gray did her part by calling officials with American Airlines and impressing on them how important it was for them to make John happy. When John and Nancy arrived at the airport check-in at Washington National Airport, they greeted him by name and showed him much courtesy. John and Nancy had seats in the smoking section. Once the plane took off, John felt brave enough to look out the window at the ground, and comment 'It's pretty smooth up here.' The date was November 5, 1979.

"Because I was carrying my bass fiddle, they had given me and my bass seats in the first-class section. They let me pre-board with the bass and put it in a big first-class window seat. About an hour into the flight, John was feeling more comfortable, and got up and wanted to see what it was like up in first class. He walked up the aisle, still carrying his lighted cigarette, which was forbidden, and checked out my digs. The flight crew let him get away with it. John's fear of flying was gone. We booked our first week-long tour of the west coast from San Diego, California to Vancouver, British Columbia in February and March of 1981.

Penny Parsons, who helped promote The Seldom Scene when they were on the Sugar Hill label and co-produced the 1989 *Duffey Waller Adcock & Gray—*

*Classic Country Gents Reunion* album, also confirmed that John eventually didn't mind flying.

And according to John's friends, Shawn Nycz and Thelma Williams, he was an avid Atlanta Braves baseball fan. Although the games were televised locally, he and Nancy would fly to Atlanta for games and sit just a few rows from Braves owner, Ted Turner and his wife, Jane Fonda. They would frequently talk together.

The running gag in The Seldom Scene was that nothing stands in the way of Duffey's Monday night out bowling.

"He'd miss a night of pickin' to go bowling," said his wife, Nancy.

Tom Carrico, a D.C. music promoter and band manager remembered that one season Duffey had to change his bowling night. This change in John's availability created a multi-band domino rescheduling among bands in several clubs.

Eddie Adcock cited bowling as a major reason that Duffey quit the Gents. "He was bowling heavy. John was fixing to go 'pro.'"

Duffey would argue that The Seldom Scene, unlike most pop groups that are hit-oriented, doesn't need to involve itself in a grueling pace.

*"Once a bluegrass group like ours makes it and establishes itself, you're there as long as you want to be,"* he said. *"That's pretty much the way it is, which is a great thing about it. It's the type of music which is not Top 10. It never dies. With other music, if you don't have a hit, you're out of business; or if you do have a hit and not have one the next week, they say, 'What's that name again?'"*

"He said he was just tired of playing with The Country Gentlemen, but we proved that incorrect time and time again with the many reunions and shows we played together after he left. Charlie, John and I held our relationship and the emotional connection to The Country Gentlemen until the day Duffey died. It just so happened that the three of us could crap on one another and still like each other. We were just buddies," said Eddie Adcock.

Tom Gray recalled, "As John Duffey was preparing to quit The Country Gentlemen in 1969, Herschel Sizemore was chosen to be his replacement. But it never happened. On John's last night with the Gents, at the Shamrock, Herschel was sitting in the audience with Len Holsclaw, soon to be the Gents' manager. Herschel had moved from his home in Alabama, where he played with the Dixie Gentlemen, to take the Gents job. The joint was packed with adoring fans of John's, savoring everything he played or sang or spoke. John was at the top of his game, and the crowd loved him. Herschel got intimidated by all the adoration for John and wondered if he'd ever be able to fill his shoes. To make it worse, it was John's birthday. Someone supplied a birthday cake and shared it with people in the room. By the end of the night, Herschel decided not to take the job.

"An emergency choice had to be made and soon. The Gents needed a mandolin player-tenor singer. Jimmy Gaudreau was asked to come to D.C. and audition. He had been playing electric guitar in a country band back in Rhode Island. Jimmy eventually would serve three stints as a Country Gentlemen member. Herschel Sizemore did stay in Virginia, and soon became a member of the Shenandoah Cut-Ups and other bands. Herschel and John Duffey would go on to become good friends, visiting each other at the many festivals where both were booked. I wonder (but would never ask) if they ever talked about that night at the Shamrock in 1969."

Local D.C. banjo player and later owner of Urban Recording, Dick Drevo recorded the last two nights that John Duffey played with The Country Gentlemen down at The Shamrock. The performances are intense.

## Jimmy Gaudreau

In a 2000 interview with G.T., Jimmy recalled, "I was fortunate to be born on July 3, 1946, in Wakefield, Rhode Island. Jimmy admits he is, "both a Yankee and a baby boomer."

Jimmy first heard bluegrass at the Newport Folk Festival. He started at age ten learning acoustic, and electric guitar and took up the banjo at age fourteen when he heard Flatt & Scruggs.

"I was also fortunate to be exposed to a great banjo player from Eastern Connecticut named Fred Pike. Fred was a Country Gentlemen fan and knew Eddie, John, and Charlie. The Gents became my favorite group."

Jimmy first met John in 1966 at Watermelon Park. "John was very cordial, but he didn't know I was a mandolin player. Once he figured that you were a musician, he tended to mess with you a little more."

When John left the Gents, Jimmy got a call from Rebel Records distributor Earl Pike, saying, "you may be getting a call from [Rebel's owner] Dick Freeland," to audition for the vacancy. He got the call, and it wasn't something he could think over and get back to them.

"It was a pressure situation. The Gents had engagements booked," Jimmy explained. "They were looking for someone who could sing the parts, play the mandolin and knew the material. I could do all three because at that time I was very up on The Country Gentlemen. I said yes, I'll be right down to try out. I figured if I don't make the grade I'll be coming home."

Dick Freeland picked Jimmy up at National Airport and drove to Charlie Waller's trailer motorhome in Alexandria, Virginia. Jimmy with Eddie Adcock, Ed Ferris, and Charlie got into an immediate jam session and played for two hours. Jimmy said he wasn't nervous because they put him at ease.

Eddie looked at Charlie and said, "This guy can do it." He turned to Jimmy and asked, "Do you want the job?" Jimmy's answer was yes.

Gaudreau explained, "John Duffey graciously stayed away from the Shamrock for a couple of months after I joined the Gents to let me get my bearings and feel more comfortable in that job. He knew I'd be completely intimidated. When he came one night the whispers 'Duffey's in the house' went around. Duffey is such a commanding presence. You can't miss him. I had to call on all of my resources to hang in there that night."

After the show John approached Jimmy with a strong hand shake and said, "Congratulations. Your mandolin's great and I think you're going to have a nice career in bluegrass music."

And then added, "But let me give you a little advice. I think you're going to have to sell it a little more because right now you are more of a technician than a salesman. And being able to sell it will take you a long way and serve you well in this business."

Jimmy said he took this advice to heart because Duffey was his mentor. "Coming from him, I was definitely listening."

In subsequent years John's friends including Tom Gray would hear Duffey call Gaudreau "the best mandolin player out there." Jimmy was very flattered that John would say that. "John would come up to me over the years and shake his head and say, 'Great mandolin player. You're still my favorite.'"

"I would blush and not be able to say anything when that happened," Jimmy admits.

When asked to describe John Duffey's legacy in bluegrass music, Gaudreau said, "John was one of the first to seriously research the music. He went to the archives and came up with tunes that had been completely overlooked. He would put his touches to them and the next thing you know they were with the times and outstanding musical pieces. A magical transformation.

"Also, first and foremost, The Country Gentlemen were not a mountain group. They lived in the Washington area. They performed for the yuppies of the day."

[Jimmy pauses at this point in the interview to collect his thoughts]

He resumes, "Again The Country Gentlemen were playing for the urbanites, and I'm sure this shaped his attitude toward performing. He didn't want to be, for example, Ralph Stanley or Bill Monroe, who were 'country-fried' bluegrass acts and mountain-type people with that sound. John also loved to be the heckler. If anybody came to the show to 'out-Duffey' him, they were doomed. It just could not be done.

"The Country Gentlemen with another group The Greenbrier Boys from New York City were developing urban bluegrass. John intended to entertain beyond what folks had ever seen before. I sure admired how he led the charge," admitted Gaudreau.

# Chapter 13: Seldom Scene, Often Heard

(l to r) Starling, Eldridge, Auldridge, Gray and Duffey at Indian Springs MD bluegrass 1974 festival sponsored by *Bluegrass Unlimited* Magazine. © Carl Fleischhauer

*The Seldom Scene was a band that didn't evolve slowly. I was out of the music business working my instrument repairs and gluing guitars together. Cliff Waldron was playing at the Red Fox Inn in Bethesda, Maryland with Mike Auldridge and his brother Dave on guitar. I had met John Starling before he went to Vietnam and when John came back, he moved back to Bethesda.*

*Ben Eldridge was teaching banjo at the music store where I had my repair shop. Ben, Mike and*

*Starling used to get together in Ben's basement to play. I think it was Starling who called me one time and invited me to this little social, a party. I said 'sure.'*

*I didn't even have a mandolin at that time, and Starling had a 3-point round hole that wasn't worth a shit, but it was something to play. So, we stood up and started singing. It was kind of fun.*

*About two weeks later, Ben called and invited me to another little social at his house and here we go again in the corner.*

JD

**W**est Virginian Cliff Waldron grew up poor. Cliff said in 2006, "We didn't have electricity until I was eight years old around 1949. We farmed with a horse and mule. There wasn't no tractor. We'd keep our fresh milk and butter in the spring water coming from the mountain to keep them from going bad. Everything was fresh We butchered hogs and canned our vegetables. It was hard work."

When Cliff was ten, he began to listen to the lunchtime radio show *Farm and Fun Time* on Bristol, Virginia station WCYB. It was a live show where acts like the Stanley Brothers and Bill Monroe would play in the radio studio not far from the Bristol train depot. The FCC approved WCYB to increase their signal from 1,000 to 5,000 watts which significantly reached new households. "We'd come in from the fields and listen to our radio. That's where I first heard music that would be later called bluegrass," Cliff recalls. "I fell in love with it."

Waldron worked extra jobs to slowly save the ten dollars he needed to order a guitar from the Sears Catalog. By seventeen he had learned enough on guitar and mandolin to play in local bands. He never imagined playing music for a living, but he was determined to escape becoming a coal miner.

To find work, Cliff took a few barber school lessons and headed for Falls Church, Virginia where he had cousins. One of his cousins was a country music fan who knew the D.C. players and where they played.

"The first show I saw around 1963 was Bill Emerson and the Yates Brothers, Bill and Wayne. My cousin told them I played guitar. Four years later Bill asked me to join his band. I knew a lot of country songs and worked with Bill to turn them into bluegrass," said Cliff. "The first was Merle Haggard's 'Working Man's Blues.'"

John Duffey wound up performing at shows with Emerson and Waldron and he recorded on three albums for Rebel Records with Emerson and Waldron. Charlie Waller helped also. "I'd play guitar with John on mandolin, or I'd play mandolin when Charlie played with us. These shows were at bars." Cliff recalled. During this time, Cliff got to know John Duffey very well.

"Some people didn't care for Duffey because he had an air about him. He'd rub some people the wrong way. But John and I spent hours just talking and pickin' together. When he and Adcock got together, they were crazy and brought the comedy. I think John was watching the Smothers Brothers and other folks like that and was quick enough to make up things on stage. Other mandolin players could play rings around John, but John could sell it onstage."

There were many iterations of the of the Emerson and Waldron band during the late '60s. Bill Poffinberger on fiddle added much. Cliff feels that with Tom Gray on bass and vocals this was the best band line-up.

In 1969 Tom invited Cliff and Bill Emerson to a party. There, Cliff met Mike Auldridge and his brother, Dave. "Mike and Dave were singing Everly Brothers

really good in another room when Bill and I got there,"
recalled Cliff. "Mike played Dobro with us that night,
and Emerson offered him a job, which Mike declined
because of his day work with the *Evening Star*
newspaper."

A few months later Emerson and Waldron, as they
were known, with Bill Poffinberger started playing at the
Red Fox. Mike and Dave joined them. Emerson asserted
that, "Adding Mike on Dobro improved our sound. Tom
had quit, and we got Ed Ferris, who was better for us.
Tom plays a lot of stuff, but I'd rather have a quieter
bass player."

Cliff left D.C. to play a short stint with the Bluegrass
Cut-Ups but returned to the Red Fox, where Ben
Eldridge began working with Cliff and Mike and brother
Dave singing tenor and playing rhythm on mandolin.
"Ben was really bashful at that time. I hate to say it, but
he was," Cliff said.

Dave, Mike and Cliff's voices blended well. Cliff
would tout Dave Auldridge as having one of the best
tenor voices. He also noted that Mike Auldridge was
playing mostly Josh Graves-style Dobro in the
beginning.

"Uncle Josh" Graves is credited with introducing the
resonator guitar to bluegrass when he switched from
bass to Dobro in the 1955 Foggy Mountain Boys. When
Josh played with Flatt & Scruggs, the trade name was
just Dobro [a contraction of the company's owners and
inventors, the Dopera Brothers]. Years later, the Gibson
Company bought out the Dobro company, and now
owns the patent and the trademark for the Dobro.

Cliff said, "Mike Auldridge started playing new leads
on the Dobro because I was singing new things, and not
just the old bluegrass tunes that had similar chord
patterns. I believe that's how Mike developed his style."

Cliff began getting jobs in Oklahoma, and Canada and this travel schedule again didn't work for Mike and Ben's day jobs. "Mike had his wife and kid and *Evening Star* job, and Ben had a great job [with the Applied Physics Lab], so they really couldn't take time off to travel. I had a government job as a supervisor so I could do whatever I wanted," explained Cliff.

During this time Ben Eldridge began his informal "basement band" get-togethers at his house with an array of pickers including Pete Kuykendall, Gary Henderson, Tom Gray, Len Holsclaw, Dan Haapala, Bruce Barnes, and others. John Duffey attended a few.

On Oct. 13, 1971, when Cliff Waldron was unable to make his weekly gig at the Red Fox, the owner, Walt Broderick asked Ben to bring his basement band to fill in for one night. The band that night was Ben Eldridge, Mike Auldridge, Dave Auldridge, John Starling, Tom Gray and Bruce Barnes (mandolin). Walt liked the band and recommended them to the Rabbit's Foot owner, who asked Walt to recommend a bluegrass band for his off nights, Mondays. By the time the Rabbit's Foot gig started, John Duffey had joined the as-yet-unnamed basement band.

**Rumor Has It**

In the summer of 1971 a rumor was started by The Country Gentlemen's manager, Len Holsclaw, who had played bass with Ben's basement band. The rumor was that a new band was being formed that would include John Duffey, Mike and Dave Auldridge, Ben Eldridge, and a new singer-guitarist, John Starling.

Dr. Starling remembers the next step: "I got a call from Ben. He said there was a rumor going around that John Duffey was thinking about getting back into music. Len's story was that John with Ben, Mike and I were going to start a band together. This was the first I had heard about this plan. I thought 'sure, that's great,' but I had a lot on my plate. I also wondered if I was good enough. These guys were professional, and I'm not.'"

"I had played music with Duffey at a party at Len's house. I wasn't used to how loud he sang. I tried to compete with him, and after two songs I had to give up because I had no voice left. It was a complete disaster. And Ben had John over to one of our pickin' sessions and John seemed not very interested. So, after the rumor, we kept waiting for a call from Duffey, but we never got one. Mike and I started playing back in Ben's house, and we're all thinking this band idea is pretty good. What can we do? Should we go over to John's house and kidnap him and bring him over to Ben's house? Finally, we got up the nerve to call him."

"Yeah, I heard that rumor, too," said John.

"Well, do you want to get together some night and see what we sound like?" Ben asked.

"Yes, I might like to do that," said John.

They gathered at Ben's house and discussed who might play bass. Starling suggested Len Holsclaw and called Len telling him, "This band might happen, and you were the one who had the idea for the band. So, do you want to play bass with us?"

Len was working in the police force in Arlington, Virginia and lived in Warrenton, Virginia. [Len worked for the Arlington County Police Department from 1956-83 retiring as chief of the Investigations Division] He was also managing The Country Gentlemen. Len thought about it, and said, 'I just can't do it.' John Duffey then said, 'Call Tom Gray.' Tom said "yes, I'll be over."

Charlie Waller had heard about the new band also and went to visit Duffey at his repair shop at Arlington Music. Charlie asked about this new group, but nobody had seen them, so he said they must be Seldom Seen, as it was not yet spelled "scene." John said, "Hey, I like that name."

Tom offered a footnote to the band name: "There was a short-lived rock band in D.C. with the name Seldom Scene, spelled the same way, that had played with The Country Gentlemen at The Brickskellar club on 21st St. NW. This planted the seed in Charlie's memory of the name," said Tom.

When discussing the origins of The Seldom Scene band name, John Starling recalled, "John [Duffey] said that one of the reasons we got the name Seldom Scene was John always regretted the name Country Gentlemen. They tried to combine the fact that they were doing an offshoot of country music, but they weren't country guys, so they were Country Gentlemen. But John said no matter how hard they tried that word 'country' in their name ended up costing them. At least he felt it did. So, The Seldom Scene—you know Charlie Waller named us when he heard what we were doing and we were just gonna play part time and just for fun he said, 'well, you should call yourselves The Seldom Seen (sic)' and we sat around and thought, 'well it was a good enough name as any' but we decided to use a slight play on words and use scene instead of seen just to try to get away from any kind of mountain boys, river—that kind of thing. Once again on the premise that don't doom yourself with the way you name the band on the get go."

Tom Gray remembered, "Before we formally adopted the name, we first made sure the original Seldom Scene rock band was no longer in business. Then we registered a trademark on it."

John Starling confessed that that the new band struggled for a while. "We really didn't know what we wanted to do. We started with cover songs and the same songs everyone else knew. But the thing that impressed me about our direction was when Duffey told us his conditions on starting the band."

**Band Rules**
Duffey told his new group, "I just have two rules: One is no big deals. And rule two: We are not going to do "Roll In My Sweet Baby's Arms" over and over again."

John Starling said, "This set the tone for our band. We were going to do this for fun. And if it stopped being fun, then we weren't going to do it. Everyone kept their day job. We will play one night a week in a club to have an audience and experiment playing something new. John's credo was that within the confines of bluegrass style and high quality, 'be different at all costs.'"

The Red Fox Inn was booked every night, so the fledgling Scene got a Monday night at the Rabbit's Foot, a D.C. bar on Wisconsin Ave, north of Georgetown. Ben described it as a, "Smoky stinky rock and roll bar down on Wisconsin Avenue about six or eight blocks below Western Avenue across from the Volvo dealership." In 1971 the owner Bruce Patterson described his bar as holding a mostly college crowd of 200 from Maryland in the 18-22 age range. Bruce described them as "well-behaved, and we're really proud of them. Apple wine is big with the crowd." But bluegrass not so much because the band's wives and girlfriends were the only crowds the Scene had the first night they played. Indeed, John Starling looked around the half-empty room and dedicated the song "I Wonder Where You Are Tonight" to the audience.

Sam Bush with members of his band, The New Grass Revival attended some of The Seldom Scene's first performances at the Rabbit's Foot.

## Duffey's view of the Rabbit's Foot fiasco

*Dave Auldridge had played there and called to say the owner wanted a bluegrass band. This lasted about six weeks. Around December, '71 we played a Monday night when the Redskins were playing the Rams on TV.*

*In front of us was a dance floor but they covered that with tables when we played. On this night the owner put a color TV next to the stage. And the game was blasting, and we were supposed to be playing. A friend of ours came in and asked the bartender to turn the game down, and they said our friend was drunk and threw him out.* [The friend was Richard Dress, a bluegrass fan, who held pickin' parties at his house]

*We said 'what the hell is this? You know goddamned well he isn't drunk. The bartender gave us some shit and we said, 'fuck you' and we left.*

*Besides that, we all wanted to watch the game, too. I ran home and flipped it on, and Starling and Ben went up to the Red Fox Inn to watch the game there. They started talking to Walt Broderick and wound up getting us a night there. We decided we'd wait until after New Year's and started the second Tuesday of January, 1972. When we started playing the Red Fox, a few calls came in. People were curious to see if I could still play. We didn't expect it, but The Seldom Scene just sort of mushroomed into something."*

## Dave Auldridge

Around the same time The Seldom Scene quit the Rabbit's Foot in December 1971, Dave Auldridge, who was an original member of the Scene going back to their basement band days, also decided to quit the band. In 2006, G.T. interviewed Mike and Dave Auldridge together in Dave's home in Alexandria, Virginia. Dave recalled, being the short-lived sixth member of The

Seldom Scene. "They [The Seldom Scene] started playing The Rabbit's Foot so I was with them for three weeks or something like that and I felt so unnecessary because I got the world's greatest tenor John Duffey doing what I used to do over in Ben's basement and I wouldn't want to sing any tenor parts on any song they did because there's no way I could compete with Duffey.

The only part I liked was singing tenor. So, I quit and a couple weeks later went back with Cliff and he said, 'if you ever quit me again, I'll kill you.' [Mike and Dave laughed] And that made me feel like I was needed. So, I enjoyed playing with him [Cliff] for the next I don't know, I guess three or four more years."

When discussing why he quit the Scene, Dave continued, "it was mainly because Duffey was so good that if I sang tenor it would put The Seldom Scene back about thirty years. I knew I couldn't possibly do what he was doing, and I just felt they would be better off without me. I'm just a guy standing back here taking money and standing at the back end of the stage keeping time. It was fun but when I was with Cliff at least I had a part."

Mike reacted by saying, "I think that was part of it. Cliff needed you."

Dave responded, "Oh, and Cliff needed me."

Mike agreed, "Yeah, that's a big deal."

When Dave was asked if he ever regretted quitting The Seldom Scene he responded, "I never really regretted leaving The Seldom Scene because I knew that I wasn't to the quality singing wise or instrumentally to compete—to compare with them. If anybody listened to me alone, they would think this guy just—he don't know what to do. He can't even keep time. He can't hit the right string." Mike was sitting right next to Dave during the interview and seemed very surprised to hear Dave saying that. Mike said, "Well, you're being too modest. I think it was just a different feel. You know? That's all."

Mike said, "It was like Curly Seckler going to work with James Taylor." Dave said, "Yeah right. I only knew how to sing Curly Seckler type stuff and John Duffey could sing like at Carnegie Hall and fill the auditorium up without a microphone. Or he could sing so quiet and so high that it was like a hummingbird making a noise or something. You just can't—nobody can do that stuff but John Duffey. He was better than the Osborne's. They would sing something, and he would sing tenor to them or he would sing high baritone to their stuff and they couldn't possibly even reach that."

Mike added, "And then he would sing bass."

Dave replied, "And then he would sing bass. And he was a showman. They just don't come along like that every day. Maybe one or two in their lifetime you will find someone like Duffey. But I didn't regret leaving them because I didn't feel I had any fun with that group just standing back there playing and keeping time with 'them. I went back with Cliff and I enjoyed the music just like it was with Ben and Mike there because he had Jimmy Arnold and he had Steve Wilson. Both of them were just as great as they could be. So, I was right back in heaven again and we did a lot of traveling around and had a lot of fun."

In 2008, Dave Auldridge passed away after a long illness. At Dave's funeral, Mike, along with John Starling and Jimmy Gaudreau played "Sing Me Back Home," "Heaven" and "The Maiden's Prayer."

Mike Auldridge reflected, "The first week we played, the Red Fox lines were waiting outside. By the second week, people were bringing their own chairs to sit in the aisles." Veteran mandolinist Jack Tottle reported the following incident at the Red Fox in a 1974 *Bluegrass Unlimited* magazine article:

One evening at the Red Fox a rather spaced-out longhair hippie was periodically weaving up to the stage to repeat his request for some ludicrously inappropriate song. This, as any seasoned bluegrass club-goer is abundantly aware, is the type of behavior which most musicians rate as slightly more obnoxious than clapping along out of rhythm with a fast tune or boogying to "Mother's Not Dead, She's Only A-Sleeping." Finally, the individual in question meandered up again in the middle of the song and sat down on the edge of the stage in front of John. The tune ended, and an anxious hush descended on the crowd as John set his mandolin aside, approached the front of the platform and towered ominously over the oblivious hippie.

Abruptly John reached down, picked up the young man, and carried him to a nearby table.

"You don't sit on our stage," admonished John with a gentle smile, "and we won't play on your table."

Another colorful story involves country music star Faron Young. Known as the "Hillbilly Heartthrob" with hits like "Hello Walls" and "Alone With You," Young once played on a bill with The Seldom Scene at the old Capital Centre, in Landover, Maryland. The Capital Centre was the home of the Washington Bullets (later renamed the Wizards) basketball team and the Washington Capitals hockey team. Other bands like The Grateful Dead, Led Zeppelin, Pink Floyd, The Allman Brothers, and most national rock acts played there over the years. It lasted from 1973-1999. The building was demolished in 2002.

The Seldom Scene played several large shows at the Capital Centre. One that happened on October 8, 1977, was really the Grand Ole Opry playing the Capital Centre and the Scene shared the bill with Faron Young.

Faron was navigating the mazelike corridors of the backstage dressing room area—allegedly drunk—and as he rounded a corner, he nearly tripped over Phil Rosenthal's guitar case. Faron kicked it across the dressing room complaining about "these bluegrass assholes."

"I'm going to kick the ass of one of these bluegrass guys," Faron bellowed.

John Duffey heard him, stood up and got right in Faron Young's face saying, "Oh yeah? Start with me motherfucker!"

Faron backed down quickly.

Another aside about that day: Faron said, "You bluegrass guys must be important around here. They gave you as much time on the program as they gave me." Then Phil Rosenthal said under his breath, "And what did you say your name was, sir?"

In an odd coincidence, Faron Young died of a self-inflicted gunshot wound on December 10, 1996. The same day that John Duffey passed away.

The Scene played other "Country Music Spectacular (Grand Ole Opry)" shows at the Capital Centre starting with the first one in March 1979. The line-up included: Bill Monroe & the Bluegrass Boys, Doc Watson, the Osborne Brothers, Ralph Stanley, Wilma Lee Cooper, Jimmy Martin, Jim & Jesse & the Virginia Boys, Mac Wiseman, The Country Gentlemen, The Seldom Scene, Bill Harrell, the Stonemans, Fiddlin' Chubby Wise, and the Bluegrass Cardinals.

As The Seldom Scene thrived at the Red Fox Inn, another music club owner in D.C. was focusing on making them an offer they couldn't refuse.

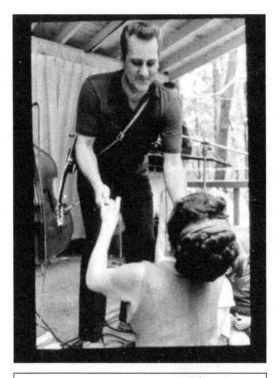

Indian Springs, 1975
© Carl Fleischhauer

## Record Deal

*Soon after we began at the Red Fox, the band, especially Mike Auldridge, started asking 'Why don't we make a record.?' I said, well, if I can't do anything else, I think I can help us get us a label and that was no problem. I called Dick Freeland and said, 'Dick, I think it's time for us to come out of the basement.'*

This was their first album, *Act 1*. It took four days doing two-track recording head-on to complete.

Starling remembered that, "John was a big believer in trying to record music live. He had a rule: we would run the track three times, and if you didn't get a recording that everyone was satisfied with then you'd

170

move onto something else and come back to it later. I learned everything from John Duffey really, including a little bit of cynicism about the music business, but we won't go into that."

*"When that Act 1 record came out you couldn't get in to the Red Fox Inn,"* John said. *"The first song we cut was the 'City Of New Orleans' by Steve Goodman."*

Their first record review in *The Evening Star* by Pat Dowell was off the hook: "Bluegrass is becoming very popular, and its fans can be split into two camps: those who prefer the traditional approach, and the newer devotees, who applaud recent developments in the style, such as the use of electric instruments and drums.

"At last, I've found an album I can recommend without reservation to both groups; in fact, it's so good that I'd recommend it to any music lover, regardless of his preferences.

"It's *Act 1*, by The Seldom Scene [Rebel SLP-1511]. Here are both old songs ['500 Miles,' 'Darling Corey'] and new songs ['Sweet Baby James,' 'With Body and Soul'] without any compromises.

"City of New Orleans" exemplifies what I'm talking about. The Seldom Scene give this hit song a treatment that makes it sound as if it was born and bred in bluegrass, rather than popular music."

An early Seldom Scene bluegrass festival appearance was June 11, 1972. *The Evening Star's* verbatim announcement was: Earl Scruggs and his review, Randy and Gary Scruggs, the Osborne Brothers, the Dillards, Doc Watson, Jimmy Martin, the Stoneman family, Mac Wiseman, John Hartford, *Hee Haw's* Grandpa Jones, the Lewis Family, J.D. Crowe, The II Generation, John Duffey, The Seldom Scene, the Shenandoah Cut-Ups, Jim Eanes, The Bluegrass Association, Clinton King,

Bluegrass 45, at the American Legion Country music Festival Park, Culpeper, Virginia 12 noon.

## Emmylou and Linda

John remembered meeting Emmylou Harris at the Red Fox during this time: *"Yea, she used to come in and sing with us. I think at the time she was really nobody, you know. We were more than she was then. Then she put her band together and started playing at the Red Fox. She got fired when she told somebody from the stage, who was being obnoxious, to 'fuck off.' Walt said, 'that's it,' which she probably had every right to say it, but that's still kind of crude, you know?*

John Starling recalls that, "when Emmylou Harris would play 'If I Could Only Win Your Love' at the Red Fox because she really liked the song, everybody got up to go to the bathroom. They didn't really care. They wanted songs they knew.

"But when she returned to Wolf Trap after she had a hit with that song, people started going crazy as soon as the opening notes started. So, you have to believe in your music and know what you're doing."

Emmylou has won 14 Grammys, and other honors including Country Music Hall of Fame induction. In 2018 she was presented the Grammy Lifetime Achievement Award.

In 2006, she told the *Washington Post,* "Obviously there was incredible musicianship, Mike being the first to take the Dobro into whole other worlds. But you had two incredibly distinct voices that you'd never think would go together: Duffey, one the great classic bluegrass tenors, and John, who is one of the most subtle, soulful singers, almost like a pop voice. John is probably my favorite singer in the world as far as restraint, intensity of emotion; I just love to hear him sing. Their voices are so different, but then you've got that cement of Mike's voice, which has a beautiful tone to it but a certain invisible quality that ties it all together with just enough texture—it's just like no other sound. They really gave bluegrass another texture, another gear." [Note: Emmylou sent this quote to us for the book.]

(l t r) John Duffey, Ben Eldridge, Linda Ronstadt, John Starling, and Mike Auldridge at the Birchmere in 1976
© Carl Fleischhauer

When asked about Linda Ronstadt, Duffey said, *"Yes, it was strange when I met Linda. John Starling knew her somehow. She was going with Lowell George and they were staying at his house for two weeks. The Scene was recording Old Train, and we were at Starling's house going over some of the numbers. Linda came*

173

*downstairs and asked if she could sing on a couple of songs with us.*

*"She was getting pretty hot then, you know, a pretty hot item. I said, 'sure, if you want to sing then fine.' Linda asked, 'are you going to do any gospel songs?' because she loves to sing gospel tunes. She knows that's not where the money is but that's one of the things she likes to do.*

*"So, we had her sing 'Old Crossroads' and 'Bottom Of The Glass.' We also did 'In The Pines' which never came out because it just didn't sound good. We left it in the can, or we didn't keep it in the can because it's long gone now.*

*"And then she tottered in to the Birchmere when we were playing and just sat down in front of us and listened for a while. Then we asked her if she wanted to sing a few, and she got up on stage. Just by some stroke of luck, the photographer, Carl Fleischhauer just happened to be there that night and he started clicking away.*

*"Afterwards, we let her dub the high baritone on 'California Earthquake.' It's funny because on the back of Old Train [their fourth album that also features Ricky Skaggs on violin] are some pictures of Linda. I had dubbed in a faint high part and everyone thought that was Linda. But it was me."*

**Carl Fleischhauer**
In 1976, photographer Carl Fleischhauer started working at the American Folklife Center at the Library of Congress and moved to Washington, D.C. The photos of the band at the Birchmere with Linda Ronstadt were made by Carl during the same month he moved. His work at the Library began to pull him away from bluegrass during the 1980s and his last photos of The Seldom Scene with Duffey are included in this book: images from the 1985 cover-photo session for the *Blue*

*Ridge* album in Chapter 24 with Jonathan Edwards and the 1986 anniversary concert at the Kennedy Center. (Chapter 14)

We thank Carl for combing through all of his John Duffey photos and offering them to us for this project. We especially thank him for sharing his personal memories at the conclusion of Chapter 26.

## Boris Weintraub

In 1972, Boris Weintraub was a feature writer for the *Evening Star*. A Northwestern University graduate, Weintraub was one of the first D.C. writers to befriend and promote The Seldom Scene through his incisive music reviews. A musician himself, he would say he first learned about bluegrass when he couldn't play Earl Scruggs's licks on his five-string banjo.

In 2018, he remembered meeting the Scene accidentally on the National Mall in D.C. as they were practicing harmonies for a nearby show possibly on the south slope of the Washington Monument with Reverend Pealy Brown in association with the Interior Department. Boris talked with them and introduced the band to his readers:

"The Seldom Scene is the quintessential modern bluegrass group. Its members are sophisticated, musically and otherwise, and they know what they are doing. And in John Duffey they have the man many hail as the father of modern bluegrass...He's a mandolin player and musical repairman who contributes high tenor vocals that are firmly rooted in bluegrass tradition, while playing mandolin in a way that brings in accents, stresses and ideas from everywhere outside it."

Weintraub became a fan and close friend of the band. Boris also discovered that artist Mike Auldridge was his co-worker at the *Evening Star*. "I would talk with

Mike during the week and find out what they were doing," said Boris in 2018. When the *Star* paper folded in 1981, Mike would never have another day job. Boris took a position at the *National Geographic* and found Tom Gray working there.

An indication of how much The Seldom Scene appreciated, and respected Boris is when they played at his and Kay Mussel's wedding reception. Kay was an American University literature professor and is today an Emeritus faculty member.

In 2018 Boris and Kay are retired, living in Boston to be near their daughters, and also living in Dingle, Ireland, where they rent an apartment. Tom Gray added, "they go to the pub to hear music 2-3 times a week, so Boris is in heaven." And, "Yes, The Seldom Scene played at their wedding, against its usual policy to not play weddings. But Boris gave us such good press, we could not refuse. It's the only wedding we ever played. It was a freebie."

One illustrative Weintraub review occurred when the Smithsonian's *American Popular Song* series produced a Seldom Scene show at the Smithsonian's Baird Auditorium in 1975. This was quite the honor for the band. The series producer B. C. May commented before the show, "we tend to concentrate on two elements of popular music history: current popular songs and the songs of the Broadway stage, and we sometimes ignore some the other contributors to the tradition."

Boris wrote, "Last night's performers were the five musicians and singers from Washington who make up The Seldom Scene. Though they are generally classified as a bluegrass group, they demonstrated many of the other strains that enter into the American popular song tradition.

Consider some of the songs The Seldom Scene performed:

- Traditional country music such as Hank Williams "Lovesick Blues" and "House of Gold" and Bob Wills' "Sitting on Top of the World." [Note: "Sitting on Top of the World" may have been done by Bob Wills but it was a 1930 blues tune written Walter Vinson and Lonnie Chatmon of the Mississippi Sheiks. It found its way to bluegrass through Bill Monroe]
- Modern Country, such as Merle Haggard's "Sing Me Back Home," Jimmy Driftwood's "Tennessee Stud,' and Norman Blake's "Last Train from Poor Valley."
- Traditional folk songs such as "Swing Low Sweet Chariot," House of The Rising Sun."
- Traditional bluegrass tunes such as Bill Monroe's "My Little Georgia Rose" and the standard "Train 45."
- Original songs of members of the group ranging from John Duffey's classic retelling of the "ghostly hitchhiker" legend called "Bringing Mary Home," to any number of fine songs crafted by John Starling.

American popular music draws from many traditions. It speaks well for the Smithsonian that it recognizes one group that draws on so many of them."

### John's aversion to a set list

John commented: *"With The Seldom Scene we never had a program, in other words, a show. It was not taped on the back of a guitar. We would ask, 'what should we start with? What do you want to open the show with?' We decide on that. Sometimes we'll go the first three* numbers. That's the furthest we've ever gone knowing what we were going to do in advance.

"And if it's three numbers, then half-way through the third number you better have five heads thinking and that's the way we do it. I'd say 95% of the time it works fine.

"Maybe 5% of the time everybody is ignoring the playing and we just stand there looking at each other

"Do you have any ideas?

"No, I have a headache.

"And nobody's brain is working. It's just like a whole ball team is going into a slump, which doesn't happen very often. But we've got five zombies up there with brains disengaged.

"I have a couple of friends who come to the Birchmere every Thursday night. I've asked them, 'Don't you get bored hearing the same songs all the time?' And they say, 'No, because we never know when we're going to hear them.' You can't set your watch by anything we do. So, I think that keeps people interested.

"A guy I know who runs three record stores in Kentucky came up and introduced himself to me at a festival to tell me that The Seldom Scene has the strangest audiences. The kids come into my stores and buy Led Zeppelin albums and ask if there are new Seldom Scene records available. He thought that was weird. He is a businessman but also a country person, and this just didn't make sense to him."

**Duffey on Wolf Trap, country music, and money**
John thought the band was getting better in 1984: "In the past few years we've been playing in places like Wolf Trap and other places like Wolf Trap in the country, like the Blossom Center in Ohio, which is damned near twice as big. And a place in Saratoga, New York, which was

*almost identical to Wolf Trap except it is made of metal instead of wood. It actually sounded better than Wolf Trap. That was amazing because I had thought the metal would bounce things around.*

*"But Wolf Trap has this natural delay out there, and on the stage it's tough to play unless you've got a really good monitor system. If you don't then you find yourself playing to the reverb coming back, and you are not playing with the band. So, it's a tough place and a beautiful place to play. There're other nice places we are playing like outside Detroit.*

*"It has now come to be where bluegrass is an acceptable art form. It's OK to say you like it. It doesn't really appeal to your run-of-the-mill redneck country music fan because today's country music is not country music. I don't know what you'd call it. With a few exceptions—and there is always an exception somewhere —most of it is sleaze. You hear 25 different artists on the air with the same band playing behind them. On all their records. It's all hype.*

*"Bluegrass has no promotion whatsoever; it just travels along on its own merits and it has fortunately become a little more than a cult thing. It has snuck outside the cult barriers with people from all walks of life enjoying it, coming to see it, and buying records.*

*"There was a day when you'd be lucky if you sold a thousand records. Here's a joke:*

*"The President of our record company called me and said, 'Your new record is doing pretty well.'*

*"I asked 'Is it going to gold?'*

*"He answered, 'No, it's turning to tin.'*

*"Unless we get hyped on MTV with how they ram music down your throat we now sell maybe 30 to 40,000 copies of a record and that is considered super in this kind of*

*music. Well, I've got sense enough not to watch MTV because I hate it."*

# Chapter 14: Surgeon Starling

Ben and Barbara Eldridge with Cynthia and John Starling in June 2018. John died of congestive heart failure on May 2, 2019 at his Fredericksburg, Virginia home, at the age of 79. © S. Moore

**J**ohn Starling was born on March 26, 1940, in Durham, North Carolina. While practicing, his medical expertise was as an otolaryngologist [head and neck surgery]. Duffey would call it *"ear, nose, and wallet."*

Here in Starling's words are his memories as recorded at the home of Ben Eldridge in 2018 and also at John Starling's medical practice by co-author, G.T. Keplinger in 1999:

"The folk boom started when I was in college at Davidson. I traveled up to Duke University to see Joan Baez. A bluegrass band opened for her. It was The New Lost City Ramblers featuring Mike Seeger.

"My fraternity had a 'record committee' and we stacked it with people who bought bluegrass records like Earl Taylor, Flatt & Scruggs etc. and it was just beginning to dawn on an age that you could admit you liked bluegrass music and not be looked down on, 'I'll go have to hide under a rock or in a closet somewhere to listen to it without being hooted at.'

"But still, it wasn't totally accepted among college kids. When I got to medical school in Charlottesville it was a different thing. The hootenannies were starting and we discovered a five-string banjo player, Alvin Breeden, who lived in Stanardsville, Virginia. We had a hard time getting him to come into town and play. And that is really when I met Ben Eldridge.

"I was at a football game and somebody invited me to a party. Ben was there with Paul Craft. I'd never met either one of them before. Paul at that time had dropped out of the University of Virginia, and was playing the five-string banjo with Jimmy Martin and The Sunny Mountain Boys at the Jamboree in Wheeling, West Virginia [Since 1933, broadcast from the Capitol Theatre, the Jamboree is the second oldest country music radio broadcast in the US after the Grand Ole Opry].

The Memphis-born Craft, who died in 2014, would go on to write several hit songs with titles like "Lean on Jesus (Before He Leans On You)," "Teardrops In My Tequila," and "Keep Me From Blowing Away", the latter appearing on the Scene's second album, *Act Two*, and a huge number one song "Brother Jukebox."

Starling continued: "At the party, we went into a bedroom with a crowd around and Ben was playing rhythm guitar and Paul was on banjo. I had never heard a banjo played that well in the same room with me before. And it blew me away. I had a few drinks too which also helped blow me away.

"I remember that my date was totally bored with the whole thing. 'Why are we listening to this awful stuff?' she asked me. I immediately became disenchanted.

"Ben had graduated but he would come back to Charlottesville on the weekends and there would be pickin' parties. We developed a friendship. I started trying to play bluegrass on a guitar but really didn't have a clue.

"There was a pecking order at these pickin' parties: The first, second, and third team—determined by how many people who would stick around to listen. The first team would play and then tire and get a drink. The second team would take over and by the time that I'd get up and play there were only a couple of people left to listen. But I didn't care. I was learning.

"Ben was on the first team because he was a good player. He taught Paul Craft how to play the banjo. I never got to play with him. One night after my sophomore year in Medical school, Ben and I were sitting on the couch and I had my guitar and all of a sudden, I thought, 'hey, I think I can play with these guys.' Ben kind of realized the same thing, too and we had a little moment there. And he encouraged me. He said, 'you ought to keep doing this (playing). You are better than you think you are.'

"So, when I finished school and moved on up to Washington to do my medical internship at Walter Reed Army Medical Center, I ran into Ben. He invited me over to his house with Mike Auldridge and his brother, Dave.

We played a little bit, and it wasn't long before we had a basement band going on Monday nights."

Another other early basement band member was Gary Henderson. Gary had joined Dick Spottswood in July 1967 to produce a half-hour bluegrass radio show on American University radio station WAMU-FM in conjunction with *Bluegrass Unlimited Magazine.* WAMU became a champion of bluegrass music in its heyday with radio broadcasters Lee Michael Demsey, Ray Davis, Jerry Gray, Katy Daley, and many others. The station hosted an annual bluegrass concert at Fairfax High School in Fairfax, Virginia as well as the yearly "Pickin' In The Glen" in Glen Echo Park, Maryland featuring performers such as Tony Rice, Alison Krauss, Hot Rize, The Gibson Brothers, and many others. In 2002 the main station transitioned away from bluegrass to an all-news and public affairs format while continuing bluegrass online and on its FM HD2 channel.

Starling continued: "Our wives would go to *Slimnastics.* [a then new type of workout–that combined cardio moves, and yoga-based toning] We got a reel-to-reel tape recorder and started doing sound-alike songs by Jimmy Martin and others to see how we sounded. We got one paying job and made $10 each playing for a friend of Mike's out on a lake. I remember that nobody would listen to us. They were all talking. This made Mike's brother real mad. He threw his guitar down and muttered some four-letter word, and we got it all on tape. Those were the painful days.

"So that was it. I finished my internship and immediately went to Vietnam for six months as an 'on the job training' doctor in an evacuation hospital. I liked the D.C. area so when I returned, I started a residency at Walter Reed for a year in ear, nose, and throat. And Ben, Mike and I got back together again.

"By that time, they were playing with Cliff Waldron's band, New Shades of Grass so there was no idea of getting a band together. So, I went down to Fort Bragg, North Carolina for a surgery residency. I played golf and sort of forgot about music."

## All Up to John

"When John Duffey and the basement band got together at my house, I lived a few doors down from Ben. We played together and realized there was something there, but it was all up to John. After a while, he told us, yes, he thought we could do something together.

"We weren't even thinking about a bass player. We just wanted to hear how our singing and playing sounded together. John did say to me: 'You know, you play rhythm guitar a little bit funny.' I think this was a nice way of saying I should work on my guitar playing.

"But one thing about John: He was always very encouraging. He was always loyal to the people he picked to play with. At that time, Ben, Mike and I had played before filling in for Cliff Waldron with Mike's brother Dave as tenor voice at the Red Fox Inn. With John coming in the band, Dave's brother dropped out.

"The second album [*Act Two*] we did at Bias, and by that time we were becoming a little bit more cosmopolitan about the recording process and realized there was something called multitrack that we had a dickens of a time getting John to accept. We would argue. I mean we had a lot of in-band little political things. There was definitely a conservative wing of the band and there was a progressive wing of the band and that's the way it ought to always be in any band. If there's not that then it's not gonna work and so we finally talked John into going to a multitrack studio.

"We did a show at Wolf Trap for the Folk Festival and the guys from Bias were there doing some live recording. We talked to them. And then as soon as John discovered the reverb pot [potentiometer] on the multitrack board where he could take his voice and add reverb to it, he was convinced particularly when he would hit those real high tenor notes and he'd take the reverb pot and go, 'waaahhh' like that. He'd go, 'I like this.' So, we did the second album at Bias on an eight track machine that used to belong to Les Paul. It was one of his original machines. Never will forget that we did it eight track.

"The third album [*Act 3*] was, I think, when we really got launched because we used an engineer named George Massenburg. On the album it says 'George Motion' but it was George Massenburg. I don't own a lot of our albums. Whenever I need one for something, I have to go and buy one. So, I went out and bought *Act 3* on CD and put it in the car CD rack and listened to it and realized now after all these years how good that CD was. I mean it was us to some degree. The material was good, but the engineering was so good. What he [George Massenburg] did with Mike's Dobro. All of a sudden, we sounded slick and we really weren't all that slick. We kind of prided ourselves in not being slick. We thought it was some kind of mortal sin to be too slick, but George made us sound slick.

"But that album sort of all of a sudden picked people's ears up that there was something going on, and of course George did *Old Train* for us which was the next album. But those two albums I think really kind of set the tone and all of a sudden, we began to realize we were we were kind of good.

"I'd sort of learned how to play the guitar by that time but there was a limit to where we were going to go.

John didn't want to fly. We were getting offers to go to California and all over the world to play and John wouldn't go. Also, I was finishing up my residency. I was finishing up my time in the Army. I had some thoughts about maybe not doing medicine and just playing music, but they didn't last very long. It was going to be very difficult for me to go into private practice and there were more and more demands on The Seldom Scene to play more and more shows and all this time they were working around my call schedule.

"I think the year before I left the band, we made maybe $15-20 thousand a piece. After I left the band, they made $60-70 thousand a piece just because they could play more.

"I actually just broached the subject with them one day because they weren't putting any pressure on me, but I began to realize what the deal was. So, I decided to bow out and let them go on. I just figured, 'run in another lead singer.' I really didn't have much to say about who it was, although I made some suggestions. And Phil was one of them just because we had done some of his songs. He was a real good songwriter. Nobody in our band wrote. I wrote some songs out of desperation because we didn't have quite enough original material to fill up a record. We were having to do too many covers and I didn't want to do that, so I wrote a few songs just because we had put a record out every year. But Phil was a songwriter. I mean he had a number of good songs and I thought that would be good. He was also much better guitar player than I was. So, I thought that that would work out, but it was up to them. I think they tried to three different people before they decided who to get, then I was gone."

**Herb Pedersen**

When The Seldom Scene were searching for material to record, it was Starling who took a leadership role. However, it was Duffey who wrote a note to Herb Pedersen to ask if Herb had any songs to contribute. Herb long admired The Country Gentlemen and was inspired by Eddie Adcock to learn the banjo.

Herb offered a group of songs written by him, alone, and also with his late wife, Nikki. It was Starling who received Herb's cassette demo tape. Starling picked his two favorites, "Wait a Minute" (H. Pedersen) and "Old Train" (H. Pedersen, N. Pedersen) and played them for Duffey. John liked both songs and they appeared on the Scene's next album, *Old Train.*

It is "Wait a Minute" that is The Seldom Scene's most popular song, and also the song Herb chooses as his best composition.

**Post Op**

In September, 1977 Starling left the band, deciding to, in his words, "do what I was originally trying to do, which was practice medicine."

In November 1986, Starling, with Birchmere owner, Gary Oelze produced The Seldom *Scene's 15th Anniversary* Concert at The Kennedy Center. This all-star tribute featured performances by artists as high flying as Emmylou Harris and Linda Ronstadt and as influential as Charlie Waller, Ricky Skaggs, and Tony Rice.

Starling choreographed the entire show, and the precisely timed program was a departure from the "no set list looseness" of the Scene. John joined in on several songs. The ensemble's swashbuckling version of the gospel classic "Take Me In Your Lifeboat" is the perfect finale.

Duffey, Ronstadt, Starling, Auldridge
at 15th anniversary concert at the
Kennedy Center
© Carl Fleischhauer

A reviewer noted that, "one group member was missing from the show and his name is Phil Rosenthal." [See Phil's story in Chapter 17] Starling returned to The Seldom Scene briefly in 1993 to fill in following the departure of singer/guitarist Lou Reid, but soon went back to his medical practice.

In 2004, following his retirement from medical practice, Starling resumed his musical career, teaming with former Scene members Mike Auldridge and Tom Gray, along with Jimmy Gaudreau and Rickie Simpkins, to form a new bluegrass band, *John Starling and Carolina Star*. For 2006 and '07, Carolina Star was Emmylou Harris' road band.

Other outstanding credits include:

- 1987: *Trio* (Dolly Parton, Linda Ronstadt, and Emmylou Harris) acoustic guitar accompanist and musical consultant
- 1992 Grammy Award for Best Bluegrass Album with Carl Jackson for their album *Spring Training.*
- 1995: *Feels Like Home* (Linda Ronstadt album) - backing vocalist
- 2006: *All I Intended to Be* (Emmylou Harris album) - lead and harmony vocalist

## Uniformity

Starling stated that, "John Duffey wanted us to wear uniforms when we started the band. He thought we all ought to have the same stuff on and we didn't much like that idea, but it was always kind of John's band. So, I remember we went out to Tysons Corner and it was a disaster. We couldn't agree on anything. We couldn't agree on the kind of pants, what kind of shirt but finally we came up with something, and I remember we had them, and we wore them for about a month and then Ben was the first one of us to start showing up in anything he wanted to. And then pretty soon Tom and John were the only two that wore the blue shirts that we bought. Finally, Tom was the only one that wore the blue shirt and then even Tom gave up.

"We just said we're not only not going to dress alike but we're gonna take advantage of the fact that we're a little off the edge here. We're different. We may not be as slick as some of them, but at least we're different. And you develop an attitude.

"I remember I talked to Bill Kirchen not long ago—Commander Cody—and you got an attitude in the 70s if you played in a band. 'I'm in a band and you're not.' Duffey has always preached, 'you got to have an attitude.'

"When he and Tom Gray played in The Country Gentlemen, Duffey overheard Tom telling somebody that his favorite band was Jim and Jesse and the Virginia Boys. After the guy moved off, John went up to Tom, and he says, 'you know they may be your favorite band but don't ever tell anybody that. Tell them The Country Gentlemen are your favorite band.'

"That's the kind of thing John taught us all about music and how to have an attitude. When we first got on stage, we were staring at the floor, and we didn't know how to entertain anybody. I barely knew how to play. John was the only one entertaining. We were fumbling with things and looking at the floor, and he said, 'don't look at the floor. Just pick out a light in the back somewhere and stare at it. The crowd will think you're looking at them.'

"I learned everything I know about music and how to perform from John Duffey, and he taught us. He was the guy. He was The Seldom Scene. He was The Country Gentlemen too, and he said that on more than one occasion."

# Chapter 15: Mathematician Ben

Ben and John at Ben's home in 2018 with co-author
Moore holding an album Duffey signed in 1984.
© Barbara Eldridge

**B**en Eldridge was born on August 15th, 1938 in Richmond, Virginia. He graduated from the University of Virginia before moving to Washington, D.C.

He remembers "flipping out" while still a toddler in his crib when his second cousin would play his harmonica on the Eldridge's front porch. Simple melody tunes like "Old Joe Clark," "Down Yonder," and "Red River Valley." Ben thinks his later preference for music over song lyrics was because of his cousin's harmonica playing.

Ben would later watch the *Old Dominion Barn Dance* country music TV show every day after grade school. An older neighborhood boy he admired, Nick Valdrighi, ["a good Irish boy," said Ben"] was playing accordion, so he asked his parents to buy him one. Since accordions were expensive, his Mom suggested a guitar instead. Ben agreed. He was nine years old.

His first guitar at the age of nine was a Gene Autry 'Melody Ranch' model for $13 purchased at the Sears and Roebucks store down on Broad Street. There's a picture of Ben on The Seldom Scene album, *Like We Used To Be* sitting with his feet in the water and his shirt off playing that guitar and holding a G chord. By the time Ben turned 12 he could play well enough to convince his parents to buy him a $75 dollar "F hole" Gibson for Christmas.

In 1949, a new Richmond radio station, WLEE AM 1480—or "WL-Double E" as it was called—signed on. Baltimore businessman Tom Tinsdale was the station owner. The "LEE" was Tinsdale's affectionate nod to General Robert E. Lee, whose large portrait hung in the WLEE's lobby at the corner of 3rd and Grace Street.

The station had a large auditorium with a grand piano, and the *Old Barn Dance* TV crew would often use it for weekend dances. Ben urged his mother to take him down to their weekend dances. "I liked the way that music felt," recalls Ben.

WLEE offered a country music show hosted by DJ "Cousin John" Moreau. "Housewives, hillbillies, and little kiddies friend" was his catchphrase. Ben loved to listen to Cousin John's show. One day a song, "I'll Just Pretend," caught Ben's ear. "I heard a little stuff going on in the background like tinkly tink, dinka, dinka,

dinka," Ben remembered. "I guessed it was a guitar. I listened carefully after the song finished to find out what band was playing. This was the first time I heard Flatt & Scruggs. When I really heard Earl play 'Foggy Mountain Breakdown' is when I flipped out. I somehow talked my father into buying me a banjo for my 16th birthday.

"It was an RB-100 Gibson that he paid $150 for, and I didn't know how to play it. There was no tablature back then. I met a guy named Bing who was about nine-months into learning. So, he came over to my house and showed me how to put on the picks, tuning, the three-finger roll and all that sort of stuff.

"I'd take Flatt & Scruggs 45rpm records and slow them down to 33rpm to figure out what they were doing. I used to have this little sunporch off of my bedroom which is where I practiced.

"One day my father came back there and opened up the door, looked at me and started shaking his head, "Son, buying you that banjo last year was the biggest goddamn mistake I ever made in my life. That thing is nothing but a cacophony of harsh and unpleasant sounds."

"At that point in time I expect he was probably right," thought Ben. "I asked, 'well, what does cacophony mean dad?' I knew what harsh and unpleasant meant. Soon after I went to University of Virginia majoring in math and partying. Mostly math. I met Paul Craft while we were students. Paul and I were both students at UVA."

After graduating UVA, Ben went to graduate school at the University of Maryland in College Park. He often returned to Charlottesville for the UVA football weekends where the pickin' parties continued. Paul Craft and Ben met a guy at one of these parties hunkered down on the floor with an electric guitar singing Johnny Cash songs. His name was John Starling.

Ben would return often on football weekends for the first couple of years after he got out of school. "John's fiancée at the time Fayssoux was a killer singer. Here's this drop-dead gorgeous lady who could sing tenor like Ralph Stanley. I thought this guy Starling must be something else if he can hook up with her. John and I got to be friends. If he and Fayssoux were coming up to D.C. for any reason they'd just stay with my wife, Betty and me, or I'd go down to Charlottesville and spend weekends with them. We became good friends."

John graduated from medical school and did his internship at Walter Reed Army Medical Center. John and Fayssoux got an apartment in D.C. and soon Ben, Mike and Dave Auldridge began to get together pretty regularly like every Monday night for pickin'.

## Knowing Duffey

Ben began seeing John Duffey almost every week in 1962 at the Shamrock with the Gents. "They played back then from nine until two o'clock in the morning. They did five sets. They were so good. The absolute best bluegrass band I've ever heard in my life. I just couldn't leave.

"I don't think Eddie Adcock remembers telling me this. Eddie said somebody told him. "If you, Charlie and Duffey are singing the trio and you hear somebody singing a little bit off? It's you." I thought that was a real cool story on Eddie.

"And I never thought their recorded stuff did them justice. I don't know whether it was just because of the quality of the recording or what but I mean in person they were just astounding.

As for Duffey, Ben didn't dare talk to him. "I was as scared of him as everyone else was," Ben admitted.

Ben said, "I knew that John at the time was an authorized Martin guitar repairman. My mother-in-law worked for the welfare community. Onc of her clients had a Martin New Yorker guitar built in the 1840s. Her client wanted to know what it was worth. His mother-in-law volunteered Ben to find out

"John Duffey didn't have a public phone number, so I went down to The Shamrock," said Ben. "I had to have a whole pitcher of beer and sit through two sets before I finally I got up my nerve. I introduced myself and explained my situation trying to estimate the guitar's worth.

"Oh, it's between the buyer and the seller," he sniffed and turned around and walked off. That was Ben's first real meeting with John Duffey. It was the Friday after John quit The Country Gentlemen that Ben really began to know him.

Vince Sims who helped start the *Bluegrass Unlimited* magazine called Ben at work and said, "listen, I know you're a chess player. John Duffey likes to play chess. Would you like to come over Friday night and just play chess with John or whatever else we're going to do?"

Ben started hyperventilating. Vince told Ben, "now, don't talk about music or anything." Ben and John ended up playing chess all night long and never mentioned music once. Ben whipped him three games. In fact, John and Ben played a fair amount of chess in the early days and Ben never lost a game to Duffey. "That's how I got to know him," Ben confided.

In early 1970 Ben taught banjo at Arlington music for six months. The little studio Ben used for teaching was opposite John's repair bay. "If I didn't have a student then I'd shoot the breeze with Duffey. I found out he was just a regular guy. At that time John wasn't playing music. He wasn't singing. He wasn't doing anything but the repair shop."

## Meeting Mike Auldridge

Tom Morgan, who had played bass with the Gents also made and fixed instruments. Tom's basement shop was in his Takoma Park, Maryland house. Ben met Bill Emerson, Frank Wakefield, Red Allen, Bill Keith, Lamar Grier and other energetic bluegrass musicians in Tom's basement, including Mike Auldridge.

Ben remembers "I was down in Tom's basement sanding necks and stuff. Mike came in with an old Gibson guitar that somebody had cut a big hole to put a resonator in and that was his Dobro at the time. He started playing and I thought 'whoa that sounds like Buck Graves.' Mike was a student at the time at the University of Maryland. Mike was playing banjo then, but when he eventually heard Ben play, Mike said, "No more banjo for me. I'll stick to Dobro."

The 1967 Monday night basement band included Gary Henderson, the beloved radio broadcaster on station WAMU, Mike and Dave Auldridge, and Bruce Barnes on mandolin. Ben had at that time an old Viking tape recorder. He'd turn it on and record everything they did. Today Ben has those tapes in the attic of his Fredericksburg, Virginia home.

Ben continues his story: "Bill Emerson was then and still is one of my all-time favorite banjo pickers. When The Country Gentlemen records came out, I would learn all the parts. Back then I played a lot like Emerson. He was a huge influence on me. Bill was working with Cliff Waldron and Mike and Dave Auldridge at the Red Fox Inn, and when Emerson left, I joined their band."

Their playlist was progressive. In addition to "Fox on the Run" which Bill Emerson gets credit for "blue grassing" an obscure song by UK's rock band, Manfred Mann, they were doing "Early Morning Rain," "Proud Mary" and other popular folk songs. Ben started with Cliff's band in July 1970 and both Mike and Ben left a year later.

"I had a family and a job, and all that sort of stuff and we were playing two or three nights a week and it was more than I could handle. It was a lot of fun. I was on three albums with Cliff in that year. Mike and I both made a little bit of a name for ourselves during that time but after about a year it was more than I could handle and so I left. Starling then was getting back from Vietnam. When it became known that Starling was coming back to the area, the rumors started that he, Mike, me and maybe even John Duffey might start a band," Ben said.

Ben remembers walking into Arlington Music in August, 1971 where John Duffey was working at the time:

Duffey said to Ben, "hey, I hear we're going to be in a band together."

Ben responded, "what?"

Duffey and Ben thought the rumor was just a "bunch of hooey."

In October Cliff Waldron was still playing at the Red Fox. Jimmy Arnold was playing banjo and Gene Johnson [later with the band, Diamond Rio,] was on mandolin. Cliff wanted to go to the DJ convention in Nashville so he called Ben and asked, "hey could you put your old basement band together?" Gary Henderson couldn't do it, so Ben recruited Tom Gray.

"I knew who Tom was because I watched him with the Gents," Ben explains. "Tom also came over to one of our Monday night deals. Tom is one of the nicest guys on the planet. We had a good time playing music. Tom called me a couple times to fill in for banjo players. I remember one time I filled in with Benny and Vallie Cain, at Jimbo's in Manassas, Virginia. Tom is really just a wonderful guy."

On break at the Red Fox they got a phone call from The Rabbit's Foot owner who was interested in trying bluegrass on Monday nights because he'd heard it had been pretty successful at The Red Fox. Ben was the one who ended up getting on the phone talking to him. Ben recalled, "He wanted somebody to come in there, starting the first Monday in November. I said, "oh hell yeah. We'll do it. Sure."

"Then I went back and asked other guys if they were interested after I'd already accepted the job. They said yeah, we'll do it. We had three weeks before we had to do this thing and I remember sitting around in my kitchen and talking to John Starling about the rumor going around. I told Starling we ought to give Duffey a call just for fun. I don't think he'll do it but why don't we give him a call so Starling said, "yeah, I'll give him a call."

"So, I can remember watching him talking to Duffey on the wall phone and him going, "oh good. Okay. Well, why don't we try to get together next week." And I'm dumbfounded because I didn't think that the Duff would really be interested but he said, "yeah it kind of sounds like fun." So, that's how it all got started. We rehearsed once or twice with Duffey and went in on the first Monday in November to play The Rabbit's Foot.

**First Scene Memories**
Ben described the making of *Act 1:* "I think it took either two or three Sunday afternoons. We did it over at Roy

199

Homer's studio two-track live head on. I think the whole album cost us about four hundred and fifty dollars to record. Part of one of those Sunday afternoons was watching a bunch of dirty movies. I think Duff, bless his heart, was into that kind of stuff and he knew Roy had some good ones.

"So, anyway we were all thrilled with it. I remember Starling had the tapes. I couldn't wait to get home from work to go to his house right up the street from me with, 'oh, put the tape on. Let's listen to this thing. And it was different from anything anybody had heard up to that point. It sounded pretty darn good. Starling's voice was just amazing, and people had really never heard John well. We had some really neat songs that attracted some attention to us. The fact that we had John Duffey attracted a lot of attention you know."

The first bluegrass festival the Scene played was Indian Springs in 1972. Ben said he was scared to death adding, "I think we were all scared to death. We get to the festival and here's all these professional bands we'd been listening to for years like Ralph Stanley and Don Reno. I don't know whether Monroe was there or not but it was a pretty substantial lineup.

"So, here's this bunch of doofuses getting up there playing. We had to back up Bill Clifton on that show too. That was strange because we had no chance to rehearse. I've got a tape of this show and it's a lot better than I remembered it being.

"John Duffey thought of himself primarily as an entertainer. Whereas the rest of us thought of ourselves as musicians. John tried like the dickens to make us become entertainers. I remember the early days of the Gents. Charlie Waller did all the emcee work and it was pretty much standard emcee work. John started taking over a lot of the emcee work when he would see people like The Kingston Trio. Half of their act went on between the songs.

"John Starling and Duffey became pretty good foils for one another because Starling was kind of straight ahead but yet he'd get up there and yak and they'd go back and forth. I never said a word for 25 years but I would make cracks in the background and not on the mic. Many of these quips would end up coming out of Duffey's mouth much to my chagrin.

"We all listened to all kinds of music and kept an ear out. 'Hey, what's something that might be fun to do?' A lot of them just happened to be things that had come in the rock era like John Fogerty, James Taylor, and The Monkees. If it's good music then why not give it a shot." Ben remembers, "John wanted us to do to try the Eagles "Lyin' Eyes." I put the quash on that because nobody can do that as well as the Eagles," Ben said strongly. "Nobody."

"There was a song that we did called "Don't Bother with White Satin." I hear that now and it gives me goose bumps on my arm. We did that maybe two times after we recorded it, but we just dropped it because it only got polite applause."

## Payoff

When asked who handled the bookings for the band, Ben replied: "John did. To his credit John would turn down a lot of jobs. John did not like to leave the house unless he was going to be appropriately remunerated. There's an interesting story the first time we had an inquiry from the West Coast. It was from McCabe's Guitar Shop. The owner called John:

McCabe's: "We are interested in having The Seldom Scene out here."

Duffey: "Fine. How much are you willing to offer us?"

McCabe's: "Well, I think I can get you a thousand dollars,"

Duffey: "Which one of us do you want?"

"Many bluegrass bands would have probably just gone out there at their own expense. When we played, it was always worth our while. We owe that to John Duffey."

## Legacy

"John was a person that once he got comfortable with something, he didn't like change. Did not like change at all. And that's just the way he was and who he was. His legacy is mammoth. Not only from the music that he left but he just touched a lot of people's lives I think with his personality and his music. He really was kind of larger than life. Once you got to know him, he was a pussycat. He really was. He could be a curmudgeon if things didn't work out the way he liked them. But usually when that happened it was because he had thought of the best way to do something and it didn't happen that way. It would bother him and he would let you know about it. But I think he'll be remembered for a long time. A very long time."

## Retirement

Ben Eldridge retired in 2016 after nearly 45 years with the Grammy-nominated band. "It was a very hard decision to make, but I've been wanting to stop for a while," Eldridge told the *Bluegrass Music Network News* at the time, "I'm 77, I don't like traveling much anymore and I'm not playing that well. My left hand is going south on me." Eldridge was the last original member of The Seldom Scene but the band continues to perform as of 2020 (see Chapters 27 and 28).

# Chapter 16: Artist Auldridge

Auldridge Sketch by Laurent
Vue © L. Vue

*Mike is pretty open with everyone and easy to talk to. His only problem is he occasionally suffers from paranoia. All of a sudden, he gets these weird ideas in his head and he thinks something's wrong, and he'll think this for a week. Then next week he's all right. I mean I love Mike. The fact is that he and I talk. We travel together and we're the*

*only two that smoke. None of the rest of the band
want to be around us.*

JD

**M**ike Auldridge gave the Dobro its first ultramodern
voice, adding a sophisticated relish to its sound. The
eighth of nine siblings, he was born in Washington, D.C.
on December 30, 1938 and moved to the suburb of
Kensington, Maryland when he was seven.

In 1999 co-author, G.T. Keplinger interviewed Mike
in his Silver Spring, Maryland home: "In those days
Kensington was a very small town, Mike said. "A lot of
farms were still around. Country music was very big
there."

Like Duffey, Mike first heard what came to be known
as bluegrass music on the radio. For Mike it was Flatt &
Scruggs. "I thought they had been around for years, but
they started their band in 1948. It was basically brand-
new music," said Mike.

By the early 1950s Mike had started on guitar and
moved to banjo. He formed a band, the South Mountain
Boys with his older brother Dave Auldridge (1934-2008),
Wayne Mason, and Wayne Damieux.

"I was probably fifteen. We got a fifteen-minute radio
show on Saturdays that had about six to eight bands in
a row on Saturday morning. We'd learn three or four
songs a week—and we'd spend all week working on
those three or four songs—it was good study habits that
I was developing on how to learn to play music."

Mike describes the first time he met John Duffey:

"John had been playing for years around
Washington and there was this place called Kramer's
Pool that was up in the country up around Olney,
Maryland. We were swimming up there one day and out
in the parking lot was this little band that was gathered

204

around the open trunk of this car and there was this guy playing a Dobro. I thought, 'Oh my gosh. There's a Dobro! I can't believe it.' I'd been in love with that sound for a long time and it turns out it was John Duffey. So, I thought of him as a Dobro player first."

Mike asked John where he could find a Dobro.

"They don't make these guitars anymore," grumbled John, blowing Mike off.

"I found out he was a mandolin player and the Dobro was a secondary instrument for him," Mike recalled. "I really didn't get into Dobro until I was about twenty. I had a cheap one that I messed around with, but I considered myself a banjo player for four or five years."

"I used to see the Country Gents at least once every five weeks at the Shamrock. I was one of the guys sitting and listening there."

When asked what about the Gents did Mike admire, he answered, "to be perfectly honest with you, my favorite bluegrass band in those days was the early Flatt & Scruggs band. When I first heard The Country Gentlemen, they were a little bit too folky for me. I admired their stage presentation—they were very entertaining guys because Duffey was just insane and Eddie Adcock was also. They were fun to watch, and that probably was the biggest thing that set them apart.

"And Duffey would go to the Library of Congress and get old folk songs basically and set them to bluegrass music. So, those two things set them apart. When I first heard them, it took me a while to develop a liking for them. To appreciate what they were doing. My love was for the real, polished sound of Flatt & Scruggs. I think Duffey's antics is probably what kept me involved with The Country Gentlemen."

Sally Gray, Tom Gray, G.T. Keplinger and Mike Auldridge at
G.T.'s parents' house in 2006. They had come over to watch a
cut of G.T.'s MFA thesis, a documentary on The Seldom Scene.
© Helen Keplinger

G.T.: What was the first record that you bought?
Mike: I think probably the first record I ever bought was
"Salty Dog Blues" by Flatt & Scruggs. I remember they
had it on a juke box in this little town I lived in. I was
about, I don't know, say twelve years old or something.
That was probably my first record.

G.T.: And did you use to listen to the record and try to
imitate them to learn how to play banjo?
Mike: Oh definitely. The one I remember trying to
imagine how somebody could do this was "Chokin' the
Strings" by Don Reno and Red Smiley. I had never seen
anybody play a banjo and it didn't occur to me that they
were playing with three picks. In my mind I was thinking

about how in the world anybody could do that with a flat pick because I had been playing guitar. (laughs)

G.T.: So, what about bluegrass music drove you to wanting to play that kind of music. What inspired you about it?

Mike: Oh gosh. There was a certain energy and feel there that just blew my mind I mean the first time I heard it. It just changed my life. I even knew it then. I loved a lot of the early swing stuff but bluegrass was the first music that just grabbed me and made me pay attention.

G.T.: And it was mostly the instrumentation of it more so than the lyrics and the message?

Mike: Oh yeah. I thought in that movie, *Bonnie and Clyde* when they showed the old cars flying along those country roads with "Foggy Mountain Breakdown" blasting away—that's how it affected me. I mean this same feeling that you get in the movie watching that did that to me when I was twelve (laughs) and that was one of the songs too actually.

G.T.: How did you decide on Dobro? That was a fairly uncommon instrument in the early days.

Mike: Very much. My uncle, Ellsworth T. Cozzens played slide guitar or steel guitar with Jimmy Rodgers in the late 1920s. My mother's brother was on Jimmy Rodgers' first sessions in 1928. [Note: In 1928, the Dobro had not yet been invented. Cozzens played an acoustic guitar with a high nut, laying horizontally on his lap, with a steel bar, just like later musicians would play the Dobro]

So, when I was seven years old, I used to see him play Dobro at our family parties and I always thought, 'boy that's a neat instrument'. And then he got into electric steel—a non-pedal steel guitar. This was in the 40s and just those sounds, you know, just watching him play. Then I heard Josh Graves, Speedy Krise, and husband and wife act, Wilma Lee and Stoney Cooper and Shot Jackson when I was discovering country and bluegrass in the late 40s. The sound of a Dobro just killed me but could never find one so I ended up playing guitar for a few years from say twelve to sixteen and then I got into banjo because of Earl Scruggs—all the while looking for a Dobro and never could find one. They were that rare in those days—I used to always ask people in music stores about them and some guy said, 'yeah, I think I have one of those things in the back that someone brought in for repairs.' The store guy brought it out and gave it to me because it had been there for four or five years. But they were really rare instruments in those days.

G.T.: And then you were in the Army? And University of Maryland?
Mike: Right. I went in the Army from 1961 to 1963 and then I went to the University of Maryland from 1963 to 1967 and studied art. I was an art major and music minor. Then I worked for a few years as a commercial artist. I worked in an art shop for a couple years and that's when I joined Emerson and Waldron which later became Cliff Waldron and the New Shades of Grass and then I worked for a few years for the Washington Star newspaper while I was a member of The Seldom Scene.

Ben was a graduate student at the University of Maryland while I was an undergrad student. I met Ben through a guy named Tom Morgan who used to build banjos here in the Washington area over in Takoma Park, Maryland. And Ben used to show up at parties, a lot of pickin' parties. I was still playing with banjo when

I heard Ben. I thought this guy knows how to play a banjo, so I think I'm going to give up on the banjo. It was the best thing I ever did because it really made me put all my energy into the Dobro which was really the sound that I loved anyway.

But, anyway, Ben and I met in college and he and Starling were college friends from the University of Virginia and we started getting together with a guy named Gary Henderson who was a bass player and a disk jockey in Washington and my brother Dave and some guy named Bruce Barnes played mandolin and we just played once a week just for fun at either Ben's house or Starling's house.

Ben had been teaching banjo in the Arlington music store where John Duffey was the guitar repair man and so he started inviting John Duffey to these parties that we were having and once we all played together, we thought, 'wow. This sounds pretty good. It's different'. It wasn't like Emerson and Waldron; it wasn't like The Country Gentlemen. It was just different because John Starling was a great singer. And his voice and Duffey's voice together were very unusual and I took up all the baritone parts in that band.

I also knew Tom Gray from before he was in The Country Gentlemen. There was kind of like this underground group of people that played this kind of music—there wasn't very many of us but there were maybe a dozen guys around Washington that I knew of and Tom Gray was the bass player. I mean, he was everybody's favorite bass player and ended up being in The Country Gentlemen.

The bad thing about bands like Flatt & Scruggs were they were still appealing to little country audiences in little schoolhouses and stuff and they had a clown playing the bass, you know, a guy with his teeth blacked out and a guy with a big pair of overalls and a pork pie hat or something and as a matter of fact when Buck Graves joined Flatt & Scruggs, he was the clown.

They started calling him 'Uncle Josh' and the bass player was 'Cousin Jake' and they were the two comedy relief guys and that was the one thing that I didn't like about that kind of music. They thought their audiences were stupid. (laughs) you know? Whereas, The Country Gentlemen, they were very urban in their thinking and in their presentation and they drew that kind of an audience—sitting out in the audience are doctors and lawyers and things and rather than guys from the farm or whatever. So, that was a big part of The Country Gentlemen.

G.T.: And their name even. They were city guys from the city. They knew that they were going to be playing to a more sophisticated audience.
Mike: Yeah. Yeah. The Country Gentlemen was the perfect name for them. They were the gentlemen of the hillbilly scene which is what it really was in those days.

G.T.: D.C. became a hotspot for bluegrass music and for the more sophisticated bluegrass music—and the Scene did cater to that same audience.

Mike: Right. Washington, D.C. became a hotbed of country and bluegrass for about four reasons. The first reason is that some disc jockeys in Washington were really great disc jockeys. There was a guy named Don Owens who was a great promoter and he brought in a lot of country and bluegrass acts. There was another guy named Curly Smith and there was a radio station owner named Connie B. Gay who started the Country Music Association. Those three guys were a big force in

Washington. The other thing, the population was coming up from the south to work in the government that had a lot to do with it and they loved that kind of music.

Bluegrass began to gain in popularity and The Country Gentlemen were a huge force in Washington. And then in the 1970s when the Scene started, we were appealing to the same audience that the Gents had. More professional people rather than farmers. For those reasons I think Washington became a huge center for bluegrass music—as a matter of fact they called it for years, "the capital of bluegrass music" for the United States, and it really was.

The truth is in those early days there wasn't the division that there is now among what people call "purists" and people that like a more modern contemporary sound. There wasn't a division because there were hardly any bands that did anything different. They all tried to sound like Bill Monroe or Flatt & Scruggs. The first generation of guys like Mac Wiseman, The Stanley Brothers, Reno and Smiley and all those guys more or less sounded the same. I mean, there were some differences amongst them, but they were all directed more at the country audience.

So, the first of the modern bands really was The Country Gentlemen. And then The Seldom Scene. I remember people saying, "you know, I don't like Dobros...You know, that's not part of bluegrass music. I used to get that a lot even though Buck Graves had been with Flatt & Scruggs since 1955, so it's like twelve years he'd been playing with Flatt & Scruggs, but people were still saying, "Dobro has no place in bluegrass music" because Bill Monroe didn't have a Dobro.

And there were some people that thought our Seldom Scene music was a little too slick. We were a little bit too polished. There's this huge division between traditionalists and people that like more modern bluegrass music.

G.T.: And you did things with the Dobro different than anyone else had done before you. In the early recordings with Dobro it was sort of a background instrument, but you would go up and take solo leads and take breaks on the Dobro in the same way a fiddle would have done.

Mike: Yeah. You know, the funny thing is, the reason I play the Dobro the way I play is because I couldn't play like Josh Graves. You end up having to play what you have in you. The Seldom Scene, Cliff Waldron, and Emerson and Waldron featured the Dobro a lot. And particularly by the time I got in the Scene, they were showcasing me basically. I was the only other Dobro player besides Buck Graves with Flatt & Scruggs. And they kind of, you know there was a big competition between Earl Scruggs and Buck Graves. Buck got some breaks, but he didn't get a break in every song whereas the whole Seldom Scene sound was kind of built around a Dobro, as opposed to a fiddle.

Duffey didn't like a fiddle because he felt it interfered with trios with the vocals. It does because it's another voice and if it's not perfect, it's awful. It's the same thing with a Dobro. One of the things that saved me was that I was one of the guys in the trio so I couldn't play and sing at the same time (laughs) so when I was singing, there was no other thing going on.

And one of my favorite things that anybody ever said to me was when Eddie Adcock in 71 said, "I don't know if you just don't know how to play very well or if you have great taste but, you know, it really fits."

The truth was I always tried to not get in the way of the singer. To us in The Seldom Scene, the vocals were the most important thing. I played a smoother style just naturally than any of the previous Dobro players. I just came along at a good time in the history of the instrument, I think.

G.T.: And what would you say that John Duffey's role is in bluegrass in general; more specifically in what people have called "newgrass?"

Mike: I think John's role was a couple of things. One was he was the first guy that brought about entertaining; the thinking of bluegrass music and your presentation as an entertainment thing rather than just stand up there and pick. I mean even the great ones of the generation before, a lot of guys that we were saying earlier the only thing they did to break the monotony of going from one song to the next was to have a clown in the band. I think that John's huge legacy was that he was the first guy that brought that to the forefront of bluegrass music.

John was really a very funny guy. For the most part I missed most of the funny things he said because I'm busy over here doing what I do. Whether you liked him or not you couldn't take your eyes off this guy. He was just a force, or a presence on stage that you had to look at. And for the most part he was hilarious, and he was an extremely quick-witted guy.

In addition to that I think his real contribution was the fact that he had a voice like nobody else really. There were certain places in the register of his voice where he could knock you down with his voice. It was just so powerful and unusual sounding.

So, yeah, his antics, his voice and the fact that he tried to bring more modern music.

G.T.: So, do you think The Seldom Scene would have gone as far as they did if they hadn't been based in the D.C. area?

Mike: I think it was fortunate that we were based in Washington for a couple of reasons. One of them is that it's a transient population. People are coming and going all the time so that's why the clubs where we worked were always filled for one thing. And it's a tourist center so that helped. Tom Gray and I and Duffey were raised in Washington, D.C. Duffey and I grew up about five miles from each other. If we had been based anyplace else it probably would never have happened.

G.T.: I'd heard that one time you said that if Duffey ever quit then that that would be the end of the Scene. What do you think about them continuing without Duffey?

Mike: I don't blame the band for going on and using the name because names are worth money. You spend twenty to twenty-five years building a name and then to just walk away from it isn't really all that smart. I don't think they're playing the same music even though they're playing the same songs. It's not the same sound that was there. I think it's a good band I just think it's a different band than it was. You know? I don't blame them for carrying with the tradition or the name. I would have.

The hardest thing about being a musician is even guessing what the future's going to bring. It's almost a day-to-day life. At the stage—at the echelon I've always been in—if you're raking in the money then you know, "well I've got enough money. If I have to, I can do anything I want to."

But I've always made just enough money so that it was like I had a job except I didn't have to go to the office every day, I could pick. I'm going to continue doing that for as long as I can because I love it.

## Chesapeake

Chesapeake had formed as a side-band with Auldridge, Gaudreau, Coleman and Klein in 1992 but did not take the name Chesapeake until 1993. They rehearsed every week, working out more advanced arrangements than the Scene. Moondi Klein had become The Seldom Scene's guitarist-lead singer during his years with Chesapeake. He had a mailing list he used to promote the band Chesapeake. He would periodically send out postcards advertising upcoming gigs and various band news. This was pre-Internet days. One of the regular postcards sent out by Moondi had the news of the Scene retiring and Moondi, Mike, and Coleman filling out the rest of their scheduled gigs with the Scene and then John Duffey and Ben had decided to retire.

This postcard was sent out in the summer of 1995. They decided to leave the Scene and do Chesapeake only at the end of 1995. The bottom line is that Mike wanted to play more adventurous music and more regularly than John Duffey.

Birchmere owner, Gary Oelze confessed in 2019, "It was very painful for me to watch their relationship deteriorate over the years. John was turning a lot of jobs down. I think it was his health. Mike was complaining to John about his not wanting to work. Duffey said to him, "Well, then get a part time job."

"Mike got Chesapeake together and the inevitable happened. The bands double booked. Duffey left Mike hanging. It cost Mike $5,000 to get out of it."

Gary said he didn't know this breakdown was happening between John and Mike at the time because he was no longer as involved day-to-day with The

Seldom Scene. "I feel very sad about it now," Gary admits. "And on a New Year's Eve show I had Duffey's Seldom Scene and Mike's Chesapeake together and it broke my heart. They weren't speaking to each other but rather talking shit about each other. It was like a couple you love getting a divorce."

Chesapeake stayed together for five years and then disbanded in the fall of 1999. Not finding the commercial success he'd hoped for, Mike told Duffey, "Man I've made a tragic mistake (quitting the Scene)."

John replied, "That's too bad, because you ain't coming back."

From 1999-2002 Mike performed with Jimmy Gaudreau and guitarist Richard Bennett as Auldridge, Bennett, and Gaudreau and they recorded two records for Rebel Records in 1999 and 2001. Next Mike performed with The Good Deale Bluegrass Band for several years. The surviving members of The Seldom Scene, with Larry Stephenson on mandolin, performed select shows as "The Seldom Sceniors" between 2001 and 2004.

From 2004 to 2008, Mike reunited with his former Seldom Scene bandmates, John Starling and Tom Gray, along with Rickie Simpkins and Jimmy Gaudreau, to form John Starling and Carolina Star. During 2006 and '07, they were the road band for Emmylou Harris. In 2009 and 2010, Mike and Tom were members of Darren Beachley and Legends of the Potomac, along with Norman Wright and Mark Delaney.

Mike Auldridge died on December 29, 2012, at home under hospice care after a lengthy battle with prostate cancer. It was the day before his 74th birthday.

He was inducted in the International Bluegrass Music Association's Hall of Fame in 2019.

# Chapter 17: Songwriter Phil

"Ladies and Gentlemen, our new guitarist is Phil
Rosenthal who we call our Kosher Connection."

JD

**W**hen Phil Rosenthal joined The Seldom Scene in 1977
replacing John Starling on guitar and vocals, the above
quote is how John would initially introduce him on
stage. John would make it funny, but this intro bothered
Phil because he didn't publicly identify himself as
Jewish, and wasn't very religious anyway. Finally,
backstage one night, Phil asked John Duffey to drop the
Kosher connection bit. Mike Auldridge, who was
Catholic, agreed with Phil and told John it was weird.
So, John said "OK."

Born in New Haven, Connecticut on September 30,
1948, Rosenthal grew up in nearby Guilford, where his
parents had a chicken farm. There was always a lot of
music in his family, listening to records and seeing
shows. Phil liked folk music and saw acts like Pete
Seeger and The Weavers as a kid. "The sound of acoustic
instruments sounded friendly and inviting to me," Phil
said. He took up "Pete Seeger" style banjo and began
lessons.

Later as he was flipping through banjo records in a
music store, he noticed some acts that also featured
banjos. He bought one of these with a picture of players
wearing suits. "It was Flatt & Scruggs and their music
drew me into bluegrass." In 1966 he first saw John
Duffey with The Country Gentlemen at the Bluegrass
Festival at Fincastle, Virginia.

There wasn't much bluegrass on Guilford radio stations back then. His father had a tape recorder where you could record multitrack "sound-on-sound," so Phil started learning guitar, writing songs by the age of 13, and making home recordings, aspiring to make professional records someday. Later he found a few kids his age who also loved bluegrass and he started a high school band.

Phil graduated from the University of Chicago in the '70s with an English literature degree. He had planned to teach, but he coupled his knowledge of storytelling with his love for music and became a singer/songwriter. After college, he worked for the New Haven Public Library, primarily creating music programs for public school children. His *Bluegrass Songs for Children* was one of the first bluegrass albums (American Melody AM 101) created especially for small fries.

In 1972, Phil saw The Seldom Scene for the first time. A photographer friend, Jim McGuire introduced Phil to Mike and Ben. Phil played them some of his songs and they asked him to put them on a cassette tape and send them so John Starling could listen.

Six months later Phil received a reel-to-reel tape containing tracks that would become the Scene's third album, *Act 3*. John Starling had called Phil to let him know they had recorded "Muddy Water." Phil was thrilled that The Seldom Scene had chosen two of his songs "Willie Boy" and "Muddy Water" to record from the cassette he had sent.

"Muddy Water" would become a standout song for the group. Ricky Skaggs was a session player on The Seldom Scene version. [Phil had originally named and sang this song as "Muddy Waters" plural but Starling and the Scene changed it to "Muddy Water" singular.]

Phil explained, "I wrote the song in July, 1972, on my way home from the Berryville Bluegrass Festival, held in Watermelon Park, on the banks of the Shenandoah River. Someone at the festival pointed out the level that water had risen just a few weeks before, when Hurricane Agnes hit the area. You could see broken branches and debris 15 feet or more up in the trees, showing how high the water had been. Driving back to Connecticut, I noticed mile after mile of the damage that had been caused, homes and farms uprooted and destroyed. I had seen The Seldom Scene perform at the festival, and I had in mind to write a song for them. "Muddy Water" was the result."

"Willie Boy," a political song about a black man living in the south with a white girlfriend was considered both daring and unusual for The Seldom Scene when the record came out. The chorus was:

*Look out Willie Boy*
*Don't raise your so head high,*
*Big man gonna get you bye and bye.*

## Old Dog

While *Act 3* was impressing the Scene's growing fans, Phil had a band called Old Dog which included his wife, Beth. Mike Auldridge told Phil, "I love your band, why don't we do an album together, half my instrumentals and half your songs."

*Mike Auldridge and Old Dog* was released on Flying Fish records in 1978 to middling reviews, but the record further cemented Phil and Mike's friendship. Mike began to lobby the band to consider Phil as a candidate to replace the departing Dr. John Starling. Mike also put Phil in touch with Gary Oelze who booked Old Dog into his club, the Birchmere.

After that Birchmere show John Duffey, Mike and Ben walked in to the dressing room.

"Can we talk to you Phil?" asked Duffey. "John Starling has decided to retire. We think you are a good musician. Would you be interested in auditioning for the Scene? If you are hired then this won't be like getting hired by Bill Monroe as a sideman. You'll be an equal member."

Phil declined this offer to audition.

John gave Phil a long stare. "Will you think about it?"

Phil's hesitation was because he had his own up and coming band. Phil remembers thinking that "taking John Starling's place didn't feel like creatively what I wanted to do. To learn all the songs that he had spent five years working up with the band. I didn't know anyone in Washington, and I didn't feel like it was my home at all obviously."

Auldridge also told Phil, "Well, think about it... because this could be a great opportunity for you. We're a well-established band and you get a chance to do your songs on records and get your material out there and really in a way that you might never be able to do with Old Dog good as the band is."

So, Phil did think about it. On the ride back to Guilford he decided that this was an opportunity he couldn't refuse.

**In The Scene**
In 1980, Duffey told *Bluegrass Unlimited* writer Don Rhodes, that, "Phil's voice is almost too smooth. Mike and I want him to take up smoking to get some gravel in his voice."

Phil recalled, "One of the first things I was surprised and disappointed to learn was that the band never really rehearsed. We'd play a song or two in the back room of the Birchmere on our Thursday night to get warmed up. The only way you could get a new song tried out was at the Birchmere before a show. One of us might say, 'Hey, let's try this' and introduce a new song. We'd take turns. I'd play one of mine and try to get Ben or Mike interested and then see if John would join in. And then someone might say, 'hey let's try that one we were doing last week,' and we'd revisit it. Eventually if everyone liked it then we'd play it in the show. And if it got a reaction, we'd keep it in the back of our minds until it came time to record."

Phil continues, "The band didn't record very often, maybe one album every year and a half. They told me that before I joined. If we had a session coming up, we might go to John's house and run over some songs but that was a rare occasion. John did not like the idea of rehearsing. He always thought that this band should be fun, so he didn't want to have to 'rehearse.' He wanted it to be more spontaneous."

Phil tried to structure some rehearsals through subterfuge. "I suggested to my wife, Beth that we could invite the band over for dinner, and then we'd rehearse afterwards." Phil tried that a few times, but John stepped in and said, "You don't really have to have us for dinner so we can rehearse together." And then the dinners were over.

Sometimes they'd go into a session and record but after listening back more objectively, they'd re-record the song. And sometimes they'd rehearse the parts in the studio. As for the structure of recording, the band would usually record a live basic track together with the vocals but leave the instrumental breaks open. And then they'd either add their solos or record over what they did on the first live track. However, it was very rare that John Duffey did any overdubs.

Phil recalls that once John got excited with a solo he did on the song, "Something in the Wind" (from the album, *Act Four*) and came back to add a second harmony mandolin part on that tune. He could enthusiastically get into recording, but that was still rare."

On the question of how much control did John have over vocal arrangements and song structure, Phil responded, "Everything pretty much needed John's approval. If John listened to something, whether it be the song or arrangement or whatever, and commented, 'Well, I don't know about that.' Everyone would usually defer to him, but not always.

One perpetual issue was that the keys Phil felt he sang the best were lower than the keys John Starling had sang. John preferred the higher keys. For example, Phil wanted to sing a song he wrote, "When a Girl I Know Gets Back in Town" in the Key of F. John wanted it two steps higher in the key of G. Both Phil and John stood their ground and it was decided that they'd record it in both keys and listen as a group to decide which version sounded best. John still preferred G, but the band thought F sounded better and that version was released on their *At The Scene* album.

Phil enjoyed when John Duffey got together with Bill Monroe: "They would both get a sparkle in their eye and kid each other. Bill would come on stage with his band, and John would say 'Let's go out there and take over the stage.'"

"One time he pushed Bill's hat over his eyes so he couldn't see and then shoved him out of the way. I took over the guitarist's microphone and we played "Rose of Old Kentucky," one of Monroe's classics. Bill would enjoy it. Several times John would reach over and cover Bill's mouth so he couldn't sing." Phil remembers.

As always, John handled all the bookings and payments to the band. They received an equal share and Phil still gets royalties for the recordings and for the albums he was on.

## Phil's Fire

One night after their regular weekly Birchmere show the band asked Phil to stick around for a band meeting. Phil sat on the couch in the back room wondering what this was all about. The band told him they had decided to go in a different musical direction. They gave Phil a two-week notice and he was fired.

"I was devastated by this news," Phil said looking back. "I thought 'what am I going to do now?' I don't remember if it was John or Mike that told me I was out. I remember thinking 'how can they fire me?' I'm one fifth of The Seldom Scene," said Phil.

Phil confirmed, there was no "full member" contract for band members so as far as Phil was concerned, if there was a problem then the band should have discussed it with him.

They said they had picked his replacement and Phil could do gigs for the next two weeks and collect the money, or they'd just give him the money and he could walk away. Someone in the music business offered Phil legal help if he decided to sue The Seldom Scene but Phil didn't want to do that.

"Mike Auldridge began pushing to fire Phil," said Tom Gray in 2018. "He wanted someone more spirited. Phil was a laid-back person who I enjoyed working with. We could ride for hours to jobs and never say a word to each other. That was fine with me. I never considered that a problem. But I could understand some of John's disappointment. Phil was using the band to promote his songwriting, which was very good. But he was straining to hit the harmony notes in the singing. He didn't have the vocal range that Duffey wanted him to have. I felt bad for Phil but understood the reasons to find someone new. We replaced Phil with Lou Reid, who like Duffey, was a tenor. Together they could sing stratospheric harmonies."

Phil felt more than frustrated because in his view the band increasingly looked to him to come up with new material, and they had liked his songs when they hired him. Now it appeared that the band was punishing him for "pushing his songs" upon them.

Phil Rosenthal and Mike Auldridge at the Rams Head Tavern in Annapolis, MD, 2011. © G.T. Keplinger

"Mike and I had a personal falling out a short time before they fired me. At one point he got really mad at me when we were on stage doing "Indian Summer," a song I had written and recorded on my solo album. Mike had also recorded it on one of his solo albums. I was trying to kill time on stage I mentioned that I had wrote it and talked about the tune. After the show Mike got in my face yelling about my talking about the song. I think he felt I was promoting myself too much. Mike and I had houses next to each other, but after our falling out, I moved to another place."

Leading up to his dismissal, John began to refer to Phil as "the wimp" behind his back. Phil and Mike had other arguments, of which Phil thought it was Mike misunderstanding things, Phil told him, "Maybe it's because I'm from the north and you're from the south, and I don't get your sense of humor."

When asked if Duffey did anything to make his dismissal less painful, Phil said, "I didn't get anything from the collective band, but I did call each of them separately to tell them how upset I was. John listened but he was very firm on the decision. Afterwards, I returned to Connecticut and heard nothing from any of them for years."

When John Starling and Gary Oelze were planning the Scene's 15th Anniversary celebration at The Kennedy Center, Mike gave the band [but not Oelze] an ultimatum: "If Phil is invited then I'm not playing." Oelze said the band told him that Phil did not want to participate. This show in November 1986, was one of the Scene's largest and most prestigious concerts.

Phil found out about the Kennedy Center concert when the album was released. In one review the writer added, "one of the people missing from the show has the initials Phil Rosenthal."

"Phil was in The Seldom Scene for the majority of those 15 years," said Gary Oelze who made sure to invite Phil to the 20th anniversary celebration at the Birchmere in 1991.

"Yes, I participated in that one and it was fun. It was like water under the bridge and they were all friendly", said Phil. John Starling and Gary also made sure that Phil was involved in a special John Duffey tribute show at the Birchmere in November, 1998, two years after John passed away. Phil discussed his performance with the current lineup of the Scene, "I went down and played and ended up doing my little part of the show with the current members of The Seldom Scene. We ran over the tunes the night before the show. And it was like instant—all we had to do is go through them once. It was sort of like, the first time when I rehearsed with The Seldom Scene, when I first joined the band. The band almost never rehearsed but we decided we better go through all these tunes at least once to make sure we got the arrangements down and it was like everything just fell into place."

Phil had a stroke [from which he recovered in 2007] and Mike Auldridge contracted prostate cancer. Phil and Mike performed together one final time at the Rams Head Tavern in Annapolis, Maryland in support of Tim and Savannah Finch and The Eastman String Band in February, 2011. Phil introduced Mike on stage as, "my old Seldom Scene band mate and one of my best friends and best musicians I've ever known." They both began long-distance consoling phone conversations to support each other until Mike's death in December, 2012. Prior to Mike's death, their once close friendship had been renewed.

We thank Phil for his help with this book. He reported he is "still living in my home town of Guilford leading several bluegrass ensembles, teaching banjo, guitar and mandolin, running my studio, doing some writing and recording, and performing solo shows.

"Beth and I visit our daughter Naomi and son Daniel, who live not too far away, and we occasionally perform with them as the Sommers Rosenthal Family Band."

In 2016, Phil began a once-a-month Internet radio show called "The Monthly Scene with Phil Rosenthal" on icrvradio.com. It's a 90-minute live program, which gets rebroadcast and then ends up in the station's archive for several months. The station is located in Ivoryton, Connecticut. He plays live music during the show, as well as recordings by his favorite musicians. Guests have included David Mallett, Roland White, Dave Kiphuth, Lisa Bastoni, Dan Tressler, and the Sommers Rosenthal Family Band.

Last 2019 Phil invited Chris Wuerth, a guitar player who produces shows in the area, and Peter Menta, harmonica player and founding member of Washboard Slim and the Blue Lights, to be guests on the show. Bobo Lavorgna, a bass player he has known for years, heard they'd be on and asked if he could join them. They played some bluegrass and blues on the show, and had such a good time, we decided to do it regularly and become a band, Frog Hollow.

Phil says, "We've got a unique blend of blues and bluegrass and have already developed a good following in Connecticut. I play banjo, dobjo and guitar. Chris plays guitar. Bobo is on upright bass and Peter plays harmonica. They take turns singing lead. Their recorded songs in Phil's studio are available on the band's website https://froghollowbluegrass.wixsite.com/home.

# Chapter 18: The Birchmere's Gary Oelze

I always say this: There wouldn't have been a Birchmere if it weren't for The Seldom Scene. They made me a legitimate club. In return, I made a decent club for them, too.

Gary Oelze

**A**nyone who has attended a music show at Alexandria, Virginia's legendary Birchmere club has already met owner Gary Oelze. Patrons with tickets receive sequential numbered cards as they arrive at the club. Gary is the friendly gentleman who calls your number that allows you to take your first-come-first-served seat inside the hall. He provides an evergreen dependable "personal touch" for grateful Birchmere fans.

In 2016, Gary with Birchmere Vice President and talent booker since 1987, Michael Jaworek, thousands of musicians, and hundreds of thousands of loyal audience members celebrated the 50th anniversary of the Birchmere.

When asked to contribute his memories in 2018 for this book, Gary began the discussion with, "Even though I'm from Kentucky, I wasn't a rabid bluegrass fan when I bought the first Birchmere in 1966."

Then that first Birchmere was a small bar and restaurant next to a grocery store in the Shirlington shopping center in Alexandria, Virginia catering to a lunchtime clientele. And with no music, either recorded or live.

Gary understood the food business because his father was a successful restaurateur. Gary boosted his customer traffic by hiring folksingers and bluegrass bands for two nights a week.

Gary explained, "At that time there was the thinking that the bluegrass pie—for both players and bar owners—was only so big. This thinking extended even to the guy with the bass fiddle strapped to the roof of his car. There wasn't an idea of sharing the pie.

"The story of The Seldom Scene is often shortened to 'then they played the Red Fox and the rest is history.' But when I started adding music to the Birchmere, there were people whose attitude was 'what the hell are you doing getting into *our* business?'

"As for the people promoting the bluegrass festivals it was basically, 'pay Bill Monroe and Ralph Stanley what they want,' and let the other bluegrass acts play for free. That was their attitude in a way of speaking.'

"The other problem then with bluegrass music was that there was no mystery to it. Elvis had left the building. The bands would play to all their friends at the bars and hang out. There was no mystique. So, I added some good bluegrass bands at the first Birchmere. One was the band, None of The Above. These were government workers who attracted good crowds.

"Another was Hickory Wind who did the same. Akira Otsuka is a great guy who always had a good band, and he played for me."

When The Seldom Scene started attracting crowds every Tuesday night at the Red Fox Inn, Gary went to see what was going on there. He wasn't impressed. "Walt Broderick, the owner, was there. You couldn't get a seat because all the friends of the bands had the seats. It seemed like a clique. They had a pool table and a bowling machine. The sound system was Shure columns and a mixer on the stage that Duffey would fool around with. The place felt like it was bowling night.

"I approached club ownership as a business. At that time, I had Don Williams, eventually with "I Believe in You" and ten other number one hit songs until his death in 2017, play the Birchmere. He only had his first record out then, but Mike Auldridge was a huge fan because Don had a Dobro player, Lloyd Green, in his group. In fact, Don Williams auditioned Mike in the back room of the Birchmere and they played together for an hour with just me sitting there listening to them. Mike told Don what money he'd need if he had to move to Nashville and Don said he couldn't afford him."

Mike and Gary became close friends. Moreover, Mike and Akira started lobbying Duffey to let Gary book the Scene at the Birchmere. Duffey said passively, "OK, I'll go over there and see."

## The Scene Play The Birchmere

Gary remembers John's first visit well: "I was still open in the daytime then. Duff came in the door and starts walking around the place and looking at things, and he scared the hell out of me. It was the first time I had met him one-on-one. Duffey was big and he intimidated a lot of people. He always had this wall he built around himself. I don't mean to exaggerate this but he was the kind of guy that when he walked in the door you took notice. After we talked, he agreed to play one Saturday night. That show produced a line around the block."

The Scene did about three Saturday Birchmere shows in 1976. Then Gary made his proposal. "I told Duffey I had talked with the band and I wanted them to play on Thursday nights. John replied, 'But we play the Red Fox on Thursday nights,' and I said I want you to quit the Red Fox and play the Birchmere.' They were making $400 a night and I offered $800."

John asked, "How are you going to do that?"

Gary replied, "Well the Red Fox charges $2.00 at the door and I intend to charge $4.00"

"You'll never get that," said Duffey.

"Well, that's my problem," Gary replied.

John said, "OK, then let's try every other Thursday." [John said in 1984, *"I didn't want to tell Walt, 'the hell with you' so we started alternating every other week"*]

And the first Thursday they played, Gary didn't make the door; in other words, he lost money. John was very upset, thinking that it had been a mistake moving to the Birchmere. Gary repeatedly told him, no it's not a mistake.

"The next Thursday they played and we sold out. And we sold out every week they played for the next 20 years," said Gary

[*"We liked the Birchmere better,"* John confirmed in 1984.]

## Quiet Please

Gary was the first bluegrass bar owner that enforced a "Quiet Please" policy at the Birchmere, taking a cue from the Cellar Door business model where respectful listening was expected. When asked if any people objected to this policy, Gary replied, "I always found that it would usually be just one guy who was entertaining his group at a table. And I'd go over a few times and ask him to be quiet. Finally, when I told him to leave, his crowd would thank me afterwards. And I always thought 'then why did you invite this asshole to begin with?'

Gary in his office in 2018 with his
Wammie Award. He is also an official
"Kentucky Colonel." © S. Moore

Gary installed a first-class sound system which
Duffey loved. In fact, Gary ran the sound in those early
years. He is proud of a Washington Area Music
Association "Wammie" award that he won in 1987 for
"Best Live Sound Engineer" for the 15th Anniversary
Seldom Scene recording at the Kennedy Center.

"People would always ask Duff if he had a sound
guy, and he'd say, 'Yeah, we have Gary,' which wasn't
always true, but I did travel with them to do sound. I did
their California tour every winter, and went to Europe
and other places with the band."

Gary calculates that he has run the sound for The
Seldom Scene in excess of 1,000 hours. "I was a good

sound guy for them because I knew what they were going to do before they did it."

"However, sometimes—and I wish they had done this more often—they might start with an old song and then play another old song, and then Tom would suggest yet another old song, and it was astonishing to watch and listen to them. They knew the music history so well. I'm sure that there wasn't a bluegrass song that had ever been written that Duffey didn't know."

## A Few Gary Tales

Two members of The Seldom Scene routinely carried concealed pistols when they left their homes. Following one road show, Gary reported to the band that the club owner didn't "make the door" and couldn't pay them. Duffey quietly pulled his Luger out of his jacket and went to talk privately with the owner. He returned telling Gary and bandmates that the, "club owner is pulling five and ten-dollar bills together, so be patient."

Another story Gary shared made him laugh out loud: In one town before a show, Mike, John and Gary were walking around the neighborhood near their hotel when John saw a porn shop. The three entered but Gary and Mike saw a regular bookstore across the street and left.

About 45 minutes later John, carrying a full shopping bag of "adult" products, came into their bookstore.

"What's that?' John asked pointing to a book Gary was holding.

"It's a James Dean biography that I'm buying," replied Gary. At that time, Gary was collecting actor James Dean memorabilia.

"Wow, this is getting to be an obsession with you," John teased.

## Swellos

In the 1970s, singer/songwriter Steve Goodman came to town to play a benefit show at the Kennedy Center for the Vince Lombardi Cancer Research Foundation. It was filmed and recorded at the Kennedy Center for a HBO telecast.

Gary recalls, "Steve Goodman called me up at the club and asked who's playing tonight at the Birchmere. I told him The Seldom Scene."

Steve replied, "God, can we come?"

"Who's 'we'?" Gary asked.

"John Prine, Vince Gill, and Rodney Crowell. Johnny Cash might come but he's got something wrong with his leg," Steve answered.

The Scene were taking a break so Gary told the band that these guys were coming over. Duffey was unimpressed. They showed up just as the band started their second set.

Prine wrote a note for the band, "I'd sure like to get up and sing with you 'swellows." Gary passed it to Mike, who gave it to John, who just continued with the show. Then Gary wrote another note, "look all these guys are here." John still ignored them.

Mike started quietly getting on John about this snub, and finally Duffey invited Prine up on stage. Gary thought, "I don't think Duffey knew who he was. He respected Monroe and those older musicians but didn't know who the younger players were."

According to Gary, when Prine started to sing, Duffey gave him a look like, 'What in the world? This guy can't sing.' But then Prine started to rag on him, and Duffey always loved that."

On that same night, John, Vince Gill and Peter Rowan attempted to out-high note each other on the song "Little Cabin Home On the Hill." Rowan just happened to be at the Birchmere that night.

Duffey stood three feet from the mic, hit the highest notes and blew them off the stage.

John Prine would become friends with Duffey and asked the Scene to open for him when he played Wolf Trap in Virginia a few years later. Gary also remembers getting Duffey to play a Handgun Control fundraiser event for a group associated with Sara Brady, the wife of President Reagan's press secretary, James Brady.

John Starling asked Gary, "How the hell did you get Duffey to play for free?"

"John trusts me," Gary answered.

Gary offered other aspects of John's personality: "John would watch Johnny Carson and Dean Martin and use a lot of their comedy lines in his shows. When he ventured into his own material would be when he sometimes became politically incorrect. His gay humor like singing "Miller's Cave" with a lisp, or "Big Bruce" was never mean spirited. Of course, you couldn't get away with that today.

"John wasn't smart, and by that I don't mean he was ignorant but rather he didn't have street smarts," said Gary. "For example, when we toured other countries, the band—especially Ben—loved getting out of the hotels to explore and see the sights, but John would just stay in his room, often with his wife, Nancy. But when we got back to the hotel John wanted to know everything we did and saw. He loved hearing about what we did but often didn't want to do it himself."

**First Player Respect**
Gary thinks that he was the first club owner to put washers and dryers in the dressing rooms for the

players. Musicians who travel in their busses really appreciated this. "You'd be surprised how many clubs treat the musicians like crap." said Gary. "They tell them to bring their own towels from the hotel. We give them our menus and they are used to having a lesser menu. 'Where's ours?' they'd ask." Gary's philosophy is that the musicians and his club are in this business together.

"We helped close a lot of bluegrass bars in the area after the Scene came to be regulars at the Birchmere," Gary said. He very fondly remembers the night Jethro Burns played the Birchmere. Near the end of Jethro's set, John Duffey, along with Akira Otsuka, Doyle Lawson, Jimmy Gaudreau, Pete Kennedy, and other mandolinists joined Jethro on stage. There were nine mandolinists in total. Jethro took it in stride and called out some tunes with nine mandolins in perfect harmony.

Over the years Gary got elected to bring the band other opportunities to perform. John would decide. Gary explained, "It made it easy for me because we had set a price."

When asked what Gary thinks of the various iterations of The Seldom Scene, including the present group which has no original members, he says, "For me it was always the original Seldom Scene. They are the band for me. In the beginning when I knew them, Mike and John were like brothers.

"Phil Rosenthal and Lou Reid stepped in and did a good job but the band is the original group in my mind. And the public sometimes is not that smart when it comes to keeping up with bands. Even after Phil and Lou came people would still ask me 'which one is the doctor in the band?' I get some of these old bands in here that only have one original member but as long as they play the songs the way they were originally recorded, it's fine.

"Speaking of Phil, he was somewhat pushed into the band because of his recording association with Mike. But Phil was very good for eight years and never properly appreciated."

When asked why Phil wasn't invited to participate in the 15th Anniversary Kennedy Center show, Gary replied, "Mike told me that Phil wasn't interested in being there."

Ben Eldridge responded to this same question with, "Mike told us that if Phil was invited then he wouldn't perform."

Gary continued, "When John died it was Mike Auldridge who called me to let me know. And neither of us were invited to the funeral. When I look back on it all I think that Ben is really the underappreciated 'forgotten man' of the Scene. Although Duffey was a team player and not always the driving force of both The Country Gentlemen and Seldom Scene, it was his perfect singing that kept it all together."

## Singing Gary's Praises

Many musicians, like Butch Smith of the East Virginia band, share how well Gary treated them. Butch says, "Gary always made the bands that played the Birchmere feel like it wasn't work. Great sound system, and audience attention, and personal attention. Our East Virginia band played there many times, and it never seemed like work."

When the club celebrated 50 years in business in the Spring of 2016, the *Washington Post* asked artists to explain what's special about Gary's music hall. Here are some selected quotes:

Chris Eldridge, Grammy winner, guitarist for the Punch Brothers and other solo and collaborative projects, and a son of Ben Eldridge:

"I basically grew up at the Birchmere. I have memories of just hanging out and eating pretzels while Dad was playing. I remember an atmosphere where music was a sacred, serious thing; people came to listen..."

Ricky Skaggs, 14-time Grammy Award-winning bluegrass mandolin player and singer: "Every January I play my first shows of the year there with Kentucky Thunder. We work on new songs to see how they fly, and that helps us set the tone for the rest of the year."

Vince Gill, country singer, multi-instrumentalist, and multi-platinum recording artist: "I've been coming to the Birchmere for 40 years... When I was in town the thing to do was go watch The Seldom Scene. When I first met those guys and started playing with them, I was partial to the late Mike Auldridge, because I was a young Dobro player in my teenage years."

Debi Smith, singer with the Four Bitchin' Babes and wife of longtime and highly respected Birchmere promoter Michael Jaworek: "When we play the Birchmere with the Babes the audiences are fabulous; nothing gets past them. They're with you from the first note that comes out of your mouth, and they get every joke. That energy comes back to you, especially in a room like the Birchmere. It's sophisticated but also has a down-home feeling."

# Chapter 19: Akira Otsuka

Co-author Moore with Akira in 2018 holding Duffey's Gibson F-12 mandolin. © S. Moore

Growing up in Japan I listened to a lot of Bill Monroe, Flatt & Scruggs and Stanley Brothers. I loved the Stanley Brothers. I still do and then The Country Gentlemen came in, and it just hit me. It's like there was nothing like it. I began to copy John's playing. I'm like, 'how did he come up with these things' you know? One note is going down the other note going up. Nobody else was doing that.

Akira Otsuka

Akira Otsuka was born in Kawasaki City, Japan in 1948 and moved to Kobe when he was eight years old. His website bio reads, "He first toured the U.S. with legendary "Bluegrass 45," the first and most influential Japanese Bluegrass band to hit these soils. Since then Akira has been acknowledged and honored in both the U.S. and Japan for his outstanding abilities on the mandolin. Highly sought as an accompanist and session player on guitar, banjo and bass as well as mandolin, Akira has shared the stage and recorded with many of the genre's greatest artists, including Emmylou Harris, Nils Lofgren, Mary Chapin Carpenter, Ricky Skaggs, Béla Fleck, Jethro Burns, Danny Gatton, Hazel Dickens, Bill Kirchen and Peter Rowan."

Akira was John Duffey's devoted fan and close friend. When he first arrived in the U.S., he briefly took the name "John." *Epilogue* is his tribute CD to Duffey released in 2018 to worldwide acclaim. Akira discussed growing up in Japan and discovering bluegrass in a 2003 interview with G.T. Keplinger and also contributed additional info in 2018:

"My brother, Uteka took Suzuki classical violin lessons for six years. I took three years. Uteka is the one who played guitar and sang lead in Bluegrass 45 when we began the band in 1967 at the "Lost City" Kobe coffee house," Akira told us.

"My next brother Josh started playing banjo, and they said: 'it's mandolin for you.'" Akira was 15 years old.

"Then there was Radio Osaka playing the *Midnight Ramble* radio show two hours a week at 12 midnight.

The second hour was bluegrass. I still see the DJ, Yukihiro Hamasaki, every time I go home.

"Three of us brothers started playing a little bit. There's a thing called Light Music Club in just about every college and university in Japan, and they might have bluegrass, country, rock and roll, reggae —well maybe reggae was not there—folk music, Dixieland, modern jazz, full band, Count Basie.

"My next brother Josh formed a Light Music Club in his school, and developed a bluegrass band. They were great, and we brothers didn't get to play as a trio that often but every time we did, we had fun.

"What inspired me is hard to say, said Akira. "Going to high school it was kind of nice to get away from studying and play mandolin or listen to LPs and take your mind off studying. And it was nice to relax and enjoy.

"We tried to copy everything we could. I was trying to learn everything that John Duffey did. We wore out LPs. Some of them were released in Japan but some were imported and expensive—$30.00 or something—and we would wear it out. We used to transfer them to open reel and then slow the tapes down and listen and pick every single note. That was hard.

"Duffey had certain licks so different from Monroe. The first album I heard was their Folkways *Country Songs: Old and New*. But when the Mercury album called *Folk Session Inside* came out, I was like, 'wow it was amazing the way they produced it.' I can still play every single note on that album. It was quite different from other groups and it had a fresh idea—kind of 'city bluegrass'. I guess Carlton Haney called it 'modern bluegrass'. John was the father of 'modern bluegrass'. Sam Bush came in and added rock-and-roll. David Grisman came in added jazz and Bill Monroe of course."

Akira's Bluegrass 45 band was discovered in Japan by Rebel Records owner Dick Freeland. They toured the United States in 1971 and were featured in the film. *Bluegrass Country Soul* (1972).

When they arrived in the U.S., they first went to the Bean Blossom festival and camped there. "We were not the first foreign bluegrass band to play at a U.S. bluegrass festival because the day before we played, the Hamilton County Bluegrass Band from New Zealand performed," said Akira.

Bluegrass 45 stayed with Dick Freeland when they returned to the D.C. area. The next morning Dick told Akira that John and Nancy Duffey were coming to dinner as were Ben Eldridge, Mike and Dave Auldridge, Bill Poffinberger and "Big" Ed Ferris.

"When John and Nancy showed up I almost peed in my pants," admits Akira. "We had dinner, and we jammed. It was pretty cool like meeting George Harrison. We had a thick songbook and I remember John saying, "that's thicker than the Sears catalog."

Akira admits John was somewhat scary at first: "He was big, and we knew he could sing. He was our idol, but once we met him, he was friendly to us. I'm pretty sure he was taken by the fact that five boys from Japan admired him so much and knew all of his music."

## Producer John Duffey

In September of 1971, Dick Freeland arranged for John Duffey to produce Bluegrass 45's second album, with Roy Homer as the engineer. The musicians were Sab "Watanabe" Inoue, banjo, autoharp; Toshio "Speedy" Watanabe, bass; Gakusei Ryo, fiddle, percussion; Tsuyoshi "Josh" Otsuka, guitar; and Akira Otsuka, mandolin, guitar.

This is the only album that John ever solely produced. The Seldom Scene started two months later in November, 1971. It is very possible that John's involvement with Bluegrass 45 encouraged his decision to jump back in the music business with The Seldom Scene.

Akira recalled, "We knew John was really precise on pronunciation. That's why I think John Duffey had a big impact on this music. Bill Monroe was from Kentucky and sang like he was from there. John never sounded like that. The biggest thing John always stressed was, 'anybody listening to me singing has to understand what I'm singing' and Bill Monroe was nothing like that."

Akira continued the story: "For the album, we recorded one early song where I messed up my mandolin break. Our fiddle player was out of pitch. I think the guitar was out of tune.

"John, Roy and Dick were in the control room listening to the take and talking. We didn't know what they were talking about. And then John came out and came up to my brother."

"Josh, 'can you say [the word] weary'?" asked John.

Josh said, "weary."

"Alright let's do it again," said John supportively.

"It was really nice of him to do that," Akira acknowledged.

When asked how the songs for that album were selected, Akira explained, "John came up with a few. He brought the Monkees' version of 'What Am I Doing Hanging Around?' He said, "hey try this." Dick Freeland had a copy of Eddie Adcock doing it before The Seldom Scene or Bluegrass 45.

"John had a song that he wrote called "Last Call to Glory." I don't know if he had it for the Gentlemen or not, but he gave it to us, and we recorded it. We wrote a few. Dick Freeland and John requested that we do a couple of Japanese songs and we did.

"John suggested a kind of gospel song. We recorded it but it just didn't work out. It exists somewhere. John suggested this instrumental number "Caravan" by Duke Ellington. It became the title tune of our album. John decided to play cymbal on it. That was neat.

"So, we got to know Duffey pretty well. He came to our apartment. We sang together. My biggest dream growing up in Kobe was just to see him play once in my lifetime. He was supposed to come with The Country Gentlemen in 1968 but I heard that he was scared of flying. He didn't want to go so he cancelled it. Then he ended up leaving the band. We were so disappointed."

In 1972 Akira graduated college and permanently moved to the U.S. a year later. Again, Dick Freeland picked him up at National Airport. Dick knew that he had no job.

"Hey, you want to go see a bluegrass show?" asked Dick.

"Sure," said Akira and they headed off to Luray, Virginia where Ralph Stanley was headlining. Cliff Waldron was playing also. Akira auditioned for Cliff and started playing with Waldron that same day.

Akira provided the above picture of the first Duck John built. He noted that he added the pickup to make the instrument louder.
© Akira Otsuka

## The Duck

John Duffey designed and built a mandolin that became known as The Duck because of its unusual "wings in flight" shape. Akira provides an excellent rundown on Duffey's mandolins in the superb 39-page booklet that accompanies his 2018 *Epilogue; A Tribute to John Duffey"* CD (Smithsonian Folkways label), co written by famed bluegrass broadcaster, Katy Daley, who shared an International Bluegrass Music Association (IBMA) award for the liner notes with Akira, Dudley Connell and Jeff Place.

In addition, Katy won an IBMA Distinguished Achievement Award in 2019 and has been a stalwart friend and advocate of John Duffey from the beginning.

If you want to hear how the Duck sounded then listen to The Seldom Scene's first four albums. Dick Freeland told Akira that he thought the Duck sounded best on their first album, *Act 1,* because the Duck wasn't completely finished. Akira is not sure about that assertion. John gave Akira this Duck. When Duffey passed away, Nancy arranged for Akira to obtain John's main Gibson mandolin.

Akira plays it at his performances these days, and gives a workshop to demonstrate both the F-12 and the Duck mandolin. He lets fans hold both instruments.

Akira shared a memory of Duffey recognizing Akira's mother from the stage. "She and my dad came to visit the U.S. a few times. My mother was wonderful and happy I became friends with John. I brought her to see The Seldom Scene several times. One time at a Cumberland, Maryland show, I said, 'John look over there from the stage,' and John yelled 'Hey!' waving at my mom. That was pretty cool."

Akira and John maintained an inspirational friendship throughout John's life. Akira traveled to Japan with The Seldom Scene on their two tours of Japan in 1985 and 1987. Akira discussed the way that John Duffey sometimes came across negatively to some people. "I know how he was to some people and it's unfortunate that some felt that way. He was a very warm person but sometimes didn't want to be bothered. I mean you can say he was selfish, but he wanted his privacy. But once you got to know him, he was a very sincere, nice person. I mean you went to his house and he would ask if you're doing okay every five minutes."

We thank Tom Travis for allowing us to include the following review he wrote for Akira's labor of love:

**EPILOGUE** *Tribute to John Duffey*
Review by Tom Travis, *Bluegrass Today*
*Smithsonian Folkways* Recordings
Producers: Ronnie Freeland and Akira Otsuka

*Sad and Lonesome Day / If That's the Way You Feel / If I Were a Carpenter / Lonesome River / Sunrise / Going to the Races / Some Old Day / Girl from the North Country / He Was a Friend of Mine / Poor Ellen Smith / Reason For Being / Ain't Gonna Work Tomorrow / Chim-Chim-Cher-Ee / Cold Wind a Blowin' / Christmas Time Back Home / Bringing Mary Home / First Tear*

When this CD dropped onto my doormat for review it made my day. Opening the package was like welcoming to my home a bunch of long-lost friends—the chief amongst them being the reason behind the production of this recording, John Duffey.

Memories flooded back from my six decades in bluegrass, like: when I first listened to The Country Gentlemen in the early sixties and heard the unmistakable voice and mandolin playing of this great man; my first impression of revulsion on hearing, in 1972, Duffey's first album, *Act 1,* with his new band, Seldom Scene; the later realization of what John was really up to with his strange antics (like saving bluegrass from a future of regional obscurity); my being won over and deciding to bring The Seldom Scene over to England to do a one-off show; the fun of interviewing John Duffey on my BBC Radio 2 programmed, *Bluegrass Ramble,* and—one of the highest spots of my bluegrass career—being invited by him to join Seldom Scene on stage to pick and sing with them. Oh happy, happy days.

There are few watershed moments in bluegrass history but when they occur, they are momentous. John Duffey, in his quest to, as he put it, *"get bluegrass out of the woods and into town,"* realized the potential of the new, urban, folk revival audiences of the 1950s and set about developing it. Now, thanks to him and the musicians with whom he worked—followed by those musicians who, after them, picked up the ball and ran with it - bluegrass music is now truly international.

Now, onto the cause of my mammoth attack of déjà vu:

The regard in which John Duffey is held, is indicated by the many musicians who willingly contributed their talents to this project. Among them: Jerry Douglas, Dobro; Sam Bush, mandolin; Béla Fleck, banjo; Tony Rice, guitar and Todd Phillips, bass. Of all the fifty-three (yes, 53) musicians who play and/or sing on this album, each is from the highest echelons of bluegrass music. They don't come better than this. The music is sublime as the chemistry between this gathering of geniuses kicks in to stimulate their creative juices—inspired harmony singing, terrific instrumental breaks and a tightness of rhythm only gained by playing at the highest level. Hearing these songs again left me with a feeling of joy, at having known John Duffey, and renewed sadness at the tragic loss of this larger-than-life character.

One of my abiding memories of John Duffey took place the year before he died. We were staying at the same hotel and breakfasting together. The waiter arrived at the table with his meal and set it down before him. "What's this!" Exclaimed John, pointing at the bacon, "Where's the fat? I like plenty of fat on my bacon. "Sorry sir," replied the waiter, removing the offending plate and heading for the kitchen. The waiter then returned and set down a plate on which was, what we would call, 'The full English,' replete with the biggest and fattiest piece of bacon I have ever seen. "Now that's better," said John, pulling his chair nearer the table, and tucking in.

When I was tasked, by *British Bluegrass News*, with writing an obituary for John Duffey, following his untimely death in 1996, I did it with great sadness. I referred to him as an incandescent light in the world of bluegrass that had flickered out. It's good to see so many respected musicians so eager to relight that flame and keep it burning. We're thinking of you John and we can hear you in the music.

Tom Travis, *Bluegrass Today*

# Chapter 20: Presidents, Pistols, and Other Tales

**J**ust before John left The Country Gentlemen, someone stole his vintage Gibson F-12 mandolin. Variations on its eventual recovery, seven years later, abound. The urban legend version of this story, repeated by various radio broadcasters and others goes like this: The stolen mandolin turned up in the hands of a "skinny musician" at the Childe Harold, a then-popular D.C. music club in the Dupont Circle neighborhood. Legend has it that John Starling came into the club one night and recognized the F-12 being played by a guy in a band.

John Starling called Duffey, and together with Rebel Records owner, Dick Freeland, Duffey barged into the bar and confronted the skinny musician who must have known he had Duffey's mandolin. The musician said, "I guess you want to see this mandolin." And John Duffey said, "Does the truss rod behind the neck bother you?"

John had modified the mandolin quite a bit, and the truss rod was showing up from the back of the mandolin. The musician said, "I guess this is yours." John got it back. The legend further claims that John's gun was somehow involved in retrieving it. The tale portrays the skinny musician as a scumbag.

When asked about the incident in 1984, John told the story a little differently:

*I didn't pull my gun on him. I just went down and took it. The poor guy had bought it hot, and he found out and he knew I was coming to get it. I don't think he ever knew it was hot when he bought it. And he didn't question it because he knew that there was no recourse whatsoever.*

*In the first place, there is no statute of limitations on stolen property and it had been gone for seven years.*

*The fact is that it never left Washington. A repair man named Baumgarten in Silver Spring had it for 3 years and he didn't steal it either. But Baumgarten knew who it belonged to. A supposedly good friend of mine knew that Baumgarten had it but he didn't tell me. I found out about it after my friend left town for Chattanooga. Nice people.*

*What happened was that John Starling had gone to see Liz Meyer's band at the Childe Harold bar in Dupont Circle. J.B. Allison played with Liz. J.B. sat down with Starling and told him he had one of my old mandolins. I went down to the club with Len Holsclaw and J.B. gave it back to me. He had another mandolin that needed work so I worked it all over for him just for the hell of it. I felt sorry for him.*

In 2018 Tom Gray added additional details: "It is my understanding that the Gibson F-12 was stolen during a Country Gents' engagement at The Brickskeller on 22nd St., a George Washington University neighborhood bar. A thief reached through an open window of the dressing room and grabbed the instrument. He probably had no clue what the instrument was or its value.

"A musician named J.B. found the instrument for sale at a pawn shop and bought it. He was not surprised when a posse of guys, including John Duffey and Len Holsclaw, came to the Childe Harold while he was performing. J.B. handed it over to John immediately. John later helped J.B. find another mandolin."

## J.B. Allison

The "skinny musician" was longtime Washington, D.C. musician, James B. Allison, who now lives in Nashville. J.B. described his involvement in the stolen mandolin affair:

"I first saw this F-12 mandolin in Jim Baumgarten's Silver Spring repair shop, fell in love with it and gave him $1,000 for it. I never knew it was stolen. There are plenty of pictures of me playing it when I was with the Liz Meyer band. One day, I was looking through albums at Joe Lee's Record Paradise in Takoma Park, Maryland and thought I recognized my mandolin in the hands of John Duffey on a Country Gentlemen's record cover.

"I did some research and went to the Red Fox Inn to talk with John Starling. And sure enough, it was Duffey's. So, I am the one who contacted Duffey to return it. I didn't have to do that. I could have altered it or just kept it out of sight. I filed a police report when I found out it was stolen but nothing came from that. Jim Baumgarten had died by that time. I take offense when others continually repeat this false story that makes me out to be a thief and a coward. And by the way, I've never been skinny and although I'm a pacifist, I have mostly been considered a tough son-of-a-bitch throughout my life. And I am not a scumbag."

J.B. also admitted that he was disappointed that he was out the $1,000 he had spent to buy the mandolin when he handed it over to Duffey. However, J.B. had bought a new Gibson model that had a thick top which didn't help the tone. In return for recovering his instrument, John helped him improve the tone by shaving the mandolin top at no charge.

## Dylan Cools His Bootheels
On a Thursday night at the Birchmere music club, the kitchen phone rang. Birchmere waitress, Mary Beth Aungier, answered the call.

"Are The Seldom Scene playing tonight?" a quiet voice asked.

"They just finished their last set," answered Mary Beth.

The man replied, "Well, Bob Dylan just did a concert, and he's in the car, and we are driving to your place. Can the band do another set so Bob can hear them?"

Mary Beth said "Hold on," and went straight to John Duffey, who always called the shots on these special requests. She relayed the message to John.

He quickly and calmly told Mary Beth, "Please tell Mr. Dylan that I have some cold beverages waiting for me at home, and if he's ever in the neighborhood early on a Thursday night then he's welcome to drop in."

When Mary Beth told the man that the band had finished for the night and were going home, the guy yelled, "BUT IT'S BOB DYLAN!

Ben Eldridge told this story a little differently to Jedd Ferris of *The Washington Post* in 2016. Ben said, "We'd be done a little after ten at the Birchmere, and John would get right out of there. One night Bob Dylan was in town, and his manager called the Birchmere and asked if we could hold the last set until 11:00 so Bob could get there and hear us. All of us were excited, but John said, 'Nope, I'm going home.' So, Bob was the one we never got to meet."

The difference between these versions is that Mary Beth said she never spoke to the other members of the band the night Dylan wanted to come, and only told the story to the band in 2010. Gary Oelze concurs but it's possible that Duffey told them about it.

## President Jimmy Carter

Ben Eldridge told this story: "First Lady Rosalynn Carter's secretary used to come hear us play at the Red Fox Inn. She was sort of instrumental in getting us down to play some functions at the White House." The first time was a dinner but the Scene didn't play.

"The second time they called to ask if we could come play for some congressional picnic on the South Lawn.

"Well, sure I think so but let me check with everybody," Ben answered. "I called Mike, Phil and Tom and everybody said yeah. I called John and he says, 'How much are they paying us?'

"Nothing, John. You know they don't pay. It's just a privilege to play at the White House."

"John answered, 'Well, I got a softball game that night so why don't you guys just go on down and play instrumentals or something. If I get done early enough, maybe I can get over there. I'll come on by.'"

Ben continued the story: "So that's what we ended up doing. They had three bands that night and they were all spread out all over the South Lawn. One band would play a song and then another band would play a song and we'd play and all we did was instrumentals. We started at five o'clock and we were done by 6:30. They invited us to stay for the picnic which we did."

Tom Gray played mandolin for that show. Mike Auldridge recalled playing for Carter: "The reason I remember is because Doc Watson was one of the other acts that was playing there and we were waiting to go on while Doc was on. People were standing around chit-chatting and tinkling glasses."

"President Carter got up and said, 'I want you all to be quiet because this guy right here is a national treasure and you need to be listening to him.' You know? Which I thought, alright." Mike nodded and laughed. "I was very proud of him."

Tom Gray recalls: "When we played the White House a second time, President Carter introduced us, telling the audience how important we were."
© Courtesy of The White House

Duffey finally showed up about 7:30 in his softball uniform with his mandolin, which he never had to take out of its case, and he got the picnic supper.

The third time was the charm as the full band played for President Carter during the last summer the Carters were in the White House. "They were very nice people," said Ben.

In the next administration, President Ronald Reagan's press secretary, James Brady, became a regular at the Birchmere at the Scene's Thursday night shows. James Brady and President Reagan were shot in an attempted assassination and Brady was left partially paralyzed. He sat in his wheelchair on the stage at the 15th anniversary of The Seldom Scene, and raised himself out of his chair when the Scene and the crowd thanked him for his loyal support.

## Eddie Adcock's President Kennedy Story

It is possible that the White House picnic wasn't Duffey's only encounter with a President. A story according to Eddie Adcock goes that The Country Gentlemen had a much earlier request from the White House.

On an otherwise ordinary day in 1961, John Duffey's phone rang.

"Mr. Duffey, I am with the Office of the White House Chief of Staff. How are you?

"So-so," answered John. "How can I help you?"

"President Kennedy wants to invite The Country Gentlemen to perform at the White House," the aide answered.

"How much does it pay?" John asked.

There was a pause.

"Well, you don't get paid when playing for the President of the United States," the aide explained.

"Nope," John said. "No pay, no play."

The conversation was over.

A few weeks later, on a Tuesday night, the President with his entourage, and accompanied by a couple of secret service agents, quietly slipped into the Shamrock bar where the Country Gents played weekly. The band didn't get a chance to meet the President because he and his people left just before their second set ended.

"I thought we should have played for Kennedy at the White House," Eddie Adcock said, "John's decision is about the only thing I ever held against him. The President still liked us enough to come and see us is the way I understand it."

Eddie sincerely spun this fantastic tale for G.T. Keplinger's video camera in 2002. However, bassist Tom Gray was on stage for every Shamrock show from 1960 through 1964. Tom would know if President Kennedy ever visited the bar. Tom had never heard Eddie's story before.

John's good friend, Penny Parsons, also has never heard the story but observed that the account of John's phone conversation sounded believable.

John goofing off on the road. © Nancy Duffey

## Weed, Whites, and Wine

During the song selection for The Seldom Scene's *Act Two* album, John Starling suggested Little Feat's song, "Willin'," written by the band's leader, Lowell George.

Again, the band liked Lowell and knew him from his relationship with Linda Ronstadt.

However, Tom Gray objected because of the lyrics: "I had three young children and I didn't want our band singing a song that glorifies drugs and illegal truckers smuggling 'smokes and folks from Mexico,'" he insisted.

John Starling suggested they might change the words. Tom recalled Duffey joking that the chorus: "But if you give me weed, whites and wine, and show me a sign, then I'll be willin'" could be changed to "But if you give me some wheats, rice, and wine."

However, the Scene deferred to Gray's objection, and it would be years later when John Starling launched his own band, Carolina Star, also with Tom on bass, that "Willin" was finally recorded with the original lyrics. Tom agreed to play that session because, "by then my kids had grown up."

### Woman Throws John Into A Bathtub

Tom Gray told this story to *Bluegrass Today* writer Richard Thompson: "In the summer of 1963, The Country Gentlemen played a two-week engagement at the Moon-Cusser Coffee House in Oak Bluffs, Massachusetts, on the island of Martha's Vineyard. It was a folk music venue which would have two acts play every night for a week at a time. One of our weeks there, we shared the bill with the Scottish folk singer, Jean Redpath. The Moon-Cusser had a big old house where they would house their entertainers. During the week we spent there with Jean Redpath, we would sit around at night after our shows and talk music and share songs. She developed a friendship with Eddie Adcock.

"Eddie was into body and muscle building and talked about how much weight he could lift. Now, Jean was a strong woman herself. So, one night when Eddie talked about lifting weights, she decided to show what she could do. She picked up Eddie over her shoulder and carried him around the house, finally dropping him in the bath tub. John Duffey had followed them into the bathroom, laughing at Eddie's predicament. So, she turned to John, said, 'What are you laughing at?' She then picked up John, threw him in the tub, and turned the water on.

John took it good-naturedly. He screamed, 'Hey,' and laughed. It was all in fun.

### John Sells Out

Ethnomusicologist and music historian, Kip Lornell, completed a bluegrass history of Washington, D.C. (*Capital Bluegrass: Hillbilly Music Meets Washington, D.C.*) published by Oxford University Press in 2020. Lornell, a faculty member at George Washington University, has published fifteen music history books, including *Exploring American Folk Music* (University Press of Mississippi) and *Virginia's Blues, Country, and Gospel Records, 1902-1943* (University Press of Kentucky). Kip generously offered encouragement and research for this book.

One story he shared involved long-time *Bluegrass Unlimited* columnist, Walt Saunders. Walt was visiting John's repair shop during the time between The Country Gentlemen and The Seldom Scene. John told Walt that he was selling his 78rpm record collection as he was through with playing bluegrass. Walt next visited John's home and ended up buying his entire collection.

Walt Saunders told Kip: "At the time I was looking for a couple of Connie & Babe singles on the *Republic* label. He had one of them, "Roll On Blues," b/w "The Lonely Waltz," but I also was looking for the other one, "How Will the Flowers Bloom," b/w "The Last Love

Letter." He didn't have the latter one. So, I was telling him about it, to see if he was familiar with the song. I said, "Do you know "How Will the Flowers Bloom?" Without blinking an eye, he said, "No I don't, but I imagine if you put plenty of cow-shit on them they'll do ok."

**Fox On The Run**
Tom Gray enthusiastically gives credit to Bill Emerson for creating the bluegrass version of the song "Fox on the Run." Tom was in the basement of his Kensington, Maryland home around 1968 when Bill brought a tape of rock songs to review for potential bluegrass material. One obscure tune was English rock band, Manfred Mann's "Fox on the Run" written by an unknown UK songwriter, Tony Hazzard. (The band's hit song was "Do Wah Diddy Diddy").

"It was a pretty boring song until Bill gave it new life as a bluegrass song," said Tom. "Bill added the fourth 'like a fox' on the chorus." Bill and Tom recorded it and later brought it to the attention of the "post-Duffey" Country Gentlemen. It soon became a standard for bluegrass bands worldwide and a requested song for John Duffey over the years, even though John never formally recorded it.

**Cardboard TV Affair**
Pete Wernick's 1980s band, Hot Rize, had a costumed alter-ego band named Red Knuckles and the Trailblazers. Pete believes the Trailblazers influenced John to start wearing his star-shaped sunglasses. During one show Waldo (Pete) and Wendell (Nick Forster) of the Trailblazers showed up on stage to interrupt the Scene's appearance at the Strawberry Festival in California to give John a "TV," actually a large

carton painted up to look like a TV. This gift was in reaction to John's persistent backstage complaints about how he was fried from lack of sleep because he had been given a motel room without a TV. Duffey said he needed a TV to help him get to sleep. Having traveled through three time zones (he had just started flying to gigs), midnight in California felt like 3:00 a.m. East Coast time. He was not a happy camper and did look exhausted according to Pete.

John was taken aback to be joined onstage by two gaudily dressed cartoon characters carrying a cardboard TV and addressing him mock-respectfully as Mr. Duffey, offering to solve his TV problem. But John quickly caught on that this was a chance to do some stage schtick, so he blearily joined in the dialogue, much to the amusement of the other Scene guys. He finished up by giving Waldo a kiss, to which Waldo responded, "WELL, Mr. *Dufty*!!"

## Marty Stuart's Hug.

Becky Johnson was born in Concord, Massachusetts into a very musical family. Everyone sang and played instruments, and Becky was no exception. It was while watching *The Andy Griffith Show* in 1960 when she was five years old that she first heard the banjo.

"I was hooked from that moment on. *The Beverly Hillbillies, Petticoat Junction*, and *Green Acres* TV shows only reinforced my desire to move one day to North Carolina," Becky said in 2018. "I finally saw my first live bluegrass concert starring Ralph Stanley & The Clinch Mountain Boys in Cambridge at the First Presbyterian Church. I was stunned! Singing lead that night was a very young Keith Whitley. They were all consummate musicians. I soon found summer bluegrass festivals all over New England, and began volunteering backstage doing anything and everything I could, while meeting the stars of the show."

At Emerson College in Boston, her Alma Mater, Becky received a B.S. in Mass Communications in 1978.

"It was natural to photograph my bluegrass heroes and the better I got to know them, the easier it became to shoot them often in candid situations," Becky explained.

Soon her photographs were being *published in Bluegrass Unlimited, Grand Ole Opry* Magazine, *Banjo Newsletter, Moonshiner* (Japan) and *British Bluegrass News.* They have also appeared in *The Washington Post,* and *U.S. News & World Report* to name a few

Her first photo book, *Inside Bluegrass, 20 Years of Bluegrass Photography* (Empire Publishing, Inc.) came out in 1998. Three of her photographs are in permanent display at the Ralph Stanley Museum.

"Mrs. Bluegrass" Becky Johnson in 2018 with her photo of John and Marty Stuart. © B. Johnson

## On John

Becky became a trusted colleague and friend of John Duffey. "He called me Loretta Lynn after taxes. He was unpredictable, unexpected and had a mysterious air about him. Over time John Duffey and The Seldom Scene got to know me as a photographer and they felt comfortable that they could be themselves around me.

"It's absolutely true that John never wanted to be beholden to anyone. He selected his friends carefully. I'd see him at festivals and there was fun and flirtatious stuff. He'd tease me from the stage when I'd go down front to take photos. I'd never snap and sit down. I'd wait for the image to come to me," Becky explained.

"I was very satisfied with the picture of Marty hugging John. This occurred very early one morning at the Winterhawk bluegrass festival in 1981. I took a walk and saw John, and then heard Marty Stuart yell, 'Oh my God, It's John Duffey.' Marty ran and grabbed him. It was magical."

When asked for a quick snapshot assessment of each of the Scene members Becky said, "I started seeing them in 1977. Mike Auldridge was one of the sweetest people I ever met. Absolutely no ego whatsoever but reserved. And also, a great dresser. Ben was like the big brown bear of bluegrass music. I mean that like a really good bear, like Yogi, with a very dry, great sense of humor. I loved Phil Rosenthal's voice and he was from New England like me. I also loved Tom Gray's playing.."

In 2017, Becky celebrated her first decade as a radio broadcaster on Community Radio's WCOM 103.5 FM "The Bluegrass Breakdown" and today hosts a second weekly radio show, "Panhandle Country" on Community Radio WHUP 104.7fm.

Becky concludes her memories of John with the last time she saw him: "Three months before John passed away the Scene played a show in Durham. The Seldom Scene was warming up, when Duffey came up to me and said, 'hey, give me a hug. Do you know where I can set up my bar?' He seemed blissed out and was the most at peace I had ever seen him."

# Chapter 21. The "New" Seldom Scene

"Without Art Menius we wouldn't have a bluegrass museum and Hall of Fame"

Carlton Haney, first bluegrass festival promoter

Art Menius was the first Executive Director of the International Bluegrass Music Association, and the first volunteer president in 1990 of The Folk Alliance. The following article by Art was originally published in the July 1987 *Bluegrass Unlimited* magazine. We greatly appreciate Art for agreeing to let us include it here in its entirety, and for his support for this project.

The Hall of Washington, D.C.'s Kennedy Center was packed with late comers happy to buy obstructed view and standing room tickets for the triple row of balconies that climb to the ceiling. Minks, tuxedos, and jewels blended with sports jackets and blue jeans as Washington's finery settled into their seats beside bluegrass fans to celebrate the fifteenth anniversary of a Washington institution on November 10th, 1986.

Bluegrass music more often may conjure images of cabin homes in Carolina than a capacity audience at the Kennedy Center. But that Monday night, the best and the brightest, headed by White House Press Secretary, James Brady, bearing a proclamation from President Reagan, gathered there to join such stars as Linda Ronstadt and Emmylou Harris in recognition of The Seldom Scene. And thus, the Scene, which has been shattering every bluegrass stereotype since 1971, continued that tradition in spectacular fashion.

Guitarist John Starling, mandolinist John Duffey, Dobroist Mike Auldridge, banjo picker Ben Eldridge, and bass man Tom Gray began The Seldom Scene during November, 1971. From the start, the group featured bluegrass standards, original compositions, and pop and rock songs given a bluegrass treatment. The band won *Muleskinner News'* awards for Band of the Year, Best Album, and Best Vocal Group for 1974, 1975, and 1976. Starling left the band in 1977, replaced first by Phil Rosenthal and then, in June of 1986, by Lou Reid, who had worked with country superstar Ricky Skaggs. The other four original members have remained with The Seldom Scene.

The group has recorded seven albums for the Rebel label and four with Durham's Sugar Hill Records. The most recent, 1985's *Blue Ridge.* More than a year after its release *Blue Ridge* remains one of the dozen top selling bluegrass records for Roanoke, Virginia distributors, the Record Depot. In fact, five of the Scene's older releases ranked among their top seventy-five best bluegrass sellers for 1986.

The Scene remains a premier show band, but the audience at the Kennedy Center saw much, much more. After the current group romped enthusiastically through a half dozen numbers, Starling's carefully choreographed show began. Starling rejoined his old comrades, then Duffey, Gray, and Charlie Waller recreated the magic of the early Country Gentlemen. Into the spotlight came "Midnight Flyer" composer Paul Craft who contributed a number of excellent titles to the list of Scene recordings. Ricky Skaggs and Tony Rice dueted on the old tunes as on their Sugar Hill album of a few years back. Skaggs stood alone with his Martin to sing his new Christmas single, later to be joined by his wife, Sharon White.

Backup musicians came and went. Bobby Hicks and Stuart Duncan fiddled, well, like Hicks and Duncan. Reid seemingly played every instrument. Alan O' Bryant, like Duncan, a member of the Nashville Bluegrass Band, added his voice and banjo. Robbie Magruder and Kenny White added drums and piano when appropriate. And the stars kept appearing. Jonathan Edwards stepped forward to perform tunes off the *Blue Ridge* project. Harris and Ronstadt, the latter in a sequined black cowgirl skirt that Patsy Montana might have worn, sang as both back up and lead vocalists. Then they joined. forces for a stunning rendition of "Hobo's Meditation," the Jimmie Rodgers cum Merle Haggard classic included on the new *Trio* album with Dolly Parton.

Some kind of birthday party for a band formed by accident by erstwhile members of The Country Gentlemen and Emerson and Waldron. I mean, they didn't even want to give up their day jobs. *National Geographic* cartographer Gray and mathematician, Eldridge still haven't.

**The Seldom Scene, At The Scene**:
If it's Thursday, it must be the Birchmere. Thursday night is a ritual activity for The Seldom Scene at the Alexandria, Virginia restaurant which has long been the D.C. area place for bluegrass and folk music. After five years of Thursdays at Bethesda, Maryland's Red Fox Inn, the Scene moved to the Birchmere in 1977.

On a snowy winter night, Eldridge stood in the dressing room displaying his recently purchased banjo —a Gibson RB-3 banjo pot to which a new neck bought in North Carolina has been affixed. Duffey, the athlete, entered complaining of an arm injury that will hinder his mandolin playing. Gary Oelze, manager of the Birchmere and sometimes booking agent for the Scene, came in with flight plans to a gig in Interlochen, Michigan and began distributing W-2 forms to the band members.

Gray sat down on the sofa beside the visitor. "You can see the reason The Seldom Scene stays together," he volunteered. "We all get paid. You wanted to know the real reason? We're growing old together. You find a groove and stay with it."

At showtime Duffey reached his microphone first, remarking, as Gray lifted his stand-up bass on stage, "Carrying that big thing around can be an advantage ... I mean the bass."

If Duffey no longer devotes as much energy to his mandolin, his magisterial tenor voice (just listen to him sing "My Little Georgia Rose") still packs more power than a chop on a Loar. Yet his greatest contribution may be as showman and spiritual leader of the pack. Duffey possesses the rare talent of saying just the wrong thing at precisely the right moment.

"Now we're going to do a gospel song," Duffey intoned. "Two new customers are at the door. I'm waiting until we get their money."

On stage The Seldom Scene conveys a sense of fun and spontaneity because, well, they're spontaneously having fun and sharing that with the audience. "We have five different personalities, and they all mesh together on stage," Gray explained following the show. "The audience sees that these five people are having a good time with each other and playing music together in a comfortable environment. Because we've played so much together, we can anticipate what each other is going to do, and if it's something different we can pick up on it and make something out of it."

That enables The Seldom Scene to perform like a solo artist, playing off the crowd rather than going through the motions of a planned show. "It is spontaneous," Gray confirmed. "We only plan the first one or maybe two songs when we go onstage. If you always do the same things in the same order you feel like you're doing your job as it has been programmed for you. As it is now, we can go out and react to the audience, see what they want."

"The attitude and the approach have always been the same," added Auldridge, whose Dobro has graced the recordings of Harris, Ronstadt, and many more, while adding steel guitar to bluegrass records by the likes of Doyle Lawson and the Lonesome River Band. "It started out as kind of a hobby. It's kind of like a party approach. It's a good-time thing. We don't take ourselves really seriously.

"There's literally no pressure on this band as far as to go out and play perfectly. John's a big asset in that if you mess up, he can sell it as something. So, it keeps it fun rather than going out to work. It's like playing at a party because of John."

"The audience is actually paying your salary," said Duffey, "so you owe them the best you can." The Seldom Scene's best has earned them a diverse, frequently urban following that shatters any image of bluegrass as hillbilly music.

"For one thing, we're not a bunch of cornballs," Duffey explained. 'We're basically city people, but yet we're city people who have been raised on this music. Possibly the choice of material [ranging from bluegrass standards to Eric Clapton], and how we present it is also trying to adjust to meet our audience on their level. We treat the people as if they have some brains."

"I think the show also enters into it," Auldridge adds. "You can go see a great bluegrass band, but if you weren't already a bluegrass fanatic, you might not appreciate it, because it's just like listening to a record. Whereas The Seldom Scene, or I might say John Duffey, is an entertainer, first. The combination of having an entertaining show and material that's either based on tradition or the latest stuff put into an acoustic style. I think is the whole reason for the success of this band. We try to make it palatable to everyone whether they're dyed-in-the-wool bluegrass fans or just the average person on the street. This has raised the standard of bluegrass music in general because people see that it can be open to a mass audience if it is done well.

"We can be accepted by all those people because we respect both audiences. We don't go too far up field from bluegrass. We all enjoy the traditional songs, and when we do contemporary songs, it's obvious where our roots are.

"We've never considered ourselves a bluegrass band We've always considered ourselves an acoustic band, and it was a good thing. That's what really set us apart."

## The Seldom Scene, *Baptizing*

The late June heat at Norman Adams' stellar Dahlonega, Georgia bluegrass festival could melt the frets off your fingerboard. Fortunately, the fans had an onsite swimming pool and a covered seating area to watch the likes of Bill Monroe, the Osborne Brothers, Jimmy Martin, Tony Rice and The Seldom Scene. The artists had an air-conditioned backstage area.

Lou Reid wiped sweat off his forehead as he talked backstage about his career and new job as lead singer, guitarist, and fiddler for the Scene. "When I was fourteen years old, I started a group with Jimmy Haley called the

Bluegrass Buddies, managed by Chuck Webster. We ended up with a group called Southbound and did a couple of overseas tours (and an album for Rebel SLP 15701) in 1977 with Auldridge on Dobro] and after we came back, we split up. Then Doyle Lawson called me and Jimmy and asked if we'd be interested in a group. So, we tried it, and Jimmy, and me, and Terry Baucom, and Doyle were the first members of Doyle Lawson and Quicksilver.

"I stayed with them for about three years. We did three albums (on Sugar Hill), and then I was asked to join the Ricky Skaggs Band. So, I joined them in 1982. I was with Ricky for four years, then I was asked to join the Scene. I tossed that around for about a year and a half, and finally I decided it's something I really wanted to do.

"It gave me the chance to be able to sing more," Reid continued. "It's a long, drawn-out story, a lot of reasons that molded into one big reason. For one thing. I was a little bit unhappy with being on the road all the time, 258 days a year and never seeing home and stuff like that. Another reason is that they're one of the biggest influences in my music back when I was first starting with John and Eddie Adcock and people like that. I listened to them more than I listened to Bill Monroe, to tell you the truth.

"I just thought, hey, it's going to give me time to breathe a little bit and be a partner in this group, and it felt good. I thought it would be good for me to be able to sing a lot more lead. I get to do a lot more than I used to, and I don't have to travel the road so much.

"I like festivals. I've been spoiled, so to speak, by playing coliseums and air-conditioned concert halls, but this is home to me. This is what I used to do all the time. It's kind of back to my roots."

271

At first, Duffey led sing-alongs—including a breathtaking interlude at Winterhawk that drew Charlie Chase away from the customers at his record table to announce, "This is what it's all about!" during parts of the Scene's sets.

The band worked up material with Reid. By the time the fifteenth anniversary rolled around, Reid had been fully incorporated into the band, singing powerfully as a perfect counterpart to Duffey, and adding material, such as John Fogerty's "Big Train from Memphis," to the Scene's sound.

**The Seldom Scene, After Midnight**: Following their show at the Birchmere, the members of the Scene talked about their past and future, while the snow made their paths home more difficult.

"I think we, the guys in the band, are like the people in the audience," Auldridge stated, "We're really typical second-generation bluegrass fans. We're not country guys. We weren't born on farms. I think we're typical of the largest population that's been exposed to this music."

"We're middle-class Americans," said Duffey, radio and television spokesman for the National Land Title Insurance Association. "I also did four spots for the IRS, and they said 'thank you' and audited me."

"The music's been on the radio around here since about 1946. It was the Appalachian influx that first brought it here since so many people migrated here during and after the Second World War. Everybody was looking for a job.

"The first generation of country fans and bluegrass fans helped establish the first market for it here, and then those of us who were born here heard it on the radio and picked up on it from there."

"I think The Country Gentlemen of the early 1960s made it respectable," Eldridge adds. "I moved to Washington from Charlottesville and Richmond in 1961. You couldn't go hear bluegrass in Richmond or Charlottesville unless you went to some really gut-bucket place.

"I used to go see these guys [Duffey and Gray] at the Shamrock, which was not quite the Stork Club; but the people in there were similar to the people you saw in here tonight. You have everyone from truck drivers to lawyers. It was amazing. I really think the Gentlemen transferred things to urban type audiences."

Does the spirit of the early Gents live on in the Scene?

"That's because of Duffey, who was the heaviest influence in that band," opined Gray.

"I promise to try and lose some weight," Duffey quipped.

Auldridge stepped in: "John's always too modest whenever this conversation comes up. I'd say there's three or four people that are responsible for the music, and Duffey's definitely one of them."

"I think one of the reasons also that bluegrass caught on with the urban audience back then was because there were groups like the Kingston Trio and Joan Baez," Eldridge said. "There was a big interest in folk music, and the Gentlemen were a really neat transition between those kinds of groups and bluegrass."

"In the early 1960s," Duffey recalled, "we were trying to sell ourselves as folk music because that was the way you could get jobs playing auditorium concerts. If you were bluegrass, you were lucky to play Watermelon Park one weekend a summer, and the rest of the time you were playing little barrooms.

"There's a revival in folk music right now that's getting hot, and I think it will have an effect on bluegrass music. I might be mistaken, but bluegrass seems to be in a recession right now. I think this folk music revival is going to do what it did in the '60s. There's a hell of an audience that's going to come into bluegrass from the folk side."

**The Seldom Scene, *Old Train*:**
But, how do you keep a band together, and sounding fresh, fifteen, going on sixteen, years in a society where people go through six or seven careers in two score and five years? "Also, the fact that it's an equal partnership," Auldridge said. "That's the main thing."

Auldridge would say, "Fifteen percent of our jobs are work, and that's a pretty good average no matter what you're doing for a living. Also, the fact that we don't travel in a bus together."

"We go to the jobs, and we get there," added Duffey. "Other than flying, we've only traveled together once in fifteen years."

"You're not on stage silently hating one person because they're making more than you are," Duffey resumed. "I think that's the biggest mistake that all bands make," Auldridge agreed.

"It's a group effort," Duffey said, "So everyone should be equally paid, beside the fact that we all have basically the same tastes in music. I always have half an ear cocked in case something comes on I think we could do something with."

"The Scene is stable," explained Gray, "because we're all comfortable with what we're doing. We're not aggressively trying to do as much as we can and travel as much as we can. We go at a comfortable pace. and we don't have a band vehicle. I'm sure if we did, there'd be some friction. As it is, we enjoy each other when we get together...there's nobody telling you what to do. It's not like a job."

"If someone was told what they had to do," Eldridge said, "then sooner or later they'd find a job someplace else when they got tired of what we're doing."

"Instead of saying we don't have a leader," Auldridge interjected, "I'd say we have five leaders. It's just weird that it works."

"Also, we're kind of willing to take a chance," Duffey said. "If it works, OK, maybe we'll try that again sometime. If it doesn't, we have brains enough to say we won't try that again, whether it's something you say or something you play."

The discussion of risk-taking among the Scene currently revolves around how to expand their market without losing what they love doing.

"That's the name of our game: Reach a bigger audience without compromising too much. Duffey stated, "you never know what's going to work. You have people saying let's get that Nashville sound, and you get a lot of people trying, and they do get it, but it still doesn't work. Why doesn't it work? Nobody knows.

"I think that we could reach a bigger audience without compromising too much," Auldridge reasons, "I mean it wouldn't be compromising at all to my tastes, if we had a real tasteful drummer and an electric bass..."

"A good sax man," Duffey interrupted,

"No, and I could play some steel on some things. Ben could play more guitar. A little more commercial sound but not to the point where it's not us. I think it can be done, whether anybody in the band agrees. I'm not talking about playing country; I'm talking about playing Seldom Scene music, but with a little more commercial sound to it. It would be more palatable to radio."

"I think it would be fun if Tom got an electric bass." added Eldridge.

"Even if it were only on some things. I would play steel on, say ten percent of our material and have a drummer on certain kinds of songs." Auldridge continued, "I think it could be done tastefully

"We've been using a drummer on the last three albums," Duffey responded.

"I mean on stage," Auldridge said. "There's enough talent in the band that if we worked at it, we could compete with anybody, but it's real hard to walk out on stage at some of these [mixed] country and bluegrass festivals. Acoustic music just sounds weak by comparison. There's no bottom end, and the same thing happens on the radio. You've got to be able to have a little stronger bottom end, rhythm wise. You could do that in a way that a song like "Old Train" wouldn't really change."

"It would have the same appeal," concluded Duffey, "But there's no guarantee it would be played [on the radio]."

You never can tell. In 1971 The Seldom Scene abandoned a gig at a local dive because the audience was more interested in Monday Night Football. In 1986 they were hometown heroes on stage of America's premier serious music venue, and the beat goes on with every mandolin chop. [*end of article*]

John with young fan, Laurie Williams
Casey. © Thelma Williams

When the Scene played their 15th anniversary show at the Kennedy Center, Tom Gray was starting to feel that his days in the band were numbered. Tom confided in 2018: "I was starting to get the same kind of treatment by the band that Phil was getting a year earlier. Our new lead singer was Lou Reid who wanted to take the group in a new direction and so did Mike. They also wanted an electric bass. They wanted to be more contemporary. Mike said, 'We are dying a slow death. We need to update our sound. We need to update our image.' And he was looking me straight in the eye when he said it."

Local D.C. musician Tom Guidera had sold Gray an electric Fender bass. Before joining the Scene, Lou Reid had played electric bass with the band, Quicksilver.

As recording sessions were beginning for the next album, Tom agreed to use the Fender bass in the studio.

Lou and Mike had a lot of opinions. Tom began to get more than annoyed about all the unwanted bass counseling he was getting.

"I was like a coiled spring," Tom recalled. "I thought if I get one more piece of unwanted advice then I'm going to blow up."

Sure enough, Tom found a spot in a song where he could add one of his fluid bass runs, and Lou interrupted him saying, "I think you ought to play that run in a lower octave." With that comment, Tom went off.

"No matter what I do on this instrument you're going to say 'I suck. And it ain't even a real bass," shouted Tom.

"You need to use the electric bass because of its sustain," countered Lou.

"Yes, it sustains like a feedback machine with no relief for your poor overburdened ears," Tom fired back.

Duffey stepped in and wisely said, "We are not going to finish these recording sessions. Our next record is going to be a live album on stage." And that album was their 15th Anniversary concert at the Kennedy Center. For Tom this was a leap from the depths of the disparaging recording session to the euphoria of the Kennedy Center where the Scene were treated like heroes, which they were.

After that show, Tom had three possible choices: He could insist that things remain as they were and he continue on the acoustic bass. Tom believes that Duffey would have backed him up if he wanted to do that because John was never part of the ones who wanted to make big changes in the band's sound.

Tom could swallow his pride and make the suggested change to electric, or he could just resign from the band

and let them hire someone who wanted to play electric bass. on electric bass, which he didn't want to do
So Tom left and T. Michael Coleman, who had played with Doc Watson, got the job.

The next album was named *A Change of Scenery* to reflect the changing membership in the band.

Coleman grew up in Leakesville, North Carolina, and played in various bluegrass and folk groups. He was the sound technician every time Doc Watson performed at his alma mater, Appalachian State University, and beginning in 1974, T. Michael played bass with both Doc and his son, Merle, and appears on 18 albums on bass with Watson. His 2016 solo album, *Pocket* featured contributions from Doc, Sam Bush, Jerry Douglas, Herb Pedersen, and other outstanding musicians.

In addition he has recorded with Johnny Cash, Marty Stuart, The Chieftains, Curly Seckler, The Smith Sisters, and others. Five projects he's been involved with have been nominated for Grammys.

Coleman is also an award-winning videographer and filmmaker, recognized for his work on *Children of Armageddon* (2008), *Broke: The New American Dream* (2009), and *Inside the Afghanistan War* (2012).

# Chapter 22: Sound Decisions

Mike Southard at the board. © Alan Grosman.

**W**hen asked to describe other people he greatly enjoyed playing music with during his career and any special shows he might like to mention, John's answer was surprising:

*Well, there have been a lot of them. Too many to list. But we played a year ago in November at the University of West Virginia in Morgantown and had the best sound man in acoustic music that we've ever run across—and we've run across a lot of them. His name is Mike Southard. Ben says he wants to adopt him. He is just absolutely the best in the business. This was in an old theater with cinderblock walls. The house was full. Mike had us sounding just like a record. It was so good like a shot of dope playing that Morgantown show.*

*Ben's wife was in the audience, and she told us it sounded just like we thought. And we could do nothing wrong. It was perfect, and so was the audience. That was a very memorable night.*

*We've used Mike in Pennsylvania, Virginia, and Tennessee and tried to hire him full time. But we can't quite pay him enough just to lay around and do nothing but exclusively our sound. But he will do our sound anytime he can.*

Mike Southard had never heard John say this before we contacted him for this book. His first reaction to Duffey's 1984 compliments was, "It is extremely cool. I would never in a million years expect to hear that coming from John, especially if you just knew him on the surface like most people knew him."

Mike was born in 1956 and raised in Harrisonburg, Virginia and is a banjo player. His story begins when he first heard Ben Eldridge play banjo on "Rider" from The Seldom Scene's album, *Live at the Cellar Door.* "I thought Ben was a god," says Mike.

It was Mike's experience as a bluegrass musician that introduced him to the challenges of providing adequate sound for acoustic instruments. "My band had terrible sound, and I became our sound guy," Mike explains. His foray into the formal business of music included a local Harrisonburg club called the Elbow Room. Mike describes, "It was an established blues nightclub with 200 seats, but in decline and was sold. I got hired as a booking agent and sound man by the new owner."

Mike began running the sound for acoustics bands 3 to 4 times a week at the Elbow Room. "I had been to the Birchmere many times and thought it was a great business model, so I tried to emulate the Birchmere at the Elbow Room."

He booked national acts like J.D. Crowe, Spectrum, Béla Fleck, Norman Blake, and others, with food and small cards on the table asking people not to talk during the music. Booking The Seldom Scene was Mike's goal to make his "little Birchmere" complete.

On his first call to John Duffey, he introduced himself and asked: "How are you?"

John answered, "Oh, So-so."

Mike thought, "Oh great, he's giving me a signal he isn't that interested in talking with me."

And Mike was right. The $1,500 he was paying most prominent acts at the Elbow Room wasn't enough for John and the band to drive the two hours from D.C.

But through persistence and subsequent calls over the next two years, Mike and Duffey gradually became more cordial and finally got the money right. John then asked the second question:

"Where are the dressing rooms?"

Mike replied, "Upstairs."

John asked, "How do you get to the stage?"

Mike said, "You walk down the steps and through the audience."

"You have to walk through the audience? Sorry we can't do that," said John.

The Seldom Scene never played the Elbow Room.

## CEO

With 40 years in the business, Mike is today CEO and founder of Southard Audio. He was a commercial pilot and flight instructor before his overriding interest in music led him into a career in live sound reinforcement. He performed in a band, taught music, and attended James Madison University. Mike maintains that, "there is still nothing more challenging than getting a bluegrass act to sound good in both the hall and in the monitors because you have low-level acoustic instruments in front of hot mics and the players need to hear what they're doing."

One day Mike had the original Dillards scheduled, and he spent two hours working with Rodney Dillard trying to make him happy with the vocals. "Certain acts are known to be very picky on sound, and nothing was working for Rodney that day. I had a regular speaker system in the nightclub, and then about 20 feet in front of the stage were two Bose 800 speakers for rear fill for the audience. Out of exasperation I got a stepladder, and turned the speakers to face the stage, patched them through the monitor system and Rodney got a big grin on his face. He absolutely loved it. It wasn't anything I had planned. It was like, "what haven't I tried?""

Mike realized that one of the things that made it difficult to get reasonable monitor sound is that all the monitors' sound came from the floor and had to pass through all the live microphones to get to the players' ears.

"So, what I did was elevate the monitors to provide side-fills so the vocals could be heard clearly. Over time I started to create two separate mixes: one for the speakers on top in the elevated monitors for the vocals, and one for the speakers on the bottom for the instruments. That enabled the players to hear their voices high and the instruments lower which made for a more natural sound for the players," This also helped Mike get more gain (volume) without feedback.

Soon after, the Elbow Room folded. Mike bought the house sound system at auction and started his own Southard Audio business.

Mike's idea for elevated or "flying" monitors won him accolades from many acoustic bands and became replicated in other clubs and venues, including the Birchmere.

It was a year later when the promoter for the West Virginia concert hired Mike to work The Seldom Scene show. Mike remembers it well. "I spent a full hour on the monitors and met John Duffey and the rest of the band at the soundcheck. I didn't introduce myself as the person who used to call him to play the Elbow Room. That came much later.

"John had such a powerful voice that he didn't worry about his voice being heard, but the mandolin was his thing. He always struggled to hear his mandolin over the banjo. And I'll admit I had everything sounding great that day. It was one of those magical shows. The audience of 1,000 loved it."

The band came to Mike when the show was over and thanked him. From that night on, John Duffey became his friend and prominent advocate. "He single-handedly moved me from the fringes of the business to work the major bluegrass festivals. He was an honest guy and had the trust of all the promoters. He'd call them up and suggest they give me a try. And they did. His endorsement propelled me to where I am now."

The Seldom Scene also hired Mike for select shows. His friendship with John grew, and John and Nancy would invite Mike over to their house. "I met Nancy, and they were just the nicest," said Mike.

## Watching the audience jump

"One funny memory of mixing the Scene were the moments that John would hit some thunderous vocal notes and watch the audience respond. What John didn't realize that sometimes these notes could reach the level of pain for the audience. There is a device called a compressor that I first used to avoid those eye-watering notes. However, the first time I used it; John came to me afterwards to complain that his voice wasn't sounding right on those notes.

Mike told him, "Yes I'm using a compressor because those notes are painfully loud out there."

"But I want them loud," said Duffey with a grin. "So, don't use the compressor."

Mike still didn't like the "glass-breaking" notes, so he modified his soundboard in a way that allowed John to hear his loud notes in the monitors, but the audience was spared and heard them compressed. This was my little secret," Mike admits.

When John knew that Phil Rosenthal was leaving the band, Duffey called Mike for advice on other guitarists who might replace Phil. That was probably the most flattering thing John had ever said to me. It was one thing to trust me with their sound, it was another thing altogether to ask my advice about adding a new member to the band. And the discussion about who might fit that role was interesting, as you might imagine.

In summary, Mike says, "John had many layers. For fans, he was polite up to a point but when you got to know him, he was a warm and loyal friend."

### In Praise of Ben Eldridge
Since his concentration on the banjo and reverence for Ben Eldridge sparked his career, Mike provided this tribute to Ben:

"As an aspiring banjo student, Ben Eldridge was among my banjo heroes, and in my opinion a vastly under-rated and under-recognized musician. There are some universal qualities shared by great players, and alongside technical ability, tone, timing, taste, and consistency, is a unique and original style of playing, one almost instantly recognizable among the hundreds of excellent players in the world.

"When you hear Ben playing, live or on a recording, you know it's Ben. He effortlessly weaves delicious melodic passages in and out of solid Scruggs style right hand technique, combining tastefully innovative and unique twists and turns, subtle and powerful.

"The great players make challenging technical pieces sound easy. As a student of the instrument, my respect for Ben's playing only grew as I attempted to learn some of his instrumental leads. Some of them sound easy to play. Few of them are.

"Ben is a consummate ensemble player. His solos are masterfully thought out, and often when listening to Ben's playing you can imagine the mathematician's brain shaking hands with an artist's soul, but his back up playing was certainly a permanent stamp on his lifelong band, The Seldom Scene. From three chord traditional bluegrass pieces to obscure blues and rock and folk genre songs that the Scene colorized in their own hues, from blazing hyper tempo drives ("Rider") to lilting waltzes ("Paradise"), Ben's playing was always just there, and it was right, and it fit as if he studied every note while in truth the music just fell off his fingers.

"As if it isn't enough to be among the early innovators and masters of the banjo, Ben is also just a great guy. Approachable, articulate, generous, and funny as hell. Ben, thanks for everything and enjoy many, many years of retirement."

**Billy Wolf**
Born near Ground Zero in Manhattan, Billy Wolf grew up in Queens, New York and New England. He first earned money playing electric bass in bands. Billy was

very aware of The Country Gentlemen and had great respect for their music. One of his roommates in college was a mandolin player and an enormous fan of John Duffey.

Billy became friends with John through his association as musician and sound man for Tony Rice, the acclaimed bluegrass musician from Danville, Virginia inducted into the International Bluegrass Music Hall Of Fame in 2013. Billy played piano on some of Rice's recordings. An authorized biography, *Still Inside: The Tony Rice Story* by Tim Stafford and Caroline Wright was published in 2010 by Word of Mouth Press.

"I had been working with Tony and David Grisman for years and while traveling Tony introduced me to Gary Oelze while playing the Birchmere. I want to say that I first met John and the original Scene backstage at the Telluride Bluegrass Festival in Colorado. It was a casual meeting and John struck me as very friendly with a good sense of humor and fun to be with.

It was when Billy moved to Virginia to run the soundboard at the Birchmere that they became close friends. "John and Nancy were very welcoming to me," Billy exclaimed. "They would have me over to their house on the holidays so I wouldn't feel misplaced. Later we'd shoot pool and watch the Atlanta Braves on TV. If people said John was shy, he was never shy with me that I noticed."

Billy recalls, "The first time I met with them to mix their house sound I thought of them like a traditional bluegrass band—like Flatt & Scruggs at Carnegie Hall. Basically, featured soloists, loud, and you hear the bass all the time is how I interpreted them."

John, Mike and Ben were all improvisational and Billy doesn't think he ever heard the exact same solos from John during the hundreds of sets as he ran the board for them. "John would play around something he had conceived for a song but his solos were never note for note (repeats)," Billy reports, adding, "I never had a set list ever, but even though they would throw in a new song or an old tune once in a while, their sets were pretty much the same songs although not in the same order."

Birchmere owner, Gary Oelze has high praise for Billy. Gary said in 2019, "Billy has engineered albums for The Grateful Dead and others. I once watched him splice a tape where the singer had mixed up two words and re-assemble the tape correcting the mistake. He ran the Birchmere board for decades and recorded most of The Seldom Scene shows. Billy is excellent."

# Chapter 23: The UK Interview
# by Tom Travis

**T**om Travis has been active in every aspect of bluegrass music since 1962. He was the organizer of the Edale Bluegrass Festival, Europe's oldest and largest bluegrass festival, for many years and brought over many leading American bluegrass bands and artists to perform in the UK. His memorabilia have filled his attic and most of the summer house in his garden.

In 1995, Tom organized a King George's Hall event where The Seldom Scene flew in, played the concert and flew back home. There Tom was given the tremendous honor of being invited by John to join them on stage and sing and pick with them.

"Their only visit to our fair shores was unfortunately brief; they were in England for about four days. In light of what happened the following year with the tragic loss of John, it's as if that visit from the greatest bluegrass band the world has ever seen, was meant to be.

Here is a transcript of Tom's interview with John, one of his last. It was broadcast on his BBC Radio 2 series, Bluegrass Ramble on 4 April 1996.

Q: John, you're a real bluegrass veteran; looking back over your many years in the music, what do remember as the high spots – those that have brought you most pleasure?
A: Mmm...Getting paid. (laughter). Well there's so many things that we just don't have the time to go into the whole thing. I remember playing Carnegie Hall in New York in September 1961.

Q: What about playing before presidents and things like that?
A: Well, there's Jimmy Carter when he was president. He invited us over three times—once, just for dinner (laughter) But we haven't heard from him since.

Q: How can you invite Seldom Scene and not have them sing—that's terrible...Just for dinner?
A: Just for dinner, yeah. I think it was neat.

Q: Well, well, that's what you call restraint. (laughter). Being a lover of bluegrass fiddle, myself, I was surprised to read in a recent article on Seldom Scene that you don't like working with fiddles. Is that true?
A: Well, back in the early days, going way back to The Country Gentlemen days, trying to get the music out of the woods and into town...it seemed as though the particular sound of the fiddle was...er...

Q: It had the wrong connotations?
A: It just didn't sound that good to people that we were to, shall we say, trying to put the music to that one particular sound, they thought, was awfully whiney and screechy. I mean, that was their opinion. I do remember, Ricky Skaggs worked with us on one occasion. I remember he got up one night... we were trying to sing...I think it was, "A Small Exception of Me," which was a quiet trio and we were all trying to hit the note and he's standing back there going about a half a tone flat...

Q: Oh dear...
A: Just to be irritating.

Q: Oh, I can't believe that. Was he doing it on purpose?
A: Oh, I'm sure he was just goofing off.

Q: He's got perfect pitch, that man.
A: Oh yeah, he was just goofing around, you know. But the total dislike of fiddles is not true. It was just a reason for it.

Q: I see. It was stopping you from furthering the music?
A: Right.

Q: And transmission to a wider audience?
A: Yeah.

Q: It's funny y' know, because when I first came into music in the mid 1950s, I used to love Hank Williams.
A: Oh yeah?

Q: And yet, I used to think, 'Oh why do they have that fiddle. It sounds awful.' So, I think that you have to be educated up to the fiddle haven't you—because I absolutely love it now.
A: Oh yeah, they're accepted everywhere now.

Q: Yes, and now I can't get enough—especially from some of the fiddlers around today. I mean, Mark O'Connor, he just blows me away.
A: He's a machine.

Q: (laughs) But you are very lucky in that you've got Mike Auldridge on Dobro who really puts in some pretty fancy licks anyway. So, maybe a fiddle might be in the way?

A: Well actually, technically, the way we are and have been for nearly twenty-four years—we really didn't need one and y' know...we don't need a sixth lead instrument.

Q: True, true—especially with a maestro like that anyway. Having been introduced to bluegrass music through Monroe, the Stanley Brothers, Reno and Smiley and their like, I remember that when I first heard a Seldom Scene album, in '72, I didn't like it. It sounded too sweet, too Avant Garde, too sophisticated. Did Seldom Scene music cause controversy with bluegrass fans in the early days?
A: Actually...I always hate to say things like this, but we're one of the reasons it started being more popular.

Q: Don't get me wrong.
A: I understand what you mean.

Q: I absolutely love it now, I mean, talking about being educated up to the fiddle, I had to be educated up to Seldom Scene.
A: Well, what we did not, like say, on purpose. It's just like mixing gun powder; you put certain things together and that's the way it comes out and it just happened to be that particular kind of sound was due to the combination – the chemicals included.

Q: Yes, it seemed so clean—the pickin' I mean—well it was the first spark of urban bluegrass, which made it different from rural bluegrass...which I'd been raised on. And I'm just an old reactionary—because it was just too new at the time—I mean it's not new to me now. I'm the guy who didn't like the Beatles the first time I heard them. So, it gives you some idea. Did you set out to change the social culture of bluegrass music? Which you most certainly have...or did it just happen as a consequence?

A: Well no, it just kinda happened...Although we did think in our minds that the one thing the music needed as a boost was it needed some new material, because it got to be bands were coming along and they just kept wearing out the same old work-horses.

Q: Singing old standards?

A: Same thing and the music did need material and one of the active things we pursued was to bring...new material in the field.

Q: The Scene is one of the most eclectic bands I've ever heard anyway, I heard you do soul... Midnight Hour...at one time you just never, ever...mind you, everybody's copying you and doing all sorts of things now.

A: Well, I guess the best thing that's happened to bluegrass music, for as far as getting out a little bit, I guess, is Alison Krauss. She still wants to play this kind of music, but she's done a few things on the side that have brought her name out more and if she continues to work with the type of band, she has...eventually that maybe some help.

Q: Having listened to it, and listened carefully, and analyzed what that band is doing, they really are breaking ground, y' know. The things that are going on between the bass and the mandolin They are just building a platform on which they can build all sorts of wonderful melodic things. And they don't exclude the banjo. So many people try to exclude the banjo to make sweet music, don't they? They do it, and recognize the bluegrass line up, and they do it well.

A: Well, she's got one thing on her side – youth. And in America, let me tell you, everything is youth, youth, youth. The Government wishes we'd all drop dead at forty, y' know.

Q: The thing is that we had the baby boom of the post war days and we now have the baby boom middle-agers. We must be a bigger market than the kids now, I should think?
A: Mmm...well you'd think so, but I don't know...I don't see it happening (Laughs).

Q: What about John Duffey and his music in the future – do you have any unfulfilled ambitions?
A: (Pause) Really none that I can think of, I mean, I'm a cheap date – I'm happy, y' know what I mean. I don't have anything I don't want to do...I don't want to, y' know, stand on the Tower of London and shout the "Muleskinner Blues!"

Q: You'll be happy just to stand up there and pick?
A: Well, I mean just more or less the way it is. I don't have any place I wanna be, or any, y'know, weird lick that I want to present to the public, or anything like that.

Q: Well, are you going to do any projects with any of your old buddies from way back, like Charlie Waller.
A: Well, we have actually two things scheduled for this year; one is in October and one in November. A little reunion show; one's on the east coast of the state of Connecticut and the other is on the west coast, in California.

Q: Are you going to record anything?
A: No, we don't have any plans to do that.

Q: Oh, what a shame, Well, maybe after you've worked together once again, you might get into the studio and lay something down?
A:Who knows? I'm just hoping that the plane stays in the air tomorrow!

Q: He's going home tomorrow folks. He's now sitting with me in Blackburn, in Britain and...you've never been to Britain before?
A: No, it's the first time we ever got invited – thank you.

Q: Ah well it a pleasure – thanks very much indeed for coming. Before we sign off, could you, maybe, give us the name of a track that you'd like us to play, that you've recorded over the years?
A: I guess...the most famous one over the years...is "Wait a Minute."

Q: Oh! I love that— a Herb Pederson song. Ahh, let's do that one!
A: Well, all right (laughs) if that's the way you feel.

Q: Thanks, John. It's been a pleasure
A: Thanks to you, Tom.

# Chapter 24: Fellow Players

*"Jonathan came into the back room of the Birchmere one night and introduced himself and said he knew some of our songs. And he did. He kept stopping in periodically, and finally somebody got the bright idea of us trying an album together."*

JD

Phil, Wayne Williams, Tom, Laurie Williams Casey, Thelma Williams, John, Ben, Jonathan, and Mike © Carl Fleischhauer

## Jonathan Edwards

Norman Rowe reported on the genesis of the album, *Blue Ridge* in the *Richmond Times-Dispatch*: "The blend of The Seldom Scene bluegrass picking and the sound of the pop singer, Jonathan Edwards found immediate favor with the (Birchmere) audience, and prompted the agent for the band, Gary Oelze, to send a cassette tape to Barry Poss of Sugar Hill Records. A few weeks later, the band and the pop singer were in the studio of Bias Recording at Springfield, VA to recreate their Birchmere jam sessions for the records."

*Blue Ridge* is a beautiful Seldom Scene album recorded with singer/songwriter Jonathan Edwards. named "Best Bluegrass Album" of 1986 by the National Association of Independent Record Distributors.

When asked how it would do commercially at the time of its release, John said, "it's really too early to predict how the LP will do. Unless you're Top 40, it takes a while for things to either catch on or bomb." In another album review, the *New York Times* called The Seldom Scene "probably the best bluegrass band in the land."

Jonathan grew up in Alexandria, Virginia on the banks of the Potomac River near Mount Vernon. In the Eighties, he lived in Springfield near Woodbridge, Virginia. For this book Jonathan described his relationship with Duffey:

"John and I were alpha dogs of the highest degree and being in his presence certainly tested my willingness to compete. Fortunately, I worked through my intimidation and any ego issues relating to the job at hand. At least I think I did.

"Our union blossomed about as naturally as growing a garden and as organically as one could imagine. Our partnership became forged in bronze and rosewood once

297

we fully realized that our relationship was based on our mutual love of the music and shared the joy of performing. Our appreciation for each other strengthened.

"I remember first seeing John live when I was playing in town. Fast-forward to the early eighties and The Seldom Scene was the Thursday night must-see at the [old] Birchmere. I was living nearby at the time, and so I would drop in to listen, and I soon couldn't help but sit-in. We were starting to sound pretty good, and John was apt to whisper to me during the applause, 'That was adequate,' and I knew I was beginning to gain his acceptance.

"One night, I mentioned that we should try to do some recording to which Mike replied, 'We were thinking the same thing but were a little shy to ask.' And so, began some of my most treasured musical moments and significant life lessons.

"We went right into the studio and started laying down tracks, and after three power-packed days, we had a nice collection of songs called, *Blue Ridge.* I became the third singer with two of the best—Mike Auldridge and John Duffey—with the most beautiful voices ever to sing a bluegrass song.

"However, I was accustomed to spending a month and six figures on album projects and assumed everyone worked like that. So, I asked John what time should we be there on the fourth day of fixing, sweetening, and mixing. He looked at me for a moment and replied as he packed up his mandolin, 'No, Jon, this is the way we sounded on a Wednesday, and that's what we're going with. OK?'"

"Thus, a valuable lesson in spontaneity, faith, and ability from a master of his art. Thank you, Alpha Dog, for your understated and at the same time outrageous example of how to do what we do. You will be forever missed especially when someone is tempted to take themselves a little too seriously.

"How did we choose the songs for *Blue Ridge*? I think everyone presented or suggested songs to consider and we tried a few, and the winners made it to the sessions. Someone had just sent me *Blue Ridge* on a cassette, and while I liked the song, I loved the song to explore with The Seldom Scene.

"I quite honestly have no idea what the sales numbers were for *Blue Ridge*. It indeed was not on my list of reasons why I wanted to record with these legendary musicians. I was just grateful for the opportunity and humbled that they would find me worthy. It seemed like a great and exciting mix and proved to be so.

"One thing I loved about the band was their willingness to try different things and not be limited by a strict adherence to tradition. I mean, look at John's pants! They were even excited to try drums on a few songs. I also suggested my dear friend, Kenny White come in and play some beautiful grand piano and they loved it, and so did I.

"We did one of their icons, "Wait a Minute," and I, for one was hooked! I met and worked with both Mike Auldridge and Herb Pedersen out in L.A. while working on one of my solo albums, so I knew the song. We also did "Sunshine" and "Little Hands" as well.

"Incidentally, even though bluegrass was one of my earliest moments of inspiration and clarity about the power and intimacy of acoustic music, I never aspired to be a bluegrass player as such. Having Bill Keith in my band, however, did open some amazing doors and deepened my love of the idiom and the people out there making it live and breathe.

## Pete Kennedy

The owner of one of the most eclectic musical resumes is Pete Kennedy. Among many other artists, Pete has played guitar and sang with Emmylou Harris and Nancy Griffith; played in orchestras for Leonard Bernstein, Bob Hope and Stevie Wonder; and served as music director for a Martha and the Vandellas' East Coast tour ("Martha Reeves signed her publicity picture, "To Pete; you thrilled my heart.") He played "Midnight Train to Georgia" with Gladys Knight—"but didn't sing the Pips' parts," he joked. His biography, *Tone, Twang, and Taste* was published in 2018 by Highpoint.Life

Pete was aware of The Country Gentlemen growing up in Arlington, Virginia. Charlie Waller lived right around the corner from him. At twelve Pete began guitar lessons at Arlington Music where Duffey had his instrument repair shop.

"John would let me hang around in his workshop. He didn't seem to mind at all," Pete recalls. "John would chat a little bit. The thing I remember that he was doing was bolting the guitar bridges down on Martin D-28 guitars for the bluegrass guys. They all used heavy gauge strings, and the bridges would pull up. He would drill holes on both sides of the bridge to bolt it down. Modifying these original Martins would drive guitar collectors to apoplexy today."

Pete started performing locally at the Monday night hootenannies held at the Red Fox Inn in 1973. First as a solo act and then with a community of folk musicians. "I got to know the owner, Walt Broderick well and he was a nice guy who liked the musicians," said Pete. The Seldom Scene played the Red Fox on Thursday nights.

By coincidence, Pete moved to the Shirlington, Virginia community where the first Birchmere was located. He would walk across the street from his house and hang out there. There he met and befriended owner Gary Oelze and later became more familiar with Duffey and the Scene when they started their residence there. "Sometimes I ran sound for Gary when he was busy waiting tables as he had a tiny staff back then," said Pete. "The Birchmere was like my family."

Pete has always been interested in roots music. "To me, that encompasses rock and roll, folk-rock, blues, Appalachian style folk, gospel, rockabilly, etc. and also jazz from before the fusion era," Pete explained.

"When Tom Principato asked me to join him in a swing jazz guitar duo, I jumped at the chance," Pete said. "Living in D.C., I had been exposed to every kind of Southern music, because at the outbreak of World War Two, people converged from all over the South, and they brought roots music with them. Roy Buchanan, Link Wray, and Danny Gatton were our local bar band guitarists, and they embodied that spirit of ecumenism when it came to music.

"Principato's idea was two guitars playing swing stuff by Charlie Christian et al. We put it together, and that happened to coincide with Danny Gatton's all-star band with Buddy Emmons and Lenny Breau. Danny called it the Redneck Jazz Explosion." Tom and Pete were the logical opening act for the Explosion. Some of these shows were at the Cellar Door.

"Mike Auldridge came one night, and he and I just hit it off," Pete remembers. "Mike wanted to learn pedal steel guitar, so I started going over to his house to play guitar with him so he could practice his steel licks. Mike was always enthusiastic about learning new music. He'd call me up and say, 'I just learned a new lick, man, so come on over and hear it,' and I'd drive from Virginia to his Maryland house to listen.

"Another time Mike called, and said I needed to come over to meet this 18-year-old guy that 'played great. I think you two will really get along.' The guy was Béla Fleck. Mike always wanted to be connected with whatever was happening in the music that was new. Mike's last band, Chesapeake was a way to do this.

"With Mike on pedal steel, we did a demo with Kathy Stone, Hank William's daughter We ended up doing Mike's Western swing album, *Eight String Swing* together." Mike used a special 8-string Dobro on this recording. Two of the cuts on the album were "Pete's Place" written by Kennedy, and the title track, co-authored by Mike and Pete.

This collaboration became an alternative sideband outside The Seldom Scene, Front Porch Swing. "We played one night a week at the Birchmere for a while in 1979. Mike played pedal steel, and Danny Gatton alternated with Tom Gray on bass. Danny on electric and Tom on up-right."

When asked if there were any tensions between Duffey and Auldridge on the commitment to playing music, Pete explains, "Tension isn't the right word. I would say there was a 'push-pull' as John seemed good with the status quo of how often The Seldom Scene was playing. Mike had wider contacts and was close to Linda Ronstadt, Dolly Parton, Emmylou Harris and people like that.

"Mike felt that The Seldom Scene could have done more if they would have gone more in a country music direction. Not necessarily commercial country but more like what Emmylou Harris was doing with vintage country music where Mike could play steel guitar some. Maybe add a Fender Telecaster electric guitar. Mike thought there were other avenues open to them. He had already persuaded John to use drums a little, but John did not like that at all."

Pete opined that John Duffey had been extremely progressive within the bluegrass genre through The Country Gentlemen. "They were the band that brought in contemporary songwriting rather than just the music Monroe, and Flatt & Scruggs had done, and you needed someone with the stature of Duffey to get away with that. People had to accept it because it was John Duffey's concept. That all started in the Shamrock. But then when it came time to push bluegrass further regarding production and the overall sound, John didn't want to go that far."

## Ricky Skaggs

Pete thinks Mike Auldridge may have been observing Ricky Skaggs as a model of what could be useful for The Seldom Scene. Born in Cordell, Kentucky in 1954, Skaggs was given a mandolin by his Dad and by age 6 had played it onstage with Bill Monroe. In his teens, he met another teen musician, Keith Whitley on guitar, and the two of them not only opened for Ralph Stanley but were invited to join Ralph Stanley's Clinch Mountain Boys. Pete continues:

"It was Charlie Waller that brought Ricky down to Washington to be a "Country Gentlemen," says Pete. In 1976, Skaggs formed progressive bluegrass band Boone Creek, which included Vince Gill and Jerry Douglas. Mike saw what Ricky did when he got his record deal and went in the direction of Emmylou's sound with the Telecaster, electric bass and drums. Ricky played in Emmylou's Hot Band for a while and wrote the arrangements for Harris's 1980 bluegrass-roots album, *Roses In The Snow.* (see *Kentucky Traveler: My Life in Music by Ricky Skaggs with Eddie Dean* (It Books).

After Ricky had success with Nashville, he said, "When I came here it wasn't that I was anti-Music Row, but it was like I was going against the grain of what everybody on Music Row was doing, and that's what has made me successful." And he also said, "The difference between the newer artists and me is that I have the history with the architects, the masters that started the music. I know where the music came from."

Pete says, "Mike thought The Seldom Scene could do Ricky and Emmylou's type of music. But John was happy where The Seldom Scene was, and couldn't be persuaded to change.

Pete continues: "D.C. was a hotbed for this music at the time. I was playing with Danny Gatton and the Rosslyn Mountain Boys. Tony Rice was in town. It was constant learning for me. One afternoon, I got a call from Gary Oelze.

"Do you want to play with Kate Wolf tonight?" asked Gary.

"Sure! And by the way, who's Kate Wolf?" Pete replied,

"The gig was packed and great. Kate, Mike Auldridge and I—with no rehearsal—sounded like we had been playing together for years. She became a fast friend, and as I started picking up more and more folk gigs, I found that most of these artists became friends. They were genuinely good people, trying to make the world a better place." To date, Pete has played the Birchmere 82 times.

Keith Whitley, who had come up influenced by The Country Gentlemen also wanted to expand beyond bluegrass. When Keith played the Birchmere in J.D. Crowe's New South band, Gary Oelze would lock the doors when the crowd left. Pete would play electric guitar with Auldridge on pedal steel, and Keith would sing old country songs by George Jones and Merle

Haggard until dawn. "Those were great nights and we did that several times," Pete recalled.

Keith Whitley moved to Nashville to become a successful country music singer with three top ten hit songs.

"J.D. Crowe was very supportive of Keith's move to country music. He wanted Keith to go as far as he could go even if it meant him leaving J.D.'s band." said Pete.

The ubiquitous picture of Keith in Confederate war uniform and John in drag with fingers in Keith's ears was done at the King's Dominion amusement park in Virginia. Tragically, Keith died of alcohol poisoning in 1989 at the age of 33.

**Duffey Legacy**

Pete agrees that The Seldom Scene helped grow bluegrass's appeal with urban white-collar workers in Washington D.C. by example—as the members themselves had day jobs that fans could relate to. "But another significant thing the band did was move away from the idea that fast instrumental prowess was the core of bluegrass. Bill Monroe wasn't a virtuoso either but rather a conceptual guy who knew a lot of these great songs. The Scene was a modern version of Monroe in a more song-oriented band with three-part harmonies.

"Like John Starling didn't care to play fiddle tunes on his guitar. He just wanted to find great songs to sing. In this way, the Scene laid the groundwork for bluegrass artists like Alison Krauss whose audience isn't just listening to how fast the banjo or mandolin breaks are played. And this is why Emmylou and Linda were so supportive of The Seldom Scene. It was all about the singing and the songs. You could see them, and if no one played any solos, it would still be fine because of the singing. For me, every time I saw them it was all about the harmonies."

## Bryan Bowers

Born near Petersburg, Virginia in 1940, Bryan Bowers came to the Washington, D.C. area at the behest of Bill and Taffy Danoff, aka Fat City. "They told me I needed to come to this bar called Tammany Hall to see a girl sing that was going to be a star. That turned out to be Emmylou Harris," Bryan said.

"Danny Gatton was playing with Liz Meyer then. I started playing solo with my autoharp around town. My first encounter with John Duffey was in the back outside bar of the old Cellar Door.

"He took one look at me with my long hair and hippie clothes and gave me a look of, 'I don't know what you are but don't come near me.' He didn't say anything. Just one look and turned away."

As Bowers played the clubs and got better known and musically respected, he was invited by Mike Auldridge to sit in with the Scene at the Red Fox Inn. Later he opened for the Scene at a Lisner Auditorium concert. "Consistency of excellent music is what I remember about The Seldom Scene, and how Duffey paced the show. After a slow, beautiful song he'd mutter to the band members, 'energy' which meant 'let's step up the next songs with some power.'"

"Duffey was a piece of work as a front man," said Bryan. "He wasn't everyone's cup of tea. Some of those gay jokes he'd throw out a couple of times a night. You could barely get by with that back then and could never today. But he didn't care if he said something tacky."

On the gay schtick, Tom Gray recalled counseling Duffey on their way to playing their first concert in San Francisco. "Don't do this at the show," urged Gray.

Of course, Duffey began the performance using his gay voice, and the audience began to hiss. Tom leaned in and said to John, "I told you not do that."

Bowers continued, "Otherwise, he was a stunning performer. And he was the leader of the band. The other guys looked to him for direction."

## Zen Gospel

The Seldom Scene liked Bowers and recorded on the first three of his albums. Bryan loved having them in the studio.

On one tune, "Zen Gospel Singing," Duffey arrived to the studio ill with a fever and couldn't sing. Nonetheless, he gave everyone their harmonies so they could record, and promised to come back when he felt better to and record his part. As soon as John set one foot out the door of the studio, John Starling and Ben Eldridge told Bryan, "Duffey must really love you because we can barely get him to record with us, and here he is sick and working to help you make your record." After that John and Bryan became pals and would begin singing harmonies on the song, "The Old Lovers" every time they saw each other. "I was very sad to hear that he died but then I thought about all the music, laughter and joy he brought to the world. I still miss him," Bryan said.

## Sam Bush

Born Charles Samuel Bush in Bowling Green, Kentucky in 1952, Sam Bush is widely regarding as one of the best mandolin players of his generation and considered by many to be the "father of newgrass." He along with his work in bands the Bluegrass Alliance and the New Grass Revival played progressive bluegrass by mixing other influences outside of traditional bluegrass into their music much like what The Country Gentlemen had done before them. Sam Bush has won multiple Grammys, several IBMA awards and an Americana Music Association Lifetime Achievement Award.

In a 2018 interview for this book by G.T., Sam spoke about The Country Gentlemen and the "father of progressive bluegrass" label.

"The Gents—they were it. They were the kings of Bluegrass to me," said Sam. "Progressive grass. I've often said, 'yes I've been called the father of newgrass, but my father of newgrass is John Duffey'. That's my father of bluegrass—of newgrass. John Duffey. The way he played.

"I bought my first Country Gentlemen record where my mother worked at Sears and they had the—I'm not sure the actual label it's on—it was called *Bluegrass Hootenanny* and there was no one pictured in The Country Gentlemen so I didn't know what anybody looked like. I bought it for 42 cents. The best 42 cents I ever spent in my life.

"When 'Nine Pound Hammer' came on with John's mandolin kickoff I was sold. That was it." Sam then convinced his parents to let him attend the Roanoke Bluegrass Festival in 1965.

"It was my first Bluegrass Festival. I read about it in *Sing Out* magazine and I saw the ad and I just begged my parents, 'Can I go to this?' and they let me go with a friend.

"When John Duffey walked on stage—I didn't know anything about them—and finally they come on stage at Roanoke with Big John and they got up there and John Duffey sang 'Muleskinner Blues' in the key of A—one key higher than Bill Monroe sang it.

"The Gentlemen just blew the roof off the place. They just blew it up that year. It was so great having The

Country Gentlemen. Now I'm a giant fan of John Duffey."

Sam graduated high school in 1970 and joined The Bluegrass Alliance band. "One of the friends I made at festivals was a great man from D.C., John Kaparakis, who was a friend of John Duffey. We, the young Bluegrass Alliance, were playing down at The Shamrock where in bluegrass circles the Gentlemen made the Shamrock club famous. I was having a problem breaking strings constantly. My friend John Kaparakis asked, 'Would you like to go meet John Duffey?' And I'm like, 'Whoa. Would I? Yes.'

"Duffey worked at Arlington Music and maybe he could figure out why I was breaking so many strings. So, I got to go in and hang with John Duffey. He worked on my mandolin a little bit and did some things and he said, 'I'd like to come down and hear you guys tonight.' And John Kaparakis told me, 'I haven't seen John Duffey in a club since he quit the Gentlemen.' Duffey told John Kaparakis, 'I want to go hear that little mandolin player.'

"That same night John came into the club and oh God was I thrilled. John Duffey's there and he listened to me play the first set. Afterwards he walked up to me and said, 'Well, I know why you're breaking all those strings.

"I replied, 'Why is that?'

"'You play too goddamn hard. The mandolin's only so big. There's only so much it'll take. You're just playing it too hard. You're going to break strings all your life if you don't soften up a little bit.'"

"And so, I took that to heart, and I did try to soften up a little but when I was playing in a band with Courtney Johnson, one of the loudest banjo players that ever lived, it is tough to soften up with Courtney. That night John got up and sat in with us. Our band at that time was Ebo Walker on bass, Lonnie Pierce on fiddle, Courtney Johnson on banjo, Tony Rice on guitar, and me on mandolin. Tony thought he could out sing John Duffey when John got up to play with us. It was such a force when he sang, you couldn't believe it.

"Just to hear him do it right on stage with him. He was three feet from the microphone not even looking at it and Tony was right up on the mic singing as hard as he could. Tony just about—he pretty much blew his throat out that night trying to keep up with John Duffey. I don't think he was worth a dang for a couple of days after trying to keep up with John. That was my first experience with John. Within a year or two, we had made friends with Ben Eldridge and John Starling."

In the fall of 1971, the Bluegrass Alliance dissolved, and the New Grass Revival was formed, and they became one of the leading bands of the "newgrass" style of bluegrass. Members of the New Grass Revival attended some of the Scene's first performances at the Rabbit's Foot in D.C. Sam remained friends with John Duffey and the Scene over the years.

"I would always see John at festivals. It was always a good time down at the Kentucky Fried Chicken festival. The Seldom Scene always played there in Louisville, Kentucky. And then when you cut to the chase of now go onwards to 1982 and it was a tough time for me. I had cancer and it was crazy. John called me while I was in the hospital with my first cancer. We'd just talk and talk about baseball, about the Braves, he was just trying to get my mind on something happier. And one of the most uplifting things that could ever happen was that John and Jethro [Burns], two of my heroes would both call me in the hospital almost daily. Duffey would just call me and rail on me and I didn't know—it took a few years to figure out that John Duffey and Jethro Burns, both of them if they liked you, they were going to butt you around. You know, you weren't even sure if they liked you or not but then I come to find out that if John Duffey didn't like you, he just wouldn't talk to you. If he liked you, he's gonna give you hell. Both John and Jethro taught me that it's OK to be irreverent. If you're gonna make fun of anybody you gotta make fun of everybody."

When the New Grass Revival started, Sam and the rest of the band deviated from the norms of the times with their long hair, casual stage attire, and their selection of material outside of traditional bluegrass. This was before John Duffey began wearing weight-lifting pants and wild bowling shirts. Even after The Seldom Scene began to wear casual clothes on stage, John Duffey kept his crew-cut hair style.

Sam recalled, "One time I told him, new wave music and punks were hitting the scene over in England. So, people are coming out with their butch haircuts and flat tops and spiked haircuts and rockabilly hair when everybody was coming out of long-haired hippie people and I said, 'Hey John. The punks over in England are wearing your hair cut now. The flat top with fenders.' And he said, 'I knew it'd come back some day.'

When speaking of John Duffey's legacy and his influence on other performers, Sam recalled, "And John Duffey knew how to sell it. He knew how to sell it. I first became aware of that phrase when I was about 17 or 18 and I was in Roy Acuff's dressing room playing the mandolin with Howdy Forrester, Roy's great fiddler and we were jamming.

"Howdy said, 'well Sammy you sure can play the hell out of that but can you sell it?' And I went, 'uh. I don't know.' And I thought about it and he goes, 'well, if you're

311

going to play it for a living, you gotta sell it. You think you want to do this for a living?' And I said, 'Yeah', 'then you gotta learn to sell it now.' And I went, 'OK.' I didn't know what he meant.

"But, John—well there's something to be said for either a singer or an instrumentalist that when you hear them it's unmistakably them. So, whether you loved or did not like John's mandolin playing you know it's him. So, yes, he had his own voice on the instrument, and you know for me, John was the person.

"A friend of mine in Louisville named Danny Jones played mandolin in the Bluegrass Alliance before I did. Danny had the great rhythm chop and I just loved it. I said, 'man your rhythm chop sounds so good' and he goes, 'I'm just doing John Duffey. Duffey's got the best chop.' John's chop was the one that I've probably most emulated as far as rhythm players go."

Sam remembered hearing examples of John Duffey's emcee work with The Seldom Scene shows. "I was in the audience once in what would have been the first show after Natalie Wood drowned. John's on stage and he said, 'you know what kind of wood doesn't float? Natalie.' And there were like groans in the audience and a couple of people yelled up at him and Duffey went, 'I suppose she was a personal friend of yours. I suppose you knew her really well. Sorry if I offended you.'"

Sam spoke of John Duffey's legacy to him personally. "There were certain solos that you know if I don't play 'em like John, they just don't sound right. So, I don't know what better tribute you could think of someone than when you play their songs that you wanna play it like them or it doesn't sound right. That's the way a lot of John's mandolin playing is for me."

# Chapter 25: A Few Reviews

Birchmere's Gary Oelze in 2018 with co-author, Moore © S.

### John Duffey: Always In Style
Review by Buzz McClain.

There's an oversized mural on a wall at the Birchmere in Alexandria, Virginia, that depicts a bluegrass band in the act. Off to the far right is a figure looming larger than the others, with a distinctive flat top buzz cut and tiny [in his large hands] mandolin. His look is one of easy authority as he seems to be finishing up a solo and handing off the melody to one of the others in the band. That the Birchmere pays homage to John Duffey, who died at age 62 in 1996, and The Seldom Scene is only fitting—the band's weekly appearances forever put the venue on the map—and now Sugar Hill does the same with a musical companion to that painting.

The album, *John Duffey: Always In Style* collects 21 songs from ten albums over twenty years. The cuts are Seldom Scene or Gents performances, but as this is intended as a Duffey career retrospective, he looms

313

larger than the rest. His crisp tenor and precise but loose mandolin solos are showcased to their best advantage in songs ranging from a crowd-pleasing version of J.J. Cale's "After Midnight" to the traditional spiritual "Were You There" to the unlikely "Girl in the Night", a Hank Thompson honky-tonk weeper spun into a Dobro-drenched bluegrass ballad.

The Scene was formed in 1971, 2 ½ years after Duffey's departure from The Country Gentlemen. Their mandate was to make bluegrass something other than the age-old sound of the hollows and hills without diverting too much from tradition. Which is why you'll find versions of Parsons/Buchanan's "Hickory Wind" and the Dill/Wilkins country standard "Long Black Veil" in the mix with Bill Monroe's "Tennessee Blues" and "Rose Of Old Kentucky". The excellent liner notes—in effect, a primer on the history of the Scene—by Jon Weisberger include quotes taken this summer from surviving band members.

But there are quibbles: The songs are not dated, and complete credits are missing from the song listings. Bluegrass aficionados will know the lineups—Ben Eldridge (banjo), John Starling (guitarist), Tom Gray (bass) and Mike Auldridge (dobro), and later Phil Rosenthal, Lou Reid and T. Michael Coleman—but their names are nowhere to be found. In fact, the re-formed band with Fred Travers, Dudley Connell and Ronnie Simpkins recorded on *Dream Scene* in 1996; three of the cuts are from that disc, with no mention of the players. Newcomers to the field will believe Duffey was the entire band. He may have loomed large, but the credit has to be shared. That aside, Duffey fans missing any of these songs will rejoice, and newcomers will find their appetites suitably whetted.

In 1984, John made these comments about The Seldom Scene's *Live at the Cellar Door* album: *The Cellar Door album was recorded Christmas week in 1974. And had two big selling points: It was very well-received, and it wasn't a haphazard job. The fact is we got this brilliant idea to do a live recording. Bill McElroy, who owns Bias Recording had a mobile truck. We got a permit from the D.C. police to park the truck on the sidewalk. We only had 8 tracks but we figured that would be enough. We ran cables to each microphone we had, and recording microphones were also added.*

*Bill recorded for two nights. He sat in the truck and in the house and never saw the show. We did six repeat songs that we had recorded before and the rest were songs we had never recorded.*

*The only thing wrong with the record is the girl screaming. She only did that once but Bill thought it was cute so he kept sticking it in through the whole damn album. I don't know. Sometimes you think people get sick of hearing live albums because it's always the same things being said and it's extremely predictable. It's bad enough to play an album and know what songs are coming but to hear the same things being said each time I would think might get on peoples' nerves. But it may have helped us to let folks know that there is more going on at our shows then just the music.*

Duffey also commented on the songs "Wait a Minute" and "Rider."

*"We still love playing those songs. Besides, we have a soft spot in our wallets for "Rider" and "Wait a Minute." Those songs have helped us make many a mortgage payment.*

*"Every time we played 'Rider,'" we're all trying to think of something when we get into it. What can I do that I haven't tried before?"*

On August 5, 1985, David Barton reviewed one of The Seldom Scene's first California shows in the *Sacramento Bee* newspaper: Over the weekend, Northern California took a giant step into the national bluegrass limelight with one of the country's finest festivals, the first Midsummer Bluegrass Festival. Presented by the Sacramento Bluegrass Society, the festival at the Nevada County Fairgrounds featured an impressive roster of talent performing from Friday afternoon to Sunday evening.... The crowd was treated to successive 50 minute sets by J.D. Crowe and the New South, Hot Rize, Tony Rice, Doyle Lawson and Quicksilver and The Seldom Scene.

Closing the show was the popular traditional bluegrass group The Seldom Scene. Switching from ballads to breakdowns, the group's delicate vocal harmonies were superseded, as was most of the evening's instrumental work, by the remarkable slide work of Mike Auldridge, whose Dobro playing was awe-inspiring and ended the terrific show on a marvelous note.

In the 1986 *Washington Times*, Lou Fournier reported that The Seldom Scene's "sound has been spreading." He wrote "The Seldom Scene, that microcosm of bluegrass proficiency and exemplar of the Washington sound, is beginning to extend its musical influence around the world in ways that have just began to be measured.

"The band has made several trips to Western Europe, where their reputation has grown with unexpected rise in popularity overseas, and it is getting ready for a tour this fall of bluegrass-enthusiastic Japan."

In *The Washington Post*, Mike Joyce reviewed the 30th anniversary Country Gentlemen show at the

Birchmere on Oct 10, 1989: "Like most 30-year reunions, musical or otherwise, The Country Gentlemen's performance at the Birchmere Saturday night evoked a lot of memories and laughter. Especially laughter. But then, mandolinist John Duffey can crack up an audience any time he's within hailing distance of a microphone...If getting these songs into gear took some collective memory-jarring, once the band kicked off, say, "Stewball, "Sunrise," "Spanish Two-step." or "Pallet on your Floor," all the pieces quickly fell into place. Waller's whiskey-smooth smooth voice, Adcock's jazz-infected solos, Duffey's decisively crisp attack, Gray's solid underpinning, and Auldridge's colorful embellishments."

# Chapter 26: Festivals Forte

John with the late Bob Cornett in 1989,
© Charles Cornett

*Mike Auldridge has a little expression he uses when we play in some shitty place or to a crappy crowd. He says 'Johnny, we're not this hungry.' But there have been some interesting places.*

"The first time we played the Great American Music Hall in San Francisco is the time where we really thought The Seldom Scene had arrived. It holds 500 people. There were two separate shows that turned over just like the Cellar Door used to do.

When we got there both shows were sold out. The tickets cost $8.00 and people on the sidewalk were selling them for $15.00, That was an ego trip. The promoters asked us to come back, and suggested they get some bucks together and have *us stop over at Denver. But the Denver gig turned out to be a Monday and the band doesn't care but I don't think Monday is a good night for a show.*

*Bluegrass has traveled along on its own merit with very little promotion. Fortunately, it snuck outside the cult barrier and people from all walks of life have enjoyed it and support it by buying records. The Lexington, Kentucky festival is just about our favorite outdoor festival. Every year the second week in June we've been playing. This (1985) will be our seventh straight year. A lot of young people come to see us and we're tickled to death to have them. Last year you would have thought the Rolling Stones came on. I swear to God we damn near caused a riot. The audience was just freaking out. One of the reasons the Lexington festival is so fun, aside from it being a great festival to begin with, is that it's hardly held in an out-in-the-woods locale. It's held in a little suburban area just outside of town, and I think there's an advantage in that.*

JD

**S**ince 1974, Lexington, Kentucky's *Festival of the Bluegrass* has been attracting talent and fans on each first full weekend of June. The festival producers, Bob and Jean Cornett and their six boys got off to a rocky start their first year despite a stellar line-up of Bill Monroe, Doc Watson, Jimmy Martin, and others.

One of their sons, Charles Cornett, recalled for this book in 2018, "the crowd was probably around 150, and soaking in the pouring rain for most of the weekend. It was a financial disaster."

For the second year, his Mom, Jean hired The Seldom Scene. Charles says, "she treated Duffey as a bit of a rock star to get them to come, offering the band more than enough money to make it worthwhile for them to fly in for the weekend.

"Despite the beautiful festival setting of the first location, Masterson Station Park, and later Kentucky Horse Park and the sense of community, my late Mom nurtured acts and guests because that second year of the *Festival of the Bluegrass* was surely a 'make or break' year," Charles recalls.

"It was the light and the energy that John and The Seldom Scene provided that let everyone see that the future was bright. The Scene closing on Saturday nights became a yearly tradition without parallel, with a crowd of thousands singing every word of many of the tunes. Word of mouth from their initial appearances —among their first outside the D.C. area—was far better than any advertising we could buy," Charles confirmed.

Charles was 15 when he first started helping out John Duvall, a local TV executive, with the stage management duties. It was a few years later when he realized that the always present cup John carried was a significant part of the equipment for the show.

Charles once asked John about his unique stage wear. John replied, "So you like my 'go to hell' pants?" Since Charles had said something a little snide about them, John's response was leading him down a path. Duffey went on, "I call them 'go to hell' pants because any little shit that doesn't like them can 'go to hell'".

Charles wanted to crawl into a box until John smiled and offered him a "trip to the trunk" where he kept his sour whiskey libations. "One of the best beverages I ever had," thought Charles.

## Duffey Memorial

At their 1997 festival they had a memorial ceremony for John after his passing some six months earlier. The ceremony preceded the band performing the for the first time without him. Charles reflected on what he wanted to as he had served as the primary emcee for the Festival of the Bluegrass from 1984 until 1995, and he estimates that he introduced John and the Scene 30 times over the years, and held that honor for another two decades.

Charles said, "I knew I had to come up with something succinct so that I might get through it, and let the crowd enjoy the Scene playing what had to have been one of their most difficult performances." Here is what he said:

"People frequently ask 'what is different at the Festival of the Bluegrass that makes it one of the most enduring festivals when so many fail?' Is it the sense of community that Mom fosters among the guests? Is it the amazing range of talent that work so hard to be there? Perhaps it is the beautiful setting of the Kentucky Horse Park. I know little of those things. What I do know beyond a shadow of a doubt is that 50 years from now, this will still be the house that John built."

John, Lou Reid, and Mike at Festival of the
Bluegrass in 1990. © G. Allred

Charles continued: "When Lou Reid joined the band, I, like the rest of the country, was in the throes of our excitement about Ricky Skaggs becoming a big star. Seeing Lou leave the band to come join the Scene was what I viewed as a surprising turn. I have since learned that there are a million different nuances about personnel changes in bands, but I boldly asked Lou about it on his first night in Lexington with the Scene. Lou seemed a little at a loss for words, trying to give me a politically correct answer, and John leaned over said, "It is like being a little fish in a huge pond, coming to be a big fish in a little pond." John was dead on, and Lou was back in his element immediately, proving an excellent counter-point to John's vocal stylings.

## Photographer Carl Fleischhauer Remembers

Carl Fleischhauer in August 1977. Photo by David Stanley, courtesy American Folklife Center.

My affection for bluegrass music goes back well before my years as a photographer. I went to Kenyon College in Ohio (class of 1962) but had friends then still attending and recently graduated from Oberlin College, including Neil Rosenberg, now well known as a bluegrass historian.

During these years I first became acquainted with John Duffey, then in The Country Gentlemen and later in The Seldom Scene.

I went to Oberlin on weekends a few times in 1961 and 1962 and, on one trip, attended a Country Gents concert. Since my Oberlin friends were pickers—Eric

Jacobsen, Franklin Miller, and Steve Gibbs—we had lengthy social and musical interactions with the band, away from the concert stage. I was profoundly impressed by the band members' musical skills, as well as by their lighthearted wit and joking manner. Duffey and Eddie Adcock were the most striking (and funny) in terms of this kind of give and take, offstage as well as on.

After Kenyon, I had a Fulbright grant to India and, when I returned, I was drafted and spent two years in the U.S. Army, discharged in 1966. During those years my contacts with bluegrass were fewer although I did attend a Country Gentlemen concert at the Sacred Mushroom coffee house in my home town of Columbus, Ohio, included in the Folkways recording *On the Road.* In 1967, I saw the Gents at a proto-festival at the Ohio State Fairgrounds. By that time, I had started photography and one of my images of the band at the 1967 event appears on page 66 of the book *Bluegrass Odyssey* that Neil and I assembled in 2001. That image reminds me of some of the "Duffey is a cut-up" photos selected for this book. In my 1967 photo, John is drinking a soft drink after he interrupted the band's set to call the soda vendor down from the stands. For me, this marked John's fun way of overthrowing the usual conventions of formal stage performance.

I photographed The Country Gentlemen a few more times in the 1960s. Like many of the band's fans, I saw Duffey's morph into The Seldom Scene as a natural evolutionary step, with John playing a central role in the new band as he had in the old. It looks like I first photographed the Scene in 1973, at Pete Kuykendall's festival at Indian Springs, Maryland. I was then working at a public television station at West Virginia University and it was a short hop from Morgantown to Indian Springs. I went a few times: two photos from the 1974 and 1975 Indian Springs festivals are in this book, and both celebrate Duffey's casual and always jesting personality: reaching across the edge of the stage to embrace a fan and, in a backstage group photo, pinching the leg of Mike. "He's a legend in his own mind," said Auldridge.

In 1976, I started working at the American Folklife Center at the Library of Congress and moved to Washington. The photos of the band at the Birchmere with Linda Ronstadt were made during the same month I moved. My work at the Library began to pull me away from bluegrass during the 1980s and my last photos of The Seldom Scene with Duffey are included in this book: images from the 1985 cover photo session for the *Blue Ridge* album with Jonathan Edwards and the 1986 anniversary concert at the Kennedy Center.

Looking back at all of this, I find myself struck by John Duffey's cosmopolitan sophistication and skills as a performer, not only in musical terms but also as comedian, including an aptitude for sight gags of a subtle sort. John's sensibility, however, was buttressed by a real respect for musical quality and the contributions of others. During the 1980s, more than once at the Birchmere, Duffey (and others including Charlie Waller) turned out for Bill Monroe concerts. They would join Bill on stage and, for me, Duffey's playing and singing on those occasions was wonderful mix of competing with and paying homage to the founder of bluegrass with his 50-year span of creative achievement. I consider it a real privilege to have witnessed this era in American music.

(l to r) Ben, Bill Monroe , John, Tom, Charlie, Mike, and Phil on stage at the Birchmere in 1981 © Carl Fleischhauer

# Chapter 27: The Scene Beyond: Side One

**W**hen Phil Rosenthal left The Seldom Scene in 1986, Lou Reid came in on guitar and vocal. Born in Moore Springs, North Carolina on September 13th, 1954, Reid listened to country music through his Dad, a guitar and banjo player but he fell in love with The Beatles in 1964. His first record was The Beatles 45 *I Want To Hold Your Hand*. He picked up the electric bass learning Beatles songs.

His father showed him things like "Wildwood Flower" and they watched Flatt & Scruggs on TV together. Lou eventually found himself in a four-piece bluegrass band called the Bluegrass Buddies.

Lou remembers the Camp Springs Bluegrass Festival held in Reidsville, North Carolina over Labor Day weekend in 1972 in a 2000 interview with co-author G.T., "we (the Bluegrass Buddies) were playing a bluegrass festival called Camp Springs that Carlton Haney put on. The very same time that the Bluegrass 45 band was over from Japan. Dick Freeland who was president of Rebel Records asked us to come on his bus.

He announced, "I've got a band that's coming out that's gonna blow the world of bluegrass away."

"Who is it," asked Lou

"Sorry I can't tell you," Dick repeated,

"I have definitely got to know. We won't tell nobody," Lou begged.

Dick gave in and mentioned John Starling and then John Duffey was in the band.

Lou had not met Duffey or Gray at this point but knew of them. He had seen Ben and Auldridge in Cliff Waldron's band. He'd never heard of Starling. When Lou heard Starling, he was blown away by his voice. Freeland had a pre-market 8-track tape and he played a little bit. "They just absolutely killed me," remembers Lou, "I loved it."

Lou talked Freeland out of the 8-track tape and took it home with him. He was the first guy to have an 8-track tape of The Seldom Scene before any fans could get their hands on it.

T. Michael Coleman, who had played bass for Doc Watson replaced Tom Gray 16 months after Lou joined the band. Lou left in early 1992 to join Vince Gill's band. John Starling came back to fill in until the band found another singer. He was enjoying himself and stayed for a whole year.

Ben Eldridge remembers that the band almost recruited Dan Tyminski, famed bluegrass vocalist and instrumentalist with Alison Krauss and her band, Union Station. "If John Starling had decided not to continue then Dan Tyminski would have been our lead singer. It's just one of those things that never happened. When John finally decided it was just more than he could handle [band plus medical practice] is when we recruited Moondi Klein."

**Moondi Klein**
Born on March 13th, 1963 in Port Jefferson, Long Island, Moondi had a classical music upbringing learning piano. "My dad was a Julliard graduate for concert piano, and he was always listening to classical music and playing it on the piano," Klein told co-author G.T. in 1999. "I was about 15 when I started playing banjo, dulcimer, and guitar."

328

Klein would later move to Washington, D.C. to start a band, Rock Creek. They liked the Scene and covered many of their songs. The first time he heard himself on radio was on one of Dick Cerri's *Music Americana* showcases he had at Ireland's Four Provinces on Connecticut Avenue in Northwest D.C. "We sang a bunch of Seldom Scene songs and he played them on his show," Moondi remembered.

"The Seldom Scene was such an interesting band just because those five people were kind of nuts and they did some interesting stuff to the music. I was always into vocals. I was in a chorus from when I was seven through high school and all of college. At 15, I started hearing bluegrass. The Seldom Scene was who I always listened to for the interesting and innovative harmony ideas.

"The Seldom Scene were those unlikely city guys with a quality in their voices that sounded Appalachian. Bluegrass people accepted them I think because of some of that. Some part of that vocal sound that John Duffey had. Some people sing and they sing notes. He made a noise. He made a really recognizable noise when he sang. Something about the way he phonated a vowel up high. You always knew it was John Duffey."

Moondi first saw the Scene live at the old Birchmere. It was a pivotal moment for him. "I didn't understand how people could be appearing to have such a good time on stage and still be considered to be performing. Duffey wasn't afraid to be silly, and to be himself. That was quite an attraction for me to the stage," said Moondi.

### John vs. John

Moondi continued: "I think the combination of John Starling and John Duffey were a little bit of opposing forces which is always good for the outer boundaries of what the music can be. You know, you have a much larger range of things that are possible if you have one person who's on one side of an issue and one person who's on another side of it. Starling was always into country while Duffey was into bluegrass for the most part but making it funny and silly. Somehow, they did that in the bluegrass Grateful Dead kind of thing.

"Everybody associates the New Grass Revival with the Grateful Dead. No, no, no—The Grateful Dead of bluegrass in my opinion was The Seldom Scene. That's where they were in that culture."

In 1992, Moondi got a call from Duffey's friend, Shawn Nycz telling him that his name had been put in for the spot to fill Lou Reid leaving. Lou had left the band quickly to join Vince Gill. Moondi recalls, "So, I called Mike Auldridge and he said, 'Well, we are playing this Thursday down at The Birchmere. Why don't you come on down and we'll get into the backroom and go over a couple songs? It'll be nice and easy and it'll be no problem.'"

"You're not gonna get me up on stage, right?" asked Moondi.

"No, no. don't worry about that. We won't do that to you," assured Mike.

During the break after the first set, Moondi is called backstage and the band start singing "Wait a Minute." Three bars into the chorus Duffey stops it.

"All right, you ready to testify?" asks Duffey, meaning 'sing with us onstage now?'

Moondi recalled, "I sort of swallowed my heart and said, 'sure, sure. I'll do it' and it was really scary. One of the Scene songs that I had always liked is "Last Train from Poor Valley." I knew their parts so all I had to do was sing the lead parts of it. So, we start the song.

"I get through the first and second verse. Then comes the first chorus. We sing the first line, [sings] 'now the soft new snows of December.' That went fine Then the second line comes and I go, [sings] 'lightly' which is the lead part. But Auldridge has jumped up onto the lead part. So, I jump down to the baritone part, [sings] 'lightly falls my cabin round.' So, I've switched parts. I decide OK I'll stay on the baritone part. Next line comes up Auldridge is back down on the baritone part so I have to jump up to the lead part. I think I'm onto them now. I've got it. So, next line I'll go back down to the baritone part so I went back down to it and no, he didn't move, so I had to jump back up to the lead part.

"This was my realization of what The Seldom Scene had been doing all those years with their harmony parts: switching voices in between registers—almost anywhere. This lent a certain color to the vocal blend that was indescribable. I think that's one of the reasons why it was so attractive to me.

"But, up there on stage you know—first time I've met the guy and I'm out there I pick a song that has reversing harmony parts and manage to get through it. The third chorus sounded great. By the third chorus I was onto it (laughs) and it went pretty well, and I did OK."

Duffey commented on this vocal technique: "*Even vocal stints, once we know a song well, one of us might think I'll try this turn here and see what happens. Just a year ago we played the Waterloo Ranch in New Jersey and all of a sudden Mike did this baritone turn at 'Small Exception of Me' which we cut in 1972, which I'd never heard before. 'Whaa? I thought 'I'll find something that will match that. Look, something different. It keeps you interested.*"

Another Moondi realization was Duffey's vocal volume: "Yeah, singing with Duffey was sometimes a shout fest. Very competitive kind of guy. He had a loud voice and he knew how to make it loud and when. He was also one of those people who when he was singing, was listening to what was happening next to him. If you started to try and sing a little bit louder than he did or put your little lick in a little bit louder one time he'd barge right in with a louder voice and then you'd end up starting to compete and that makes the music exciting. I think he and Lou Reid did that fairly well, too. They were always competing with each other which is neat. Healthy competition up on stage is a good thing."

Soon after the Birchmere audition, Duffey called Moondi: "You want to try and do this thing?" he asked. "Absolutely," was the answer.

For the record it was T. Michael Coleman and Mike Auldridge who voted against Moondi going into The Seldom Scene. Ben and Duffey said 'yeah let's get him.' "Coleman and Auldridge who later I end up in a band with are the only two who say. 'no, no, no, he won't do,'" commented Moondi.

Moondi offered his take on the postcard he sent out that was discussed in Chapter 16. The postcard announced that the Scene was breaking up and that John and Ben were retiring after the departure of Mike, Coleman and Moondi.

"We had been talking at a gig in Kentucky with Duffey and Ben and told them what we intended to do. We gave them a year warning about Chesapeake which is a good amount of time if you're in a band to give somebody a warning.

"Duffey said, 'well, I'm going to quit. I don't need to do this anymore. I don't need to go out on the road.' Ben also said, 'I don't need to do this. I've got plenty of work to do at the office.' So, I thought they were going to hang it up. I sent out the postcard with information that we were going to be leaving The Seldom Scene and that John Duffey and Ben Eldridge were going to retire. It was my greenhorn move of the century. John was rather perturbed."

One regret in the Moondi Klein story is that he never recorded with the Scene. "The highlights for me with the Scene are more along the lines of just in awe of being able to be onstage with people like that." Moondi holds the distinction of being the first member of The Seldom Scene who was a Seldom Scene fan before he was a bluegrass fan.

Moondi sums the break-up as, "We wanted to play more and Duffey wanted to play less so that's kind of why the three of us left The Seldom Scene."

Chesapeake let Auldridge fulfill his long-desired wish to add lap and pedal steel to the mix. Their music was adventurist and heavily rehearsed as they blended progressive bluegrass, rock, jazz, and influences like Little Feat and Van Morrison into their act. They stayed together for five years, three albums, and then disbanded, Jimmy Gaudreau and Moondi Klein continued to play together as a duo.

**Today's Seldom Scene**
Dudley Connell [vocals, guitar], Ronnie Simpkins [bass], and Fred Travers [Dobro, vocals] with Duffey and Ben were The Seldom Scene after Chesapeake set sail. "And that was a lot of fun when they joined," Ben Eldridge confessed, "We got back to playing bluegrass again which is what I've always liked to do anyway. I really wasn't very comfortable with a lot of the stuff that we did over the years. I didn't like some of it very much but if folks out there like it then I'll learn to like it. You know,

333

that kind of thing. But it was fun for Duffey and me when they came because we really did move back to more of a bluegrass band I think."

## Dudley Connell

The Johnson Mountain Boys were a popular bluegrass band throughout the 1980s in Washington, D.C. and beyond. From 1978 to 1993 they released ten albums and played the White House, Lincoln Center, Carnegie Hall, and the Grand Ole Opry to name a few. Today's Grand Ole Opry emcee, Eddie Stubbs joined the Johnson Mountain Boys as the band's fiddle player one week before his 17th birthday. The group played in a traditional bluegrass style. On guitar and lead vocals was Dudley Connell, born on February 18th, 1956 in Rockville Maryland.

"Yeah, I'm one of the rare D.C. natives," Connell told G.T. Keplinger in 1999. "My family lived in Rockville until 1968 and then moved to Gaithersburg. I've basically been around here all my life. My dad used to talk about all the music that he saw including bluegrass bands at D.C.'s Glen Echo Park. There was also a bar in Washington called The Famous, where they saw Jimmy Dean and Scotty Stoneman."

"What really got me started on bluegrass music was as a kid my father played banjo and my mother sang like old-time ballads like "Bury Me Beneath the Willow," "Remember Me," and songs by the Bailes Brothers, Blue Sky Boys, and other kind of mountain tunes.

Dudley proudly recalled, "I learned all the harmony parts on the 1964 *Meet The Beatles* album when I was just a kid. I had the Beatle boots. It was phenomenal. There was a lot of good music on the radio back in those days. The Stones, Supremes, James Brown and Otis Redding. I listened to all that but I always had the bluegrass and country music thing going because of my parents.

"My life changing experience with live bluegrass music was in 1974 at Ralph Stanley's Carter Stanley memorial festival in McClure, Virginia. I was still in high school. I think that's why I got into the traditional stuff so much. I went right from Jimi Hendrix to Carter Stanley in one fell swoop and because they both had that emotional edge that I like. One did it with a banjo and one did it with an electric guitar.

"I had got the Ralph Stanley bug really bad by listening to Gary Henderson's WAMU radio program. WAMU then was so strong with Gary Henderson and then Katy Daley who later on went to WMZQ. She became his partner in crime or sidekick. The bluegrass at WAMU actually started with Dick Spotswood. Bluegrass kind of built WAMU but now it seems like it's kind of in the shadows again. It looks like they kind of turned their back on bluegrass which is really unfortunate.

"In the early days of the Johnson Mountain Boys we played a lot of open mics and things like that. We played four or five nights a week and then gradually got up to the big money. $150 dollars a night to be split five ways and we thought we're doing pretty good.

"The Nitty Gritty Dirt Band put out that *Will The Circle Be Unbroken* record that knocked down all kinds of walls because they were a bunch of hip kids pot-smoking long haired blue jean wearing cool guys and everybody listened to the Nitty Gritty Dirt Band. They put that record out and everybody goes, 'wow this is really interesting. This is brand new.' It really wasn't. It was just bringing Mother Maybelle Carter, Jimmy Martin, Doc Watson and Earl Scruggs into the studio because they admired them. But that made all those players hip, too. It's a shame Bill Monroe didn't do it. I heard he was invited but he wasn't interested."

## Meeting John

"I met John Duffey at the old Birchmere. The Johnson Mountain Boys were booked to play a New Year's Eve. I was scared to death of John Duffey. John always just intimidated the hell out of me. It wasn't his fault. He had this persona that was bigger than life. I was kind of shy and afraid around him and intimidated by him.

"But he was always real friendly and nice. We sang together on one of those jam things at the end and we were singing all these Bill Monroe songs. I really liked that and I was just flattered that John would want to sing with me. And he really loved that stuff. He really could cut it. I remember singing you that song "I Hear a Sweet Voice Calling." It has this really high line in it and John was just shaking the speakers loose at the Birchmere. It was just really exciting. His passionate voice.

"By the late 80s I had really explored traditional bluegrass and was becoming more and more open to other styles of bluegrass. The Johnson Mountain Boys quit performing and I was performing with a lot of different people. John Starling came back to work with the Scene."

One of the bluegrass community's senior leaders, Kitsy Kuykendall, came to Dudley with advice. "You know, you ought to call Duffey. You should join The Seldom Scene. You should work together."

Dudley replied, "you're out of your mind. I don't know their material. I don't know John Duffey. I can't imagine he'd be the least bit interested in me as a player or anything else."

However, that thought stuck in Dudley's mind like, "wow that's an idea—really out there." But Dudley continued to play with more people and different kinds of music. And then, Dudley saw a notice in *Bluegrass Unlimited* that Moondi, T. Michael, and Mike were leaving the band and that The Seldom Scene were going to be no more.

Dudley thought, "damn that's a shame, that's a legendary group, and I just hated to see that that die." So, on a whim he called John Duffey. "I didn't ask for a job," Dudley confirms.

He told Duffey, "I sure would like to get together and sing with you sometime. I'm really sorry to hear about the band. What do you think if we just got together and just sang just to see what it sounded like?"

John said, "oh really?" Do you know any of our material?"

"No, not really." Dudley responded.

"Well, I know you can sing bluegrass but do you sing parts?" quizzed Duffey.

"Yeah. You know I could sing baritone or tenor you know whatever you needed me to do," Dudley said.

Duffey had already talked to Fred Travers, a Dobro player who had been trained by Mike. John let Dudley know that the *Bluegrass Unlimited* notice was incorrect. They weren't ready to let the band fold.

Duffey gave Dudley a half a dozen songs to learn including "Fallen Leaves," "Wait a Minute," and "A Small Exception of Me," and invited Dudley over to his house.

"We are gonna get Fred Travers and either Ronnie Simpkins or Tom Gray over, too," Duffey exclaimed. Dudley thinks John was leaning toward Ronnie because he is a killer bass player. This would have been in August or September, 1995.

337

Dudley confirms that "the music just worked right out of the chute. Neither Ben or John said much as we went through the songs. 'Yea, that sounded good' or 'let's do another one.'"

After a half an hour Dudley was standing around John's pool table playing music when Duffey said, 'well, let's try something of yours. Let's try "Blue Diamond' because he'd heard it on the radio that day. "They were all so diplomatic about it you know. They were just as interested in my stuff as I was in theirs. That made me feel good and I started to get kind of a burn that this might be something I'd really like to do. I wanted him to like me. I wanted to make it work.

"John started setting up these rehearsals like every Wednesday we'd go over to his house and play. After about a month Ronnie and I would talk every day on the phone, 'have you heard anything from John? Do you think he's going to hire us?' 'What'd Ben say?' and all this kind of stuff.

"Finally, we just all got together and sat down and asked, 'John? Ben? Do you do you want to hire us? I mean because we'd really like to do this. They said it was a given as far as they were concerned. The new Seldom Scene were going to debut New Year's Eve '95 at the Birchmere. Chesapeake would be there and even Starling. I remember being so thankful that I wore baggy pants because my legs were really shaking. I was so nervous.

"This huge round of applause happened when we came out to play. They let us know in no uncertain terms that they wanted the band to continue. For The Seldom Scene to still exist. It was a great year with John."

## Changes

"Way before I knew John personally," Dudley said, "I always heard that he hated to rehearse, wouldn't rehearse. Hated to record, wouldn't record. We had to just drag him to a recording studio, drag him to rehearsal but I'm really thankful that John was always calling rehearsals.

"We just rehearsed all the time and when we went in the studio to record, we cut everything live. It was multitrack and digital multitrack, but we cut everything just vocals, music, everything happening at one time for the most part and John loved it. I guess because he can get into the feel of it and some of those things on *Dream Scene* like "The Boatman," "Willie Roy," And "Fair and Tender Ladies," John did all that stuff in one take. He just nailed it to the wall first time, every time, just amazing, you know. I don't know, for whatever reason it seemed like it was a combination that worked personally for him as well as musically.

"I really think John came to look at Fred, Ronnie and I as almost like his surrogate kids or something. I mean he babied us and looked out after us just like we were his kids and maybe because we had so damn much respect for him, we really looked up to him like a dad. We tried not to put that kind of responsibility and pressure on him but at the same time I mean we really did look up but up to him and he knew that. I just know that he knew that. I'm real proud of that too.

# Chapter 28: The Scene
# Beyond: Side Two


Ronnie Simpkins was born on New Year's Eve, 1958 in Christiansburg, Virginia. Music was a family affair growing up with his dad on banjo and fiddle, mom and brother Rickie on guitar, and sister, Tammy on mandolin. Listening to and playing bluegrass, the driving sound and the harmonies inspired him.

Simpkins started on mandolin very young. "I learned like three chords and would chop along and play with my family," Ronnie said. He moved to the bass and his first professional job was with The Bluegrass Cardinals, traveling in their bus going across the country in 1980. This lasted four years,

He then moved to Richmond, Virginia to hook up with The Heights of Grass band with Donny Grubb, Sammy Shelor, Mark Newton, and his brother, Rickie. They became the Virginia Squires in 1983 for six years and released four albums for Rebel Records.

One year after the band broke up Ronnie got a call from Tony Rice and went to work with his band playing acoustic bass until 1995.

Ronnie spoke about hearing The Seldom Scene for the first time in a 2000 interview with G.T. "It was when *Act 1* came out. We had an 8-track of it. It was really revolutionary at the time like, 'wow man what are these guys doing?' You know, and it's just completely turned me around for sure. Their style, and the way they approached songs and the material. The whole nine yards. It had such a big impact.

"I've got to confess about Tom Gray's bass playing. He had a pretty dominant role and some of the kickoffs. Some of his lines that he played. I mean "Rider." That speaks for itself. I tuned in a lot to the bass lines he was doing and that was a big part of it for me as well, being a bass player."

Ronnie continues the story; "Well, I'd heard that the Scene was going to either disband or not disband basically. Moondi Klein, T. Michael Coleman, and Mike Auldridge had been working quite a bit with their side group, Chesapeake. They gave their notice that they were leaving. I got to thinking that Tony quit singing so that work had fell off. I knew I had to do something to stay in the music business. So, I talked with Ben Eldridge about it when we worked a show at the Bluegrass Festival in Dahlonega, Georgia.

"John Duffey finally set up a rehearsal at his house, and it was me, Dudley, and Fred. I've been playing for a long time, but I was nervous about that first meeting at John's house. So, we went in together and just had a real pleasant visit with John. Ben was the last one to arrive. We got our instruments out and just started picking, you know, doing some of the Scene's material.

"I remember getting hot in the room. I mean I guess a combination of nerves and whatnot, but nothing was really said officially. We got together several times and I remember me and Dudley would call each other back and forth, asking, 'well, have you heard anything?' 'No. Have you?'"

When asked about first meeting Duffey, Ronnie pauses, "A few years before I joined the band, I'd see John in passing [through the music scene] and he was always friendly and joking. Not the big scary guy that a lot of people thought. I didn't look at him that way. If you threw something at him, he'd throw it back at you and that's always a good sign that the person has a good sense of humor. John definitely had that.

"I think the attitude that John and Ben had toward me, Dudley, and Fred, was, that we were all treated as equals. We weren't like new people coming in and they were going to tell us what to do, or how we were gonna look up to them. It wasn't that way at all. We were part of the band.

"John would always call each individual guy whether it was about do we want to do this show, or do we want to fly here and drive from here or whatever it was, 'what do you think?' And then you would voice your opinion. But then he would suggest, 'well we could do this' and have it figured out so he always knew the best thing to do. Yet he would always ask first to see what you thought. And with Ben—it's the same now [2000]. I feel like we're part of a family, almost like a good marriage with the band now.

"Duffey had a jazz influence with the way he approached it some of the syncopations and the notes that he played. He just went for it you know? I like that 'going out on a limb', not knowing if he'll come back or not. But he wasn't scared. He would do that. I really respected him for his knowing a good song when he heard it, and he knew immediately whether it would work or not."

**Fred Travers**
The current Dobro player with The Seldom Scene was born on September 29th, 1958 and grew up outside of D.C. in District Heights, Maryland. At 12, Fred moved down to the city of Huntingtown in Southern Maryland. Today, he lives within a quarter mile of where he first moved.

Fred played with The Seldom Scene during the last year of John Duffey's life, and two of the reasons the current Seldom Scene captures both the sound and feel of the classic Seldom Scene are because of Fred's singing, and more importantly because he learned Dobro from Mike Auldridge.

In 2000 and 2018 interviews by the authors, Fred explained how this came about: "My mom and dad owned Popey's Tavern in District Heights, Maryland—(his dad's middle name was Pope)—where they had music every Friday and Saturday evenings. It was the old-time country music that I remember growing up.

"I started learning trumpet and later both French and baritone horn. I couldn't read music very well, but if I heard something, I could copy it. The Allman Brothers, especially the album, *Eat A Peach*, introduced me to Duane Allman's slide guitar. That had a big influence on me."

Around 1980, Fred, Kyle, his wife to be, and friends would sit around and play six string acoustic guitars and sing Eagles and America songs.

"My first experience with bluegrass came from going to see Doc and Merle Watson because the slide guitar that Merle was playing was what I was interested in. I was trying to learn bottleneck slide and the opening act that night happened to be this band called The Seldom Scene. When they walked out, they just floored me. Mike was playing the Dobro and that was the first time I'd ever seen a Dobro guitar. That's what I realized I wanted to play because it had that that steel sound I was looking for, yet it was acoustic. From that point I was the major Seldom Scene Mike Auldridge fan."

Fred became a regular at Thursday nights at the Birchmere. "People would line up for hours to get in to see the Scene. I wanted to sit at that table right in front of Mike and watch what he played. The Seldom Scene were the reason my wife and family started going to bluegrass festivals because we followed them around. We were pretty much fanatics. I could list forever who my favorite players are, but the Scene was the band for me."

## Lessons

Fred described a momentous story when he and Kyle got married: "I was trying to play Dobro and her wedding present to me was a lesson with Mike Auldridge. I was just knocked out by it. I'm thinking you know 'there's no way.'

"I asked Kyle, 'Well, how'd you get his phone number?'

"She said, 'It's in the phone book.'

"And I said, 'Mike Auldridge's phone number is not in the phone book. There's no way. Everybody'd be calling him all the time.'

"They probably were, and it was just so amazing I was going to be able to do a lesson with him. It actually didn't work out right away because Mike was trying to steer away from beginners. Kyle told him I'd been playing a year and he was a little bit hesitant and told her, 'maybe you ought to try this Dobro course that I have on tape for a little while and then we'll get together.'

"Kyle had already bought that tape for me, so I had already gone through that. To appease Kyle he said, 'sure I'll do it for you.' So, we finally got together, and we struck a real good relationship. We became friends and he saw that I could play a little bit. He had a real good time showing me some stuff that was a little bit more than just your basic right hand, left hand technique.

"Of course, it was great for me. I had come to my lesson with three or four pages full of questions and we went through all of them. He was only supposed to be teaching me for an hour. We did enough playing for 2-3 hours. He made a tape for me. I practiced for seven months because he gave me so much information. He was the guy who showed me how to do what I do."

It is this encouragement that helped Fred understand and reproduce the Auldridge technique and tone.

"Mike's tone was impeccable. When I hear somebody play a note on a song, I can tell you whether it's Mike or not because of the tone that he gets. His approach is also more subtle," Fred explained.

Fred had met Duffey at the Birchmere but only got to know him the first day he rehearsed with The Seldom Scene at John's house. Most of the Scene players throughout the band's history describe Duffey at first as standoffish, but not Fred.

When Mike, T. Michael, and Moondi left with Chesapeake and Ben and John still remaining there was talk through the bluegrass world that Fred might join the new Seldom Scene. People came to Fred saying, "hey man I hear you're joining the Scene. You're taking Mike's place in The Seldom Scene.'

"That just thrilled me to hear that," Fred recalled, "but no one had talked to me. I never heard anything from John or Ben or anything, so my response would be, 'well that's great. I'd love to do it, but you know I haven't heard anything from the guys.'

"Then eventually I did get the phone call from John Duffey seeing if I was available to get together. That was August 31, 1995, the first time we all met at John's house.

"That first time was obviously exciting yet nerve-wracking at the same time. I don't recall being real nervous but I'm sure I was. I'll often tell people that the timing for this for me was perfect. If the offer had come five years before I wouldn't have been ready, and I'd have been so nervous, I wouldn't have been able to do anything.

"But at the time that it did come about, I'd had enough experience with playing and recording and things out on the circuit that I really felt that I could do it. Especially with my background with the Scene and following them for so long, knowing the material, and learning from Mike. I just felt like I think I can do this, and the day was exciting."

Fred described arriving: "I got there early so I didn't want to park in front of John's house. I drove around the corner and parked at a church and here comes Dudley up the street early too. We didn't want to be late, and when we got in there, John and Ben were wonderful. They tried to make us feel at home. The first tune we did was Hank Williams' gospel tune, "House of Gold." I think they wanted to see how we would react to the different styles of music that they play and different harmony configurations that the Scene do. I never felt that I was at a tryout. They didn't want it to be that way it was just a it was a rehearsal. So, we got together to just see how everybody liked each other.

"Afterwards, John called me up and told me they thought the music was great and asked me if I wanted to be a part of it. It wasn't like what we want you to do but rather, 'are you OK with everything? Because if you are, we'd like you to be in the band.' I was ready to jump out of my seat trying to remain calm. That was the approach. It was just real laid-back."

## Playing in the band

The debut of the new [and last] Duffey-led Seldom Scene came on New Year's Eve, 1995 at the Birchmere. "The place just erupted and gave us a standing ovation for what seemed like five minutes," exclaimed Fred, "it was so cool because that just made us feel like, 'alright this is going to work.' I honestly don't remember playing the first two songs. It really struck me when we did our third song. I looked down the row and saw Duffey singing "Reason For Being." I thought 'my gosh I'm in The Seldom Scene' and it was powerful. That's one show I'll never forget. I felt like I'd almost been groomed for the spot."

Fred agrees with Dudley Connell that John was the father figure for all of them. "John would never call himself the leader, and he didn't want that position. But he was the one who took care of everything. John coordinated the bookings through the agency and took care of the flight and hotel reservations. He handled the records and mercantile stuff. He made sure our rooms were right. All the rest of us had to do was show up.

"He looked out for us, and we really appreciated that we never had to worry about any of that and could focus on trying to learn our parts and learn the songs, and try to make that band sound like The Seldom Scene. He took care of us, said nice things about us on stage and made us feel comfortable. He was sincere about it too, and that meant more than anything else."

Fred recalled the last show the Scene played before John passed away: "It was in New Jersey. We played with the Nashville Bluegrass Band and the Del McCoury Band. Del was really at the top with a bunch of awards from the IBMA. The Nashville Bluegrass Band was a great band. I thought we would open up, but we closed the show that night.

347

"When John passed away, there was about a two-week period that we didn't even talk about the band or anything. We were more concerned with losing John. When we did talk about it, we felt that we were having a lot of fun what we were doing over the last year and we got along really well. We were more like brothers. We thought John would probably want us to continue. He wouldn't want us to say we can't do this anymore without him."

Lou Reid returned to the group while Ben stepped up as the leader. Fred praises Ben as, "one of the nicest, warmest people that I've ever met. And I'm not just saying that. I mean I think just about anybody who ever met Ben would say the same thing. He's a very warm and personable guy. Great social skills, you know, he likes to be around people and talk. He's perfect."

Ben never said a word for 25 years on stage but really blossomed as the emcee until his retirement in 2016. Banjo and fiddle player, Rickie Simpkins first, and two years later Ron Stewart replaced Ben

"We really hit the jackpot when Ron Stewart agreed to join us," Fred told the authors in 2019. Ron has been a fan of The Seldom Scene since their album, *Act 1*.

The Indiana native won the International Bluegrass Music Association award for Fiddle Player of the Year in 2000 and Banjo Player of the Year in 2011.

With Stewart The Seldom Scene released a new album, the 2019 *Changes* on the Rounder label.

Fred concludes, "The last time I saw John Duffey was waving to him at breakfast as he was standing in the buffet line for more bacon. I'm really glad that I had that year and a half to spend with John and the guys. It was a lot of fun. John was unique and his role in creating a newer style of bluegrass music was immense."

# Chapter 29: Fare Thee Well

In 1996, the International Bluegrass Music Association inducted the "Classic" Country Gentlemen into their Hall of Fame. John Duffey did not attend the Gents' induction. Many of those who knew John assumed he didn't go to the award show because there was no money in it.

However, at the time, John told Tom Gray, "If we deserve an award, it should be for The Seldom Scene, not The Country Gentlemen." John also told then IBMA president, Pete Wernick, that he was going to wait until The Seldom Scene was inducted before attending any ceremonies.

Gray replied, "Hang on, that will probably happen someday." Unfortunately, John's life would end ten weeks after The Country Gentlemen's induction ceremony.

In the weeks before John's death, The Seldom Scene was rehearsing for their next record which included a new arrangement of the Muddy Waters classic, "Rollin' and Tumblin'." John told friends he was, 'the happiest playing with the Scene that he had ever been."

According to Eddie Adcock, John called him around this time and told him that he was going to die soon. Eddie replied, "Duffey, we're going to have to hit you in the head with a damn axe to get you outta here. You ain't going nowhere."

John was scheduled to play a show in Englewood, New Jersey and went to his barber for a haircut. His barber asked him how he was doing as John sat in the chair.

"Not great," John said. "I couldn't sleep last night."

"How come?" his barber asked.

"I just felt cold. And I never feel cold," replied John.

The Englewood, New Jersey show went on and John was exceptional. Fred Travers affirms that the band played and John sang really well. "The last tune we did was an encore song, "Walk Through This World with Me." It was his final performance. I have the great privilege of singing that song with the band now."

On December 10, John experienced a severe myocardial infarction around 12: 30 am at his home. This sudden deprivation of circulating blood to the heart muscle was caused by the coronary artery disease John had been secretly battling for a decade, according to his medical records.

He told Nancy that he was having a heart attack. When the paramedics arrived, John was lying unconscious on his bedroom floor.

He was rushed to the Arlington, Virginia hospital. There, doctors and nurses were able to resuscitate him repeatedly over the course of three hours before he was pronounced dead of cardiac arrest. A nurse told family that it was compassionate that he passed, because the considerable loss of oxygen to his brain would have left him severely disabled had he survived.

He was interred at Columbia Gardens Cemetery in Arlington, Virginia. Nancy, passed away at age 70 on July 17, 2002. They share one modest burial plaque with their names together.

The day after John died, music writer Richard Harrington wrote the following moving obituary for the *Washington Post.* It was introduced into the Congressional Record. We thank Richard for letting us include it here.

# *A Mandolin For All Seasons*

## by Richard Harrington

© Becky Johnson

**T**he *National Observer* once dubbed John Duffey "the father of modern bluegrass," a paternity that suited the muscled, buzz-cut mandolinist and high tenor who was co-founder of both The Country Gentlemen in 1957 and The Seldom Scene in 1972. Those two seminal acts not only helped popularize bluegrass worldwide but made Washington the bluegrass capital of the nation in the '60s and '70s.

Already reeling from the recent death of bluegrass patriarch Bill Monroe, the music and its fans may be excused for feeling orphaned right now. Duffey, who died yesterday at the age of 62 after suffering a heart attack at his home in Arlington, was, like Monroe, a towering figure, physically and historically.

Duffey was also one of the most riveting and riotous personas in bluegrass, as famous for his (generally politically incorrect) jokes and onstage shenanigans as for ripping off fiery mandolin solos and then flinging his instrument behind his back when he was done— because, well, he was done,

"John was one of the half-dozen most important players ever in this industry," fellow musician Dudley Connell said yesterday. "He helped redefine how people looked at bluegrass, made it acceptable to the urban masses by his choice of material and style of performance."

Connell, founder of the critically acclaimed Johnson Mountain Boys, joined The Seldom Scene just a year ago when several of that band's longtime members left to devote themselves to a band called Chesapeake. That changeover represented a third act for John Duffey, the Washington-born son of an opera singer whose forceful and unusually expressive voice was once described— quite accurately—as "the loudest tenor in bluegrass."

"John Duffey had such a presence onstage you just had to watch him," noted bluegrass and country music radio personality Katy Daley. "It wasn't just that high tenor, either. He had such flair that he made the music a joy to watch at a time when so many bluegrass groups would just stand straight-faced at the mic."

In terms of stubbornness and steel will, Duffey was not unlike Bill Monroe, but where Monroe was a tireless proselytizer for bluegrass, Duffey chose a different course that left him far less famous.

"He was proud but didn't want to pay any of the prices—interviews, travel, rehearsing, recording," says Gary Oelze, owner of the Birchmere, the Virginia club put on the world entertainment map by virtue of The

Seldom Scene's 20-year residency there on Thursday nights.

"He hated to rehearse, and would only pull out his mandolin when it was time to play," Oelze recalled yesterday. "And he hated the studio, where his theory was, "If I can't do it right in one take, then I can't do it right at all." He's like Monroe in that both were set in their own ways. John was a big dominating character and cantankerous old fart. It's hard to imagine the big guy gone."

John Starling, a Virginia surgeon who was for many years The Seldom Scene's lead singer, concedes that Duffey was "sometimes difficult to deal with from a professional standpoint, but he was also true to himself and he never changed. John was one of a kind."

Starling first encountered Duffey while in medical school at the University of Virginia in the mid-'60s; at the time, Duffey was with The Country Gentlemen and Starling would venture to Georgetown to catch them at the Shamrock on M Street. "I never dreamed one day I'd play in the same band," Starling says, adding that "everything I know about the music business—especially to stay as far away from it as possible—I learned from John."

"Left to our own devices, The Seldom Scene would have cleared a room in 10 minutes without John," Starling says with a chuckle. "He was the entertainer, the rest of us were players and singers. He did it all."

Duffey's career began with a car wreck in 1957 that injured a mandolin player, Buzz Busby, who fronted a bluegrass group. Busby's banjo player, Bill Emerson, quickly sought substitutes so the band could fulfill a major club date.

Emerson found a young guitar player named Charlie Waller and a young mandolin player named John

Duffey. And so, on July 4, 1957, what would soon be The Country Gentlemen played their first date, at the Admiral Grill in Bailey's Crossroads. They liked their sound, and decided to strike out on their own. It was Duffey who came up with the name, noting that a lot of bluegrass bands at the time were calling themselves the so-and-so Mountain Boys. 'We're not mountain boys," he said. "We are gentlemen."

And scholars. At least Duffey was, spending hours at the Library of Congress's vast Archive of Folk Songs, looking for unmined musical treasures. Duffey was a product of the first American folk revival, which had introduced urbanites to rural culture. And he in turn passed it on. "John was one of those people who brought rural music to the city," says Joe Wilson, head of the National Council for the Traditional Arts. "He was concerned with authenticity even though he didn't share the [rural] background."

What came to be known as the "classic" Country Gentlemen lineup was settled with the addition of banjoist-singer Eddie Adcock in 1959 and Tom Gray in 1960. Duffey (tenor), Waller (lead) and Adcock (baritone) created one of the finest vocal trios in bluegrass history. The band's repertoire deftly melded bluegrass, folk and country tunes in a way that was both tradition-oriented and forward-looking. And they began adapting popular songs in the bluegrass style.

Duffey "gave bluegrass accessibility to lawyers and accountants and people who worked on Capitol Hill," says Wilson. "He was an interpreter in the finest sense of the word, bringing grass-roots culture to an elite."

Along with Flatt & Scruggs—a duo introduced to mass television audiences by the *Beverly Hillbillies* theme song—The Country Gentlemen probably made more bluegrass converts in the '60s than Bill Monroe himself. They were criticized in traditional bluegrass circles for being too "progressive"—for playing what was dismissively dubbed "newgrass." But on the emerging bluegrass festival circuit and in venues as un-Shamrock-like as Carnegie Hall, their approach made them the music's most successful ambassadors.

By 1969, however, John Duffey was frustrated with traveling, terrified of flying, and generally down on the music business. He retired to an instrument-building and repair business in Arlington. In weekly gatherings at Bethesda, he played with other gifted musicians who didn't want to give up their day jobs. These sessions blossomed in 1971, into a band with a modest name: The Seldom Scene.

The Country Gentlemen survived Duffey's departure, enduring 40 years around Waller, its lone survivor. Perhaps The Seldom Scene will go on, too. But John Duffey was so much the focus, the showman, the entertainer—that huge man with his fingers flying over his tiny mandolin—that it's hard to imagine the band, or bluegrass, without him.

# Appendix 1: John Duffey's Roots By Robert Kyle

John's wit, smile, personality, story-telling and love of music left no doubt his ancestors were Irish. According to the *Ireland Roots* website:

"In Irish the Duffy surname is O'Dubhthaigh, from 'dubhthach' meaning dark, black or swarthy. The name was born by a 6th century saint who was also archbishop of Armagh. The original homeland of the Duffys was Monaghan, where the surname is still very popular, and they are also found in Donegal, Mayo and Roscommon. The Donegal Duffys were centered on the parish of Templecrone, where they were powerful churchmen for almost 800 years.

The variations in spelling also include O'Duffy and Duffe.

John was indeed a Donegal Duffy. His ancestors arrived in America in the 1700s, likely in Philadelphia. From there Catholic Duffys trekked more than 300 miles across the state to an area just north of Pittsburgh. They named their settlement Donegal in 1804.

Protestant Duffys, of Scots-Irish descent, settled in what is now Lancaster County. Their Donegal township was established in 1722. It was later divided into East and West Donegal.

John Duffey's great-great grandfather, John M. Duffey, was born in Pennsylvania in 1770, according to several sources, including the census. He married Catherine Waldeck about 1810. She was born on February 25, 1790, in Frederick County, Maryland, to German parents.

Because Frederick County is located just southwest of Lancaster County, Pennsylvania, it is likely John M. Duffey is related to the Donegal Duffeys of this region and not those to the west near Pittsburgh.

John and Catherine moved to Jefferson County Virginia just across the Potomac River from Frederick County, Maryland. The 1810 census shows them without children. At the outbreak of the War of 1812, it is written that John signed up with Captain Samuel Colville's militia.

The 1820 census tells us they had six children under age 10 and had moved to Middletown (now Gerrardstown) in adjacent Berkeley County. They added four more children so that by 1830 their total was 10. By 1840 the total was down to four children, as most had grown and left home. By this time, they had moved to Washington Township in Shelby County in western Ohio near Indiana.

John's occupation was school teacher, according to a biography of his grandson, Amos Duffey, that appears in "Huntington County, Indiana, History & families, 1834-1994."

By 1850 the census shows John M. Duffey, now 80, is living with his daughter Ellen, 25, who has married George Morris, a tailor, in Washington Township, Miami County. With them is Ellen's unmarried sister Elizabeth, 22. Their mother, and John's wife, Catherine, age 60, lives nearby with her daughter Lydia, 28, in Spring Creek, Miami County. A widow, Lydia had been married to immigrant Benoni Hollis, a wheelwright who died at age 34 in 1848. He left three young children. Lydia eventually married Cyrus Boyden, a shoemaker, and had four children. One can surmise Catherine Duffey moved in with her widowed daughter to help with the children.

A decade later Catherine, now 70, moved in with her daughter Catherine, who married Joseph Severns. They are farmers, have four children, and live in Union Township, Mercer County. Catherine is still living there in the next census, 1870. She is about 80 years old.

Exact death dates of John and Catherine Duffey are not known, but they had significant longevity for the period. They are the great-great grandparents of John Duffey.

The attention now shifts to one of their sons: John W. Duffey, born February 1, 1811, in Moorefield, Hardy County, Virginia. Catherine Raimer, born March 25 1813, became his wife on April 17, 1837. They were parents of three sons and seven daughters. Catherine, however, died in 1863 at age 49. John married Arthalinda Bauers on Oct, 17, 1865. They had two children.

An ambitious businessman and civic leader, John operated one of the town's two hotels, which included a popular gathering spot, Duffey's Tavern. When Moorefield became incorporated in 1854, John was one of the trustees. When the Civil War erupted, John was among few in town to side with the Union. Moorefield became part of the new state of West Virginia when it was formed on June 20, 1863. His family lived in his hotel.

Around this time John served as sheriff of Hardy County and in 1868 won election as a Republican in the House of Delegates. He was an investor and board of directors member for the local bank. In 1869 the others formed a railroad company. The 1870 census shows his occupation as post master. At age 76 in 1887 he closed his tavern. He died two years later. He and his first wife are buried in Olivet Cemetery in town.

John's first born son, Jefferson Waite Duffey, would become one of the most prominent persons in the region. In 1864, at age 18, he enlisted in a local band of fighters called McNeill's Rangers. They were an independent military force commissioned under the Partisan Ranger Act of the Confederate Congress.

John Hanson McNeill and his son Jesse formed the Rangers. Each man would furnish his own food, clothing and weapon. Writer Simeon Miller Bright in 1951 described the Rangers this way:

"It must not be assumed that all the McNeill Rangers fought solely or mainly out of loyalty to the Confederate cause. It is true that most of them were attracted to the principles of the Confederacy, and to the way of life in the slaveholding South, and many felt a personal devotion to Captain McNeill. But love for adventure and loot, and the desire for a good fight lured many Valley men into the ranks of the McNeill Rangers. It might be said in passing, that the opportunity to drink freely any amount of hard liquor they could attain attracted some men to the Partisan rangers. Captain McNeill himself indulged in this mode of enjoyment."

And so young Jefferson Duffey exchanged his cozy room in his father's hotel for a life of hit and run fighting, bushwhacking, sleeping in the woods and barns, and living off whatever he could capture and forage.

When Captain McNeill was accidentally killed by one of his own men in November 1864, his son Jesse took over. In February 1865 he led a daring raid to downtown Cumberland, Maryland, where surrounded by encamped Union soldiers his men entered the Barnum Hotel and snatched two Union generals, Kelley and Crook, from their rooms.

"This most daring episode of the Civil War created a great sensation all over the country, as at the time several thousand Union troops were stationed in Cumberland," wrote Simeon Miller.

Many years later Jefferson Duffey would write about the raid in a 22-page account that still sells reprint copies today. He also wrote a second book, "McNeill's Last Charge: An account of a Daring Confederate in the Civil War."

The expectation that Private Duffey, if he survived the war, would work in his father's hotel and tavern was dispelled when the young man attended a local church on New Year's Day, 1865. A 1930 tribute to him at Baltimore Conference of the Methodist Episcopal Church, South stated:

"He was converted January 1 1865, in Hebron Lutheran Church, located upon Capon River, Hampshire County, West Virginia, Reverend Peter Miller being pastor of the church, and two months later he was received into the Methodist Episcopal Church, South, in Moorefield by Reverend James Beaty. He was licensed to preach by the Quarterly Conference of Moorefield Circuit September 28, 1867."

Jefferson enrolled in the Methodist college, Randolph-Macon, in Ashland, Virginia. A student from 1867 to 1870, he returned to Moorefield where he married school teacher Nancy Hyder on July 10, 1872. His 50-year career as a clergyman saw him preside over at least 15 churches in Maryland, Virginia, West Virginia and Washington, D.C. In 1901 his alma mater awarded him an honorary Doctor of Divinity degree. The Duffey United Methodist Church in Moorefield was named for him in 1922.

"Dr. Duffey had many qualities that made him one of the outstanding preachers of his day," continued the memoir in the 1930 Baltimore conference program. "People everywhere loved him and this was because he loved them. His supreme gift was probably in the sphere of personal contacts.

"It is to be doubted if he ever made an enemy. He had marvelous grace in the sick room and here all the tenderness and interest, and care of the shepherd heart was instinctively given to those of his flock who were passing through the dark shadows."

Jefferson lived his final years in Washington, D.C. He died on November 9, 1929, at age 82. His wife, whom he called Nannie, died in 1941, age 94. They are buried at Arlington National Cemetery in the Confederate section.

They had four children: Sue P., born 1874, Mary K., born 1877, John H., born 1879, and Hugh S., born 1887. Sue and Mary never married and lived with their mother until she died. Mary was a nurse, Sue, a clerk for the federal government. Hugh went into education like his mother. He served as a school principal and superintendent of schools in Winchester, Virginia. Later, he lived in Washington D.C. and worked as a statistician for the census bureau. He married Vera Lynch in 1915. He died in 1964 at age 76.

His older brother John Humbird Duffey is shown on the 1900 D.C. census as employed as a clerk on the railroad. He was 20 and soon would be singing a different tune. In a mere 10 years his life would change dramatically. In 1920 he was a star opera singer living in Manhattan with a wife and two children.

His first marriage was not without controversy, and news of it made headlines across the country.

"Widow of Californian Weds Oratorio Singer, Surrenders Big Fortune for Man of Her Choice" wrote the Los Angeles Herald on August 11, 1907. The reason?

"First Husband's Will Provides That Money Should Revert to Other Heirs in Event of Remarriage" was the sub-headline. The article states:

"Charmed by his voice, Mrs. Frederick R. Hoyt, the young widow of a California mining man, has given up a $250,000 fortune to marry J. Humbird Duffey, a choir and oratorio singer…'I love my husband so much more than the fortune which our marriage has cost me,' the bride said to an intimate friend, 'that I am absolutely happy to give it up.'"

The article says after Fred Hoyt, 25, died in 1900 his will stated his widow, the former Margaret Stewart, would receive $250,000 (equivalent to about $4 million today) if she refrained from a second marriage. "Friends of Mrs. Duffey say that renunciation of her fortune appeared inevitable to her as long ago as November 1903 when for the first time she heard Mr. Duffey's voice at a concert at Carnegie Hall," the article explained.

"She was sitting in a box near the stage when a smooth-faced, blue-eyed, flaxen-hair young man appeared beside the orchestra leader and began to sing 'Wotan's Farewell' from Wagner's 'Walkure.'"

The newspaper reported that John Humbird Duffey urged her to take the fortune instead of him. She reluctantly did so. Fate intervened several months later when the pair unexpectedly met in Switzerland when each had chosen that place and time to visit the home of composer Wagner.

They married in New York City on June 27 1907. Daughter Allan Stewart soon followed, then son Jefferson Humbird Duffey was born the following March. But by 1920 the census shows Margaret and daughter Allen are renting a room elsewhere in the city because of a divorce. A decade later Margaret met a tragic end. The New York Times reported on March 6, 1930:

"Mrs. Margaret Duffey, 45, of New York City, was burned to death in the home of her daughter, Mrs. Allen Deppe, at Phoenix last night. She had been in Arizona as guest of her daughter...for two months. She is said to have escaped from the burning house and returned evidently to save $10,000 worth of diamonds."

John had since remarried, to Florence Ryan of Washington, who was divorced from Herbert Reamy. Their only child was John Humbird Duffey, Jr., born on March 4, 1934.

Not long after leaving D.C. for New York, John Sr. landed a role in a Broadway play, *Love's Lottery*, which opened in October 1904. Then followed a whirlwind of performances in New York and around the country with various opera companies in productions such as *The Mikado, Three Musketeers, The Chocolate Soldier*, and *Pirates of Penzance*. His name on early credits was John H. Duffey, then he preferred J. Humbird Duffey.

His name began appearing in Washington newspapers in 1902. One review on March 7 of that year was in the *Evening Star*. A piano and song recital at the Willard Hotel spoke of John's "fine baritone" and that he was taking voice lessons. He was 23 at the time.

"Mr. Duffey has been a pupil of Otto Torney Simon for three years, during which time he has made marked improvement. He has a voice of much power and good compass, and his enunciation is remarkably distinct. His efforts last night were loudly applauded."

The *Evening Star's* review of a show on April 25, 1903 at New York's St. Bartholomew Church praised the young singer. "Mr. Duffey's work created a sensation, and some of the musical people speak of him already as being a great artist."

A June 26, 1915, ad for a New York vocal studio in the Musical American publication praises its prize student:

"Another Arens Pupil Wins Triumph," it proclaims. "J. Humbird Duffey, Leading Tenor in Strauss' *A Waltze Dream* Capitvates Thousands in St Louis." By this time he had switched from baritone to tenor.

In the 1930s, in his early 50s, his New York years behind him, John Sr. returned to Washington. Still involved in music, an ad in the December 2, 1938, *Evening Star* revealed the singer had taken on new roles.

A Woodward & Lothrop full page ad included: "You are invited to hear a 15-minute program of songs presented by the Potomac Electric Power Company glee club, under the direction of Mr. John Humbird Duffey." He participated in many of these glee club events around town and also served as choir director of Washington's Fifth Baptist Church.

The D.C. 1940 census shows John Sr., now 61, has a day job with Census Bureau. John Jr. is age six and never had the opportunity to see and hear his father in his peak years on the New York stage. Fortunately, John Sr. lived to be almost 94 years old, plenty of time to fill his home with songs and his son with dreams that he, too, might delight audiences everywhere.

# Appendix 2: Duffey Discography

*We'll close our show with a gospel selection. We asked Jimmy Swaggart to sing along, but he said, no thanks, I'll just watch.*

John Duffey

Chronological listing of John Duffey's recordings.

**Luke Gordon**
Late 1954/ Early 1955, Luke Gordon session, Producer Ben Adelman, Ben Adelman Studio, 323 Cedar Street, N.W., Washington, D.C.
[01] Goin' Crazy (Luke Gordon) LP-0014
[02] Goin' Down the Road Feelin' Bad LP-0014
[03] Take Me for the Fool That I Am (Luke Gordon) LP-0014
[04] On the Banks of the Old Pontchartrain (Luke Gordon)
[05] Is It Wrong (Luke Gordon) LP-0014
Luke Gordon, vocals, guitar; Buzz Busby, mandolin; John Duffey, Dobro; Scotty Stoneman, fiddle; Oscar James "Jimmy" Stoneman, bass

**Luke Gordon**
1955, Luke Gordon session, Producer Ben Adelman, Ben Adelman Studio, 323 Cedar Street, N.W., Washington, D.C.
[01] I Believe I'm Entitled to You (Carlisle, Foree, Rice) LP-0014
[02] Swing Wide Your Gate of Love (Hank Thompson) LP-0014
[03] Let This Kiss Bid You Goodbye (Luke Gordon) LP-0014
[04] When It's Time for the Whippoorwills To Sing (Alton Delmore) LP-0014
[05] Lonely Hearts (Luke Gordon) LP-0014
Luke Gordon, vocals, guitar; Buzz Busby, mandolin; John Duffey, Dobro; Scotty Stoneman, fiddle; Oscar James "Jimmy" Stoneman, bass

## Luke Gordon
1955, Luke Gordon session, Producer Ben Adelman, Ben Adelman Studio, 323 Cedar Street, N.W., Washington, D.C.
[01] Don't Say Goodbye If You Love Me (Luke Gordon) LP-0014
Luke Gordon, vocals, guitar; Buzz Busby, mandolin; John Duffey, Dobro; Scotty Stoneman, fiddle; Oscar James "Jimmy" Stoneman, bass

## Buzz Busby
1955, Jiffy session, Producer Ben Adelman
[01] Lost (Busby) Jiffy 207BCD-16425
Buzz Busby, mandolin; Charlie Waller, guitar; Don Stover, banjo; John Duffey, Dobro; Scotty Stoneman, fiddle; Lee Cole, bass

## Lucky Chatman & The Ozark Mountain Boys
Early 1956, Lucky Chatman Studio, Frederick, Maryland
[01] I've Waited So Long 45-573A
[02] Blue Grass (Duffey) 45-573B
Lucky Chatman, guitar, vocals; John Duffey, mandolin, vocals [on 01]; Bill Berry, bass; Bill Poffinberger, fiddle, Bill Blackburn, banjo;

## The Country Gentlemen
October, 1957, Dixie session, Producer, Don Nelson, Radio Station WARL, Arlington, Virginia
[01] Going to the Races (Stanley) No number
[02] Heavenward Bound (Duffey) No number
John Duffey, mandolin, vocals; Charlie Waller, guitar, vocals; Bill Emerson, banjo, vocals; John Hall, fiddle; Tom Morgan, bass

## The Country Gentlemen
December, 1957, Starday session, Producer Ben Adelman, Ben Adelman Studio, 323 Cedar Street, N.W., Washington, D.C.
ST 2609 Backwoods Blues (Emerson, Davis) 45-344 SLP-283ST
ST 2711 Yesterday's Love (Duffey)ST-3510
John Duffey, mandolin, vocals; Charlie Waller, guitar, vocals; Bill Emerson, banjo, vocals; Carl Nelson, fiddle; Roy Self, bass

## The Country Gentlemen

December, 1957. Starday session, Producer Ben Adelman, Ben Adelman Studio, 323 Cedar Street, N.W., Washington, D.C.
ST 2608 Dixie Look Away) (arr. Emerson) (inst.) 45-344SD 3510
ST 2610 It's the Blues (Duffey) 45-347 GT 6020SD 3510
John Duffey, mandolin, vocals; Charlie Waller, guitar, vocals; Bill Emerson, banjo, vocals; Carl Nelson, fiddle; Pete Kuykendall, bass

## Bill Clifton

March, 1958, Mercury-Starday session, Producers, Bill Clifton, Don Pierce, RCA Victor Studio, 1611 Hawkins Street, Nashville, Tennessee
ST 16318 You Go to Your Church (Arr. Clifton, York) 111BCD 16425
ST 16319 Are You Alone (Clifton) SLP 159 BCD 16425
ST 16320 Another Broken Heart (Carter) SLP 111BCD 16425
ST 16321 When You Kneel at Mother's Grave (Liley, Clifton)
ST 16322 Corey (Clifton, York) SLP 159BCD 16425
Bill Clifton, guitar, vocals; Jimmy Self, guitar; Ralph Stanley, banjo; Curly Lambert, mandolin [on 18, 19, and 21], vocals; John Duffey, mandolin [on 20 and 22], Dobro [on 18, 19, and 21], vocals; Tommy Jackson, fiddle; Benny Martin, fiddle; Junior Huskey, bass

## The Country Gentlemen

May, 1958, Starday session, Producer Ben Adelman, Ben Adelman Studio, 323 Cedar Street, N.W., Washington, D.C.
ST 2780 Orange Blossom Fiddle (Fenton) 45-440SLP-104SD 3510
ST 2781 High Lonesome (Duffey) 45-367 SLP-136SD 3510
ST 2783 Mountaineer's Fling (Emerson) 45-440GT 6020SD 3510
ST 2784 The Church Back Home (Duffey, Davis) SLP-105
John Duffey, mandolin, vocals, bass [on 2781], vocals; Charlie Waller, guitar, vocals; Bill Emerson, banjo, vocals; Carl Nelson, fiddle, bass [on 2784]; Pete Kuykendall, mandolin [on 2781], lead guitar [on 2784], Roy Self, bass

**The Country Gentlemen**
May, 1958, Starday session, Producer Ben Adelman, Ben Adelman Studio, 323 Cedar Street, N.W., Washington, D.C.

ST 2782 Hey Little Girl (Duffey)45-367SLP-115SD 3510
Charlie Waller, guitar, vocals; John Duffey, mandolin, vocals; Bill Emerson, banjo, vocals; John Hall, fiddle; Roy Self, bass

**Bill Clifton**
August, 1958, Starday session, *Mountain Folk Songs* album, Capitol Transcription Service, 1120-A Connecticut Avenue, N.W., Washington, D.C., Producer Bill Clifton

052 3098 Dixie Mountain Express (Clifton) SLP 111BCD-16425
052 3099 When Autumn Leaves Begin to Fall (Clifton) SLP 111
052 3100 Walkin' In My Sleep (Clifton) SLP 111 BCD-16425
052 3101 Dixie Darling (Gillespie) SLP 111 BCD-16425
Bill Clifton, guitar, vocals; Johnny Clark, banjo, vocals; John Duffey, mandolin, Dobro, vocals; Roy Self, bass; Carl Nelson, fiddle; Cal Newman, fiddle; Mike Seeger, autoharp, banjo

**The Country Gentlemen**
November 6, 1958, Starday session, Producer Ben Adelman, Ben Adelman Studio, 323 Cedar Street, N.W., Washington, D.C.

ST 2856The Devil's own (Duffey, Davis) 45-415SD 3510
ST 2587Rollin' Stone (Roberts, Hill, Davis) 45-415SLP-136SD
Charlie Waller, guitar, vocals; John Duffey, mandolin, vocals; Bill Emerson, banjo; Pete Kuykendall, vocals; John Hall, fiddle; Roy Self, bass

**Bill Clifton**
December, 1958, Capitol Transcription Service, 1120-A Connecticut Avenue, N.W., Washington, D.C., Producer, Bill Clifton
060 3245 You Don't Think About Me (When I'm Gone) (Clifton, Clayton)45-498SLP-159 BCD 16425
060 3246 Mail Carrier's Warning (Clifton) 45-498BCD 16425

Bill Clifton, guitar, vocals; Johnny Clark, banjo, vocals; John Duffey, mandolin, Dobro, vocals; Roy Self, bass; Carl Nelson, fiddle

**Bill Clifton and The Dixie Mountain Boys**
February, 1959, Capitol Transcription Service, 1120-A Connecticut Avenue, N.W., Washington, D.C., Producer, Bill Clifton
062 4554 Little Darling Pal of Mine (Carter)unissued BCD16425
063 4555 Railroading on the Great Divide (Carter) 45-529   SLP-170 BCD-16425
064 4556 Bed on the Floor (Carter)45-529 SLP 159 BCD-16425
Bill Clifton, guitar, vocals; Johnny Clark, banjo, vocals; John Duffey, mandolin; Roy Self, bass; Carl Nelson, fiddle; Mike Seeger, autoharp, banjo

**The Country Gentlemen**
May 13, 1959, Starday session, Producer: Ben Adelman, Ben Adelman. Empire Studio, Takoma Park, Maryland
ST 2905 Nine Pound Hammer (Travis) SD 3510
ST 2906I Never Will Marry (Duffey, Davis) 45-434SLP-168SD
ST 2907 Travelin' Dobro Blues (Duffey, Davis) 45-434SLP-109SD
ST 2908 Nobody's Business (Country Gentlemen) SLP-174SD
Charlie Waller, guitar, vocals; John Duffey, mandolin, Dobro [on 2906] vocals, bass [on 2907], vocals; Bill Emerson, banjo; Pete Kuykendall, banjo, guitar [on 2905], bass [on 2906]; Tom Gray, bass [on 2908]

**The Country Gentlemen**
June 30, 1959, Starday session. Engineer Mike Seeger or Ed Behr, Capitol Transcription Service, 1120-A Connecticut Avenue, N.W., Washington, D.C.
ST 3003 New Freedom Bell (Osborne) (alternate take) SD 3510
ST 3003 New Freedom Bell (Osborne) 45-455SD 3510
ST 3004 The Hills And Home (Duffey) 45-455SLP-136SD 3510
Charlie Waller, guitar, vocals; Eddie Adcock, banjo, vocals; John Duffey, mandolin, Dobro, vocals; Jim Cox, bass; Mike Seeger, autoharp [on 3003]

**Lucky Chatman & The Ozark Mountain Boys**
July 26, 1959, Lucky Chatman & The Ozark Mountain Boys
session, Producer Joe Bussard, Joe Bussard Studio, Fleming
Avenue, Frederick, Maryland
[01] Put My Little Shoes Away 617-B
[02] Blue Grass (Duffey) 617-A
[03] I've Waited So Long
Duffey is spelled "Fuffey" on the A side and correctly spelled on
the B side
John Duffey, mandolin, vocals; Lucky Chatman, guitar, vocals;
Bill Berry, guitar; Bill Poffinberger, fiddle

**The Country Gentlemen**
Late, 1959, Folkways session, *Country Songs: Old and New*
album, Engineer Mike Seeger, Capitol Transcription Service, 620
11th Street, N.W., Washington, D.C.
ST 3217 Roving Gambler (Arr. Duffey) FA 2409
ST 3218 The Little Sparrow (Arr. Duffey) FA 2409
ST 3219 Drifting Too Far (Arr. Duffey) FA 2409
ST 3220 Weeping Willow (Arr. Duffey) FA 2409
ST 3221 Tomorrow's My Wedding Day (Arr. Duffey FA 2409
ST 3222 The Story of Charlie Lawson FA 2409
ST 3223 Turkey Knob (Adcock) FA 2409
ST 3224 Paul and Silas (Arr. Duffey) FA 2409
ST 3225 Poor Ellen Smith (De Graaf) FA 2409
ST 3226 The Long Black Veil (Dill, Wilkin) FA 2409
ST 3227 Honky Tonk Rag (Duffey) FA 2409
ST 3228 Jesse James (Arr. Duffey) FA 2409
ST 3229 Have Thine Own Way (Arr. Duffey) FA 2409
ST 3230 A Good Woman's Love (Cobin) FA 2409
ST 3231 The Double Eagle (Arr. Waller) FA 2409
ST 3235 Darling Alalee (Arr. Duffey) FA 2409
Charlie Waller, guitar, vocals; Eddie Adcock, banjo, vocals; John
Duffey, mandolin, vocals; Jim Cox, bass, vocals.

**The Country Gentlemen**
January, 1960, Starday session, Engineer Mike Seeger, Capitol
Transcription Service, 1120-A Connecticut Avenue, N.W.,
Washington, D.C.
ST 3143 A Letter to Tom (Duffey) 45-487SLP-174SD 3510

ST 3144 Darling Alalee (Duffey) 45-487FA 2409SD 3510
ST 3155 Tomorrow's My Wedding Day (Arr. Duffey) SEP-229
Charlie Waller, guitar, vocals; Eddie Adcock, banjo, vocals; John Duffey, mandolin, Dobro [on 3143], vocals; Jim Cox, bass

**The Country Gentlemen**
April 20, 1960, Starday session, Engineer Mike Seeger, Capitol Transcription Service, 1120-A Connecticut Avenue, N.W., Washington, D.C.
ST 3382 Helen (Godsen) 45-515REB 2201
ST 3383 Blue Man (Self) GT 6020
ST 3384 Remembrance of You (Kuykendall) GT 6020
Charlie Waller, guitar, vocals; Eddie Adcock, banjo, vocals; John Duffey, mandolin, vocals; Jim Cox, bass

**Red McCoy And The Sons Of The Soil**
1961 Rodel Studio, 1028 33rd St., N.W. Washington, D.C.
[01] Let Jesus Come Into Your Heart (Morris) MVM-157
[02] I Heard My Savior Calling (William) MVM-157
[03] I Want To See My Mother Again MVM-157
[04] Be Careful of Your Father's Name MVM-157
[05] Rainbow Joe MVM-157
Wayne "Red McCoy" Busbice, guitar, vocals; Buzz Busby, guitar; John Duffey, Dobro; unknown, piano; unknown, steel guitar; Carl Nelson, fiddle; Jack Stoneman, bass

**Red McCoy And The Sons Of The Soil**
1961 Rodel Studio, 1028 33rd St., N.W. Washington, D.C.
[01] Tragic Love Affair (Busbice) SSU-308
[02] Darling Do (Busbice) SSU-308
[03] She's Coming Home Today (Busbice) SSU-308
[04] Farther Along SSU-308
[05] When God Called Daddy Away (Busbice) SSU-308
[06] By and By SSU-308
[07] Let's Grow Old Together (Busbice) SSU-308
[08] What's the Use (Busbice) SSU-308
[09] What a Friend We Have In Jesus SSU-308
[10] Never AloneSSU-308

Wayne "Red McCoy" Busbice, guitar, vocals; Buzz Busby, guitar; John Duffey, Dobro; unknown, steel guitar; Carl Nelson, fiddle; Jack Stoneman, bass

**The Country Gentlemen**
February, 1961, Folkways session, *Sing & Play Folk Songs and Bluegrass* album, Engineers, Mike Seeger, Pete Kuykendall, Producers John Duffey, Pete Kuykendall, Capitol Transcription Service, 1120-A Connecticut Avenue, N.W., Washington, D.C.
[01] Train 45 (Arr. Duffey) FA 2410
[02] Remembrance of You (Kuykendall) FA 2410
[03] The Fields Have Turned Brown (Stanley) FA 2410
[04] They're At Rest Together (Arr. Duffey) FA 2410
[05] Will The Circle Be Unbroken (Arr. Duffey) FA 2410
[06] Behind These Prison Walls of Love (Bolick, Gerard) FA 2410
[07] Wear a Red Rose (Duffey) FA 2410
[08] I'm Coming Back (But I Don't Know When) (Monroe)
[09] Come All Ye Tender Hearted (Arr. Duffey, Kuykendall)
Charlie Waller, guitar, vocals; John Duffey, mandolin [all but 01], Dobro [on 01], vocals; Eddie Adcock, banjo [all but 05], vocals; Tom Gray bass [all but 05], vocals; Kenny Haddock, Dobro [on 08]; Wayne Yates, mandolin [on 01 06]

**Bill Clifton**
March 13, 1961, *Carter Family Memorial* album, Producer, Bill Clifton, Capitol Transcription Service, 1120-A Connecticut Avenue, N.W., Washington, D.C.
081 4746RE I'll Be All Smiles Tonight (Lulu Belle and Scotty)548 SLP 146 BCD-16425
082 4747RE My Clinch Mountain Home (Carter) SLP 146 BCD-16425
083 March Winds (Clifton) BCD-16425
084 4744RE Bring Back My Blue-Eyed Boy To Me (Clifton) 561 SLP 146 BCD-16425
085 4764 I'm Rollin On (Clifton) 548SLP-159 BCD-16425
086 4732RE No Hiding Place Down Here (Clifton) SEP-186SLP 146 BCD-16425
Bill Clifton, guitar, vocals; Johnny Clark, banjo, vocals; Mike Seeger, banjo, guitar, autoharp; John Duffey, mandolin, Dobro, vocals; Roy Self, bass; Benny Martin, fiddle

**The Country Gentlemen**
March 19, 1961, Folkways session, *Sing & Play Folk Songs and Bluegrass* album, Engineer Pete Kuykendall, Capitol Transcription Service, 1120-A Connecticut Avenue, N.W., Washington, D.C.

ST 4992 Red Rocking Chair (Duffey, York) SLP-169FA 2410
ST 4993 If That's the Way You Feel (Stanley, Stanley) GT 6020
[03] Strutting on the Strings (Adcock) FA 2410
[04] Southbound (Duffey)FA 2410
[05] Standing In the Need of Prayer (Arr. Kuykendall) FA 2410
[06] Handsome Molly (Arr. Duffey, Kuykendall) FA 2410
[07] Victim to the Tomb (Duffey)FA 2410
[08] Little Bessie (Arr. Duffey, Kuykendall) FA 2410
Charlie Waller, guitar, vocals; John Duffey, mandolin [all but 01], Dobro [on 01], vocals; Eddie Adcock, banjo [all but 05], vocals; Tom Gray bass [all but 05], vocals; Kenny Haddock, Dobro [ST 4992, 03, 04, 06, 07, 08]

**The Country Gentlemen**
August, 1961, Folkways session, leased to Starday, Capitol Transcription Service, 1120-A Connecticut Avenue, N.W., Washington, D.C.
ST 4996I Know I've Lost You (Price) 45-558SLP 174
Charlie Waller, guitar, vocals; John Duffey, mandolin, vocals; Eddie Adcock, banjo, vocals; Tom Gray bass, vocals; Kenny Haddock, Dobro

**The Country Gentlemen**
September 16, 1961, Carnegie Hall, *Country Gentlemen On The Road And More*
[01] I Ain't Gonna Work Tomorrow (Louvin, Louvin) SFW
[02] A Letter to Tom (Arr. Duffey) SFW CD 40133
[03] John Hardy (Arr. Adcock) SFW CD 40133
[04] The Fields Have Turned Brown (Stanley, Stanley)
[05] These Men of God (Eliis, Williams, Williams) SFW CD 40133
[06] Little Sparrow (Arr. Duffey) SFW CD 40133
Charlie Waller, guitar, vocals; John Duffey, mandolin, vocals; Eddie Adcock, banjo, vocals; Tom Gray bass, vocals; Kenny Haddock, Dobro

**The Country Gentlemen**
November 6, 1961, Starday session, *Bluegrass at Carnegie Hall* album, Engineer Pete Kuykendall, Capitol Transcription Service, 1120-A Connecticut Avenue, N.W. Washington, D.C.
ST 5131 Two Little Boys (Duffey, Davis) SLP 174
ST 5132 Willie Roy, The Cripple Boy (Country Gentlemen)
ST 5133 Sunrise (Duffey) 628SLP 174
ST 5134 Silence or Tears (Gray, Stuart) SLP 174
ST 5135 Country Concert (Duffey, Adcock) SLP 174
ST 5136 These Men of God (Ellis, Williams, Williams) SLP 174
ST 5137 Down Where the Still Waters Flow (Kuykendall)SLP 174
ST 5138 Nobody's Business (Country Gentlemen)SLP 174
Charlie Waller, guitar, vocals; John Duffey, mandolin, vocals; Eddie Adcock, banjo, vocals; Tom Gray bass, vocals; Kenny Haddock, Dobro; M. Jackson, Vibroharp.

**The Country Gentlemen**
1962, Design session, *Hootenanny* album, Wynwood Studios, Engineer Pete Kuykendall Falls Church, Virginia
[01] Nine Pound Hammer (Travis)DLP 613
[02] Eddie on the Freeway (Adcock)DLP 613
[03] 500 Miles (West)DLP 613
[04] The Knoxville Girl DLP 613
[05] Redwing DLP 613
[06] Nearer My God to Thee DLP 613
[07] Katy Dear DLP 613
Charlie Waller, guitar, vocals; John Duffey, mandolin, vocals; Eddie Adcock, banjo, vocals; Tom Gray bass, vocals

**The Country Gentlemen**
April 13, 1962, Folkways session, *Country Gentlemen On The Road* album, Antioch College, Yellow Springs, Ohio. Live Concert recording
[01] Handsome Molly (Arr. Duffey, Kuykendall) FA 2411
[02] The Sunny Side of Life (Bolick) FA 2411
[03] Poor Ellen Smith (De Graf) FA 2411
[04] The Long Black Veil (Wilkin, Dill) FA 2411
[05] Grandfather's Clock (Work. Arr, Gray, Adcock) FA 2411
[06] Ain't Got No Home (Henry) FA 2411

Charlie Waller, guitar, vocals; John Duffey, mandolin, vocals; Eddie Adcock, banjo, vocals; Tom Gray bass, vocals

**Bill Clifton**
Early-September, 1962 (two days), *Soldier Sing Me a Song* album, Producer, Bill Clifton, Engineer Pete Kuykendall, Wynwood Studios, Falls Church, Virginia

087 5810 There's a Star Spangled Banner Waving Somewhere
088 5811 A White Cross Marks the Grave (McHan) SLP213    089
5812 Spanish Flandang (Bill Clifton) SLP 213 BCD-16425
090 5813 Jimmy Will Be Slain (Wynn) SLP 213 BCD-16425
091 5814 Drink Your Glasses Dry (Wynn) SLP 213 BCD-16425
092 5815 The Battle of Quebec (Clifton, Clayton) SLP 213 093
5816 This Old Cold War (Clifton) SLP 213 BCD-16425
094 5817 The Sinking of the Maine (Clifton, Clayton) SLP    213
095 5818 I Want to Go Home (Clifton, Clayton) SLP213
096 5819 The Sailor on the Deep Blue Sea (Clifton) SLP    213097
5820 Faded Coat of Blue (Clifton) SLP 213 BCD-16425
098 5821 Uniforms of Grey (Clayton) SLP 213 BCD-16425
099 5822 Tim (Clayton) SLP 213 BCD-16425
100 5823 Volunteer's March unissued BCD-16425
Bill Clifton, guitar, vocals; Paul Craft, guitar, banjo, vocals; John Duffey, mandolin, vocals; Tom Gray, bass; Curtis Lee, fiddle; Carl Nelson, fiddle; Mike Seeger, autoharp, guitar

**Bill Clifton**
Mid-September, 1962, *Soldier Sing Me a Song* album, Producer, Bill Clifton, Wynwood Studios, Engineer Pete Kuykendall, Falls Church, Virginia
101 5833 San Juan Hill London HAU-8325 [UK] BCD-16425
102 5834 The Marine's Hymn (York)SLP-213 BCD-16425
103 5821RE Uniforms of Grey (Clayton)unissuedBCD-16425
Bill Clifton, guitar, vocals; Paul Craft, guitar, banjo, vocals; John Duffey, mandolin, vocals; Tom Gray, bass

**The Country Gentlemen**
November 1, 1962, Rebel session, Wynwood Studios, Engineer Pete Kuykendall, Falls Church, Virginia
111621 Christmas Time Back Home (Duffey, Hill) F 236RLP

111622 Heavenward Bound (Duffey) F 236 REB 1476
Charlie Waller, guitar, vocals; John Duffey, mandolin, vocals;
Eddie Adcock, banjo, vocals; Tom Gray bass, vocals

**The Country Gentlemen**
November 17, 1962, Rebel session, Producer Pete Kuykendall,
Wynwood Studios, Falls Church, Virginia

[01] Philadelphia Lawyer (Guthrie) SLP 1527
[02] The White Rose (Traditional P.D.) RLP 1475
[03] The Gentlemen Is Blue (Adcock, Duffey) RLP 1476
[04] Paddy on the Turnpike (Jackson) RLP 1473
[05] Sunrise (Sparks)SLP 1535
Charlie Waller, guitar, vocals; John Duffey, mandolin, vocals;
Eddie Adcock, banjo, vocals; Tom Gray bass, vocals

**Lee Moore**
1963, (maybe 1961 or 1962), Producer, Lee Sutton, Radio
Station WWVA, Wheeling, WV
[01] Mother's Call (Arr. Moore, Sutton) LP-463
[02] Vacant Cabin (Arr. Moore, Sutton) RRLM-137LP-463
[03] Paul's Ministry (Travel) RRLM-137LP-463
[04] I Have Dusted Off The Bible (Kyle, Bailes)LP-463
[05] Legend of the Dogwood Tree (Moore) LP-463
[06] Give Me Your Love (Arr. Moore, Sutton) LP-463
Lee Moore, guitar, vocals; John Duffey, mandolin, dobro; Charlie
Waller, guitar; Eddie Adcock, banjo; Tom Gray, bass

**Pete Pike**
1963, Producer, Charles R. "Dick" Freeland, Wynwood Studios,
Falls Church, Virginia
REB-4000 [01] In the Pines (Eleanor MacGregor) R-1473
[02] Train 45 R-1474
[02] Down In the Willow Garden R-1476
[03] I'll Meet You at the Portals Unissued
[04] John Henry R-1473
[05] Put My Little Shoes Away (Eleanor MacGregor) R-1474
Pete Pike, guitar, vocals; John Duffey, mandolin, Dobro, vocals;
Lamar Grier, banjo; Billy Baker, fiddle

## The Country Gentlemen

January 6, 1963, Folkways session, *Country Gentlemen On The Road* album, Sacred Mushroom, Columbus, Ohio. Live Concert recording

[01] Heartaches (Hoffman, Klenner. Arr. Adcock) FA 2411
[02] Little Glass of Wine (Stanley, Stanley) FA 2411
[03] Walking In Jerusalem (Just Like John) (Arr. Duffey, Adcock)
[04] I Am a Pilgrim (Travis) FA 2411
[05] A Letter to Tom (Arr. Duffey) FA 2411
[06] Raw Hide (Monroe) FA 2411
[07] Blue Ridge Mountain Blues (Hess) FA 2411

Charlie Waller, guitar, vocals; John Duffey, mandolin, vocals; Eddie Adcock, banjo, vocals; Tom Gray bass, vocals

## The Country Gentlemen

March, 1963, Rebel session, Engineer, Pete Kuykendall, Wynwood Studios, Falls Church, Virginia

[01] I Am Weary (Let Me Rest) (Kuykendall) REB 4002
[02] Sad and Lonesome Day (Traditional P.D.) REB 4002
[03] The Bluebirds Are Singing (Duffey, Kuykendall) REB 4002

Charlie Waller, guitar, vocals; John Duffey, mandolin, vocals; Eddie Adcock, banjo, vocals; Tom Gray bass, vocals

April, 1963, Rebel session, Engineer, Pete Kuykendall, Wynwood Studios, Falls Church, Virginia

[01] The White Rose (Traditional P.D.)REB 4002
[02] The Gentleman Is Blue (Adcock, Duffey) REB 4002
[03] Philadelphia Lawyer (Guthrie) REB 4002

Charlie Waller, guitar, vocals; John Duffey, mandolin, vocals; Eddie Adcock, banjo, vocals; Tom Gray bass; Pete Kuykendall, open tuned guitar [on 02]

## The Country Gentlemen

April 11, 1963, Starday session, Engineer, Pete Kuykendall, Wynwood Studios, Falls Church, Virginia

ST 6218 Copper Kettle (York, Duffey) 628SLP 1494
ST 6219 Night Walk (Adcock) SD 3510

Charlie Waller, guitar, vocals; John Duffey, mandolin, vocals; Eddie Adcock, banjo, vocals; Tom Gray bass; Pete Kuykendall, Pepsi bottle and nail

## The Country Gentlemen

April 14, 1963, Design session, *Hootenanny* album, Wynwood Studios, Engineer Pete Kuykendall, Falls Church, Virginia
[01] You Left Me Alone (Gray, Stuart) DLP 613
[02] East Virginia Blues (Duffey) SLP 1527
[03] Make Me a Pallet On The Floor (Duffey) SLP 1535
[04] Katy Dear (Traditional) SLP 1494
Charlie Waller, guitar, vocals; John Duffey, mandolin, vocals; Eddie Adcock, banjo, vocals; Tom Gray bass, vocals

## Bill Clifton

August 5, 6, and 7, 1963, *Code of the Mountains* album, Producer, Bill Clifton, Wynwood Studios, Engineer Pete Kuykendall, Falls Church, Virginia
104 6556 Going Back to Dixie (Clifton) SLP 271 BCD-16425
105 6557 Your Mother Still Prays For You Jack (Clifton) SLP 271
106 6558 Moonshiner (Clifton, Clayton) SLP 271 BCD-16425
107 6559 Just a Smile London HAU-8325 [UK] BCD-16425
108 6560 Lonely Little Cabin (Clayton) SLP 271 BCD-16425
109 6561 Dream of the Miner's Child (Clifton) SLP 271 BCD-
110 6562 Groundhog Hunt (Clifton) SLP 271 BCD-16425
111 6563 Engine Twenty Three (Clayton) SLP 271BCD-16425
112 6564 Jim Hatfield's Son (Clifton, Clayton) SLP 271 BCD-
113 6565 Saturday Night (Clifton) SLP 271 BCD-16425
114 6566 Lonesome for You (Clifton) SLP 271 BCD-16425
115 6567 Lazy Courtship (Clifton, Clayton) SLP 271 BCD-16425
116 6568 Across the Shining River London HAU.8325 [UK]
117 6569 Roll the Cotton Down (Wynn) SLP 271 BCD-16425
118 6570 Take Me Back (Clifton) SLP 271 BCD-16425
119 6571 Lonesome Field (Lee) SLP 271 BCD-16425
Bill Clifton, guitar, vocals; Charlie Waller, guitar, vocals; Eddie Adcock, banjo, vocals; John Duffey, mandolin, vocals; Tom Gray, bass; Paul Justice, fiddle; Roy Justice, fiddle; Mike Seeger, autoharp, guitar, banjo

## Bill Clifton

September 3 and 4, 1963, *Going Back to Dixie* album, Producer, Bill Clifton, Wynwood Studios, Engineer Pete Kuykendall, Falls Church, Virginia

120 6640 Little Green Valley (Clifton) NLP 2018 BCD-16425
121 6641 When I Lay My Burdens Down (Clifton) NLP 2018
122 6642 At My Window (Clifton) NLP 2018 BCD-16425
123 6643 Gonna Lay Down My Old Guitar (Clifton)NLP
124 6644 Where the Willow Gently Sways (Barrett, Clifton)
125 6645 When I'm With You (McHan) London   HAU-8325   [UK]
126 6646 My Nights Are Lonely (Clifton) NLP 2018 BCD-16425
127 6647 Lamp In the Window (Clifton) NLP 2018 BCD-16425
128 6648 Louis Collins (Hurt) London HAU-8325 [UK]
129 6649 I'll Be Satisfied (Clifton) NLP 2018 BCD-16425
130 6650 Old Ruben (Clifton) NLP 2018 BCD-16425
131 6651 My Cindy Girl (Clifton) NLP 2018 BCD-16425
132 6652 Dixie Ramble (Bluegrass Ramble) (Clifton) NLP
133 6653 Big Bill (Clifton) NLP
134 6654 Bringing Mary Home (Kingston, Duffey) NLP2018
Bill Clifton, guitar, vocals; Charlie Waller, guitar, vocals; Eddie Adcock, banjo, vocals; John Duffey, mandolin, vocals; Tom Gray, bass; Paul Justice, fiddle; Roy Justice, fiddle; Mike Seeger, autoharp, guitar, banjo

**The Country Gentlemen**
September 27, 1963, Mercury session, "Folk Session Inside" album, Producer, Pete Kuykendall, Wynwood Studios, Falls Church, Virginia
2 30593 The Bluebirds Are Singing For Me (Duffey, Kuykendall)
2 30594 Sad and Lonesome Day (Arr. Duffey, Kuykendall) SR
2 30595 The Girl Behind The Bar (Stanley) SR 60858
2 30596 Can't You Hear Me Calling (Monroe) SR 60858
2 30597 The School House Fire (Dixon Brothers) SR 60858
2 30598 Night Walk (Adcock) SR 60858
2 30599 The Galveston Flood (Rush, Duffey, Adcock) SR 60858
2 30600 The Young Fisherwoman (McHan) SR 60858
2 30601 This Morning At Nine (Campbell) SR 60858
2 30602 I Am Weary (Let Me Rest) SR 60858
2 30603 Aunt Dinah's Quilting Party (Fletcher, Kyle) SR 60858
2 30604 Heartaches (Hoffman, Klenner, Adcock) SR 60858
[13]Dark As a Dungeon (Travis) CCRS 7008
Charlie Waller, guitar, vocals; John Duffey, mandolin, vocals; Eddie Adcock, banjo, vocals; Tom Gray, bass, vocals

**The Country Gentlemen**
June – July, 1964, Mercury session, Engineer, Pete Kuykendall, Wynwood Studios, Falls Church, Virginia
[01] Electricity (Murphy) CCC 0111
[02] She's Long, She's Tall (Blue Yodel #3) (Rodgers) CCC 0111
[03] Nashville Jail (McHan) CCC 0111
[04] This World's No Place To Live (But It's Home) (Duffey, Hill)
[05] Azzurro Campana (Adcock, Duffey) CCC 0111
[06] Brown Mountain Light (Wiseman) CCC 0111
[07] A Cold Wind's A Blowing (Duffey, Hill)CCC 0111
[08] Uncle Joe (Adcock) CCC 0111
[09]Theme From Exodus (Gold)
[10] Flowers By My Grave Side (Allen, Duffey) CCC 0111
[11] Are You Waiting Just For Me (Tubb) CCC 0111
Charlie Waller, guitar, vocals; John Duffey, mandolin, vocals; Eddie Adcock, banjo, vocals; Tom Gray, bass, Ed Ferris, bass on 06

Tom Gray added the following notes about this session: A few confusing things about this June - July 1964 session. It was to be our second album for the Mercury label, but then Mercury decided they didn't want any more bluegrass. Therefore, these tapes just sat on the shelf for 26 years until Gary Reid at Copper Creek records got the rights to release it on CD in 1990.

We included what we thought was "Blue Yodel # 4," because that's what the label on Bill Monroe's record of it from the 1940s said. It was mis-labeled. The song that Monroe recorded was actually Jimmy Rodgers' "Blue Yodel #3 (She's Long She's Tall). Rodgers' Blue Yodel #4 was California Blues. The Gents never played that song.

**The Country Gentlemen**
August 18, 1964, Rebel session, Engineer, John Rogers, Moon-Cusser Coffee House, Martha's Vineyard, Massachusetts. Live concert recording
[01] Tom Dooley (Arr. Duffey) SLP 1521
[02] Pretty Polly (Sparks) SLP 1535
[03] M.T.A. (Steiner, Hawes) SLP 1535
[04] I Never Will Marry (Sparks) SLP 1521

Charlie Waller, guitar, vocals; John Duffey, mandolin, vocals; Eddie Adcock, banjo, vocals; Ed Ferris, bass

## The Country Gentlemen

August 21, 1964, Rebel session, Engineer, John Rogers, Moon-Cusser Coffee House, Martha's Vineyard, Massachusetts. Live Concert recording

[01] These Men of God (Eillis, Williams, Williams) SLP 1535
[02] This Land Is Your Land (Guthrie) SLP 1527
[03] Columbus Stockade Blues (Duffey, Waller) SLP 1527
Charlie Waller, guitar, vocals; John Duffey, mandolin, vocals; Eddie Adcock, banjo, vocals; Ed Ferris bass

## The Country Gentlemen

November 1, 1964, Folkways session, leased to Starday, *Going Back To The Blueridge Mountains* album, Producer Edgar Sanford, Folk Gallery Club, Syracuse, New York

ST 8162 Brown Mountain Light (Wiseman) FTS 31031
ST 8163 Electricity (Murphy) FTS 31031
ST 8164 Daybreak In Dixie (Napier) FTS 31031
ST 8165 Mary Dear (Arr. Duffey) FTS 31031
ST 8166 Sad And Lonesome Day (Arr. Duffey, Kuykendall)
ST 8167 Cripple Creek (Arr. Duffey, Adcock) FTS 31031
ST 8168 Don't This Road Look Rough And Rocky (Arr. Duffey)
ST 8169 Mule Skinner Blues (Rodgers) FTS 31031
ST 8171 Going Back To The Blue Ridge Mountains (Delmore Brothers) FTS 31031
ST 8172 Going To the Races (Stanley) FTS 31031
ST 8173 Azzurro Campana (Blue Bells) (Adcock, Duffey)
ST 8173 Dark As A Dungeon (Travis) FTS 31031
ST 8174 Copper Kettle (Arr. Waller, Duffey) FTS 31031
ST 8175 Billy In The Low Ground (Arr. Waller, Adcock, Duffey)
ST 8176 I Saw The Light (Williams) FTS 31031
ST 8177 Tom Dooley #2 (Arr. Waller, Duffey) FTS 31031
Charlie Waller, guitar, vocals; John Duffey, mandolin, vocals; Eddie Adcock, banjo, vocals; Ed Ferris, bass

**The Country Gentlemen**
February 23, 1965, Rebel session, *Bringin' Mary Home* album,
Producer Charles R. "Dick" Freeland, Engineer, Gary Sanford,
H.B. Crouse Hall, Syracuse University, Syracuse, New York
8391 Spanish Two Step (Wills) F-265RLP 1478
8382 Bringing Mary Home (Duffey, Mank, Kington)
[03] The Convict And The Rose (Chapin, King MacDonald)REB
8385 Banks of The Ohio (Traditional P.D.) RLP 1478
Charlie Waller, guitar, vocals; John Duffey, mandolin, vocals;
Eddie Adcock, banjo, vocals; Ed Ferris, bass

**The Country Gentlemen**
February 24, 1965, Rebel session, *Bringin' Mary Home* album,
Producer Charles R. "Dick" Freeland, Engineer, Gary Sanford,
H.B. Crouse Hall, Syracuse University, Syracuse, New York
8383 Down Where The River Bends (Anglin, Peck, Wright)
8384 Battle Hymn of The Republic (Howe) RLP 1478
8388 This World's No Place To Live (Duffey, Streeter)
8392 Uncle Joe (Adcock) RLP 1478
Charlie Waller, guitar, vocals; John Duffey, mandolin, vocals;
Eddie Adcock, banjo, vocals; Ed Ferris, bass

**The Country Gentlemen**
February 25, 1965, Rebel session, *Bringin' Mary Home* album,
Producer Charles R. "Dick" Freeland, Engineer, Gary Sanford,
H.B. Crouse Hall, Syracuse University, Syracuse, New York
8387 Northbound (Duffey, Adcock)F-267. RLP 1478
8393 Let the Light Shine Down (Swan)RLP 1478
8390 The Girl from the North Country (Dylan)RLP 1478
8390 A Cold Wind A' Blowin (Duffey, Hill) F-257RLP 1478
[05] Swing Low, Sweet Chariot RLP 1478
Charlie Waller, guitar, vocals; John Duffey, mandolin, vocals;
Eddie Adcock, banjo, vocals; Ed Ferris, bass

**The Country Gentlemen**
June or July, 1965, Rebel session, *Christmas Time Back Home*
album, Recordings Inc., Baltimore, Maryland
40052 Jingle Bells (Pierpont) F-264 RLP 1477
[02] Silent Night (Gruber, Mohr) RLP 1477
[03] We Three Kings (Hopkins) RLP 1477

Charlie Waller, guitar, vocals; John Duffey, mandolin, vocals; Eddie Adcock, banjo, vocals; Ed Ferris, bass

**Bill Clifton**
July 26 and 27, 1965, Producer, Bill Clifton, Wynwood Studios, Falls Church, Virginia
137 Jug of Punch (Traditional) BFP-15121 BCD-16425
138 Keep That Wheel A-Turning (Traditional) BFP-15121
139 Baby Lie Easy (Traditional) BFP-15121 BCD-16425
140 Green To Grey (Goulder) BFP-15121BCD-16425
Bill Clifton, guitar, vocals; Eddie Adcock, banjo, vocals; John Duffey, mandolin, vocals; Tom Gray, bass; Zeke Dawson, fiddle

**The Country Gentlemen**
November 15, 1965, Starday session, Engineer Pete Kuykendall, Wynwood Studios, Falls Church, Virginia
ST 7869 Home Sweet HomeSLH 52ST 3510
ST 7870 This Land Is Your Land (Guthrie) SLH 52ST 3510
ST 7871 My Old Kentucky Home SLH 52ST 3510
ST 7872 Take This Hammer SLH 52ST 3510
ST 7873 Auld Lang Syne SLH 52ST 3510
ST 7874 Goodbye Katy SLH 52ST 3510
ST 7875 Camptown Races SLH 52ST 3510
ST 7876 Red River Valley SLH 52ST 3510
ST 7877 Oh, Susanna SLH 52ST 3510
ST 7878 Long Journey Home SLH 52ST 3510
ST 7879 500 MilesSLH 52ST 3510
ST 7880 Free Little Bird SLH 52ST 3510
ST 7881 Rose Connelly SLH 52ST 3510
ST 7882 Blowin' in the Wind SLH 52ST 3510
Charlie Waller, guitar, vocals; John Duffey, mandolin, vocals; Eddie Adcock, banjo, vocals; Ed Ferris, bass

Note: these recordings remained unissued until the 2002 CD release *Country Gentlemen - High Lonesome - the Complete Starday Recordings* ST 3510

**The Country Gentlemen**
June 15-16, 1966, Rebel session, *The Traveler* album, Producer, Charles R. "Dick" Freeland, Engineer, George Motion (Massenburg), Recordings Inc., Baltimore, Maryland

35382 Blue Bell (Adcock, Duffey)F-263
[02] It's All Over Now, Baby Blue (Dylan)F-265SLP 1481
[03] Matterhorn (Burch, Tillis)F-267SLP 1481
[04] Dark as a Dungeon (Travis)SLP 1481
35381 Big Bruce (Duffey)F-263
Charlie Waller, guitar, vocals; John Duffey, mandolin, vocals; Eddie Adcock, banjo, vocals; Ed Ferris, bass

**The Country Gentlemen**
July 3, 1966, Rebel session, Engineer, Richard N. Drevo, Roanoke Bluegrass Festival, Fincastle, Virginia. Live Concert recording
[01] Roanoke (Monroe)SLP 1527
[02] Windy and Warm (Loudermilk)SLP 1527
Charlie Waller, guitar, vocals; John Duffey, mandolin, vocals; Eddie Adcock, banjo, vocals; Ed Ferris, bass

**The Country Gentlemen**
September, 1966, Zap (Rebel) Records session, Carlton Haney's Bluegrass Festival, Fincastle, Virginia. Live Concert recording
[01] Nine Pound Hammer ZLP 101
[02] Make Me a Pallet On The Floor (Duffey) ZLP 101
[03] Battle Hymn of The Republic F-267ZLP 101
[04] Lonesome Day (Sparks) ZLP 101
[05] Two Little Boys (Duffey) ZLP 101
[06] Copper Kettle ZLP 101
[07] The Fields Have Turned Brown (Stanley, Stanley)ZLP 101
[08] Blue Bell ZLP 101
[09] Mule Skinner Blues ZLP 101
[10] Big Bruce (Duffey) ZLP 101
Charlie Waller, guitar, vocals; John Duffey, mandolin, vocals; Eddie Adcock, banjo, vocals; Ed Ferris, bass

## Jim Eanes

February 5, 1967, Zap (Rebel) Records session, *Your Old Standby* album, Baltimore, Maryland

[01] Your Old Standby (Eanes, Perry)Rebel REB-4000MLP-102
[02] Lady of Spain (Reaves, Evans)MLP-102
[03] Precious Memories MLP-102
[04] No One To Love Me Now (Hypes)Rebel REB-4000MLP-102
[05] Nobody's Darling MLP-102
[06] 51267 Donna Lynn (Benedict)MLP-102
[07] It's a Weary, Weary World (Eanes) MLP-102
[08] Step It Up And Go (Bucke)MLP-102
[09] Somebody Touched Me MLP-102
[10] Jimmie Brown MLP-102
Jim Eanes, guitar, vocals; Charlie Waller. guitar; John Duffey, mandolin, vocals; Walter Hensley, banjo; Russ Hooper, Dobro, vocals; Ed Ferris, bass

## The Country Gentlemen

May 30, 1967, Rebel session, Engineer, Bob Lloyd, Bob Lloyd Studios, Riverdale, Maryland
[01]When They Ring Those Golden Bells (DeMarbelle) REB 4002
Charlie Waller, guitar, vocals; John Duffey, mandolin, vocals; Eddie Adcock, banjo, vocals; Ed Ferris, bass

## The Country Gentlemen

September 3, 1967, Rebel session, Engineer Gary Sanford, Watermelon Park, Berryville, Virginia. Live Concert recording
[01] Are You Waiting Just For Me? (Tubb) SLP-1521
[02] Long Black Veil (Dill, Wilkins) SLP-1521
[03] Under The Double Eagle (Waller) (instrumental) SLP-1521
[04] Get In Line Brother (Flatt) SLP-1521
[05] Cripple Creek (Sparks) SLP-1527
[06] Heaven (arr. McSpadden) SLP-1535
Charlie Waller, guitar, vocals; John Duffey, mandolin, vocals; Eddie Adcock, banjo, vocals; Ed Ferris, bass

## The Country Gentlemen

January 9, 1968, Rebel session, *The Traveler* album, Engineer, Roy Homer, Roy D. Homer & Associates, Clinton, Maryland

[01] Buffalo Girls (Traditional P.D.) F-275SLP 1481
[02] A Beautiful Life (Golden) SLP 1481
[03] I'm Working On a Road (Flatt) SLP 1481
Charlie Waller, guitar, vocals; John Duffey, mandolin, guitar [on 03], vocals; Eddie Adcock, banjo, vocals; Ed Ferris, bass, vocals

**The Country Gentlemen**
January 10, 1968, Rebel session, *The Traveler* album, Engineer, Roy Homer, Roy D. Homer & Associates, Clinton, Maryland
63952 Border Incident (Spanish Is A Loving Tongue) (Clark)
22668 Johnny Reb (Kilgore)F-275SLP 1481
Charlie Waller, guitar, 12 string guitar [on 22668], vocals; John Duffey, mandolin, vocals; Eddie Adcock, banjo, vocals; Ed Ferris, bass

**The Country Gentlemen**
January 17, 1968, Rebel session, *The Traveler* album, Engineer, Roy Homer, Roy D. Homer & Associates, Clinton, Maryland
[01] Many a Mile (Skye) SLP 1481
[02] Amelia Earhart (McEnery) SLP 1481
[03] Lord I'm Coming Home (Kirkpatrick P.D.) SLP 1481
[04] The Traveler (Duffey) SLP 1481
Charlie Waller, guitar, vocals; John Duffey, mandolin, vocals; Eddie Adcock, banjo, vocals; Ed Ferris, bass

**The Country Gentlemen**
January 24, 1968, Rebel session, *The Traveler* album, Engineer, Roy Homer, Roy D. Homer & Associates, Clinton, Maryland
[01] Silver Bell (Arr. The Country Gentlemen) REB 4002
[02] Theme From Exodus (Gold)F-285 SLP 1481
[03] Love and Wealth (Louvin Brothers) REB 4002
Charlie Waller, guitar, vocals; John Duffey, mandolin, vocals; Eddie Adcock, banjo, vocals; Ed Ferris, bass

**The Country Gentlemen**
March 16, 1968, Rebel session, *Let the Light Shine Down* album, Engineer, Bob Lloyd, Bob Lloyd Studios, Riverdale, Maryland
[01] When They Ring Those Golden Bells (Duffey)SLP 1521
Charlie Waller, guitar, vocals; John Duffey, mandolin, vocals; Eddie Adcock, banjo, vocals; Ed Ferris, bass

**Emerson And Waldron**

1968, Rebel session, *I'm Bound to Ride* album, Engineer, Jim Hall, Roy Homer, Unity Recording Studios, Washington, D.C.

[02] I'm Bound To Ride (Emerson, Waldron) SLP-1485
[03] Red Wings (Emerson) SLP-1485
[04] You Didn't Say Goodbye (Emerson, Waldron) SLP-1485
Cliff Waldron, guitar, vocals; Bill Emerson, banjo, vocals; John Duffey, guitar [on 01], mandolin, vocals; Ed Ferris, bass

**The Country Gentlemen**

March, 1969, Rebel session, *Play It Like It Is* album, Producer: Charles R. "Dick" Freeland, Recordings, Inc., Baltimore, Maryland

[01] He Was a Friend of Mine (Arr. The Country Gents) SLP 1486
[02] Daybreak In Dixie (Napier) SLP 1486
[03] Some Old Day (Certain, Stacey) SLP 1486
[04] Raggy Mountain Shakedown (Adcock, Duffey) SLP 1486
[05] Banana Boat Song (Attaway, Burgess) SLP 1486
[06] Going to the Races (Stanley) SLP 1486
[07] Waiting For the Boys To Come Home (Presley) SLP 1486
[08] Darling Little Joe (Traditional P.D.) SLP 1486
[09] El Dedo (Adcock)SLP 1486
[10] I'll Be There Mary Dear (Sterling, von Tilzer) SLP 1486
[11] Blue Ridge Cabin Home (Certain, Stacey) SLP 1486
[12] Take Me In a Lifeboat (Southern) SLP 1486
Charlie Waller, guitar, vocals; John Duffey, mandolin, vocals; Eddie Adcock, banjo, vocals; Ed Ferris, bass, vocals

**Emerson And Waldron**

1970, Rebel session, *Bluegrass Session* album, Producer, Charles R. "Dick" Freeland, Engineer. Roy Homer, Roy Homer and Associates, Clinton, Maryland

[01] Early Morning Rain (Lightfoot) SLP 1493
[02] Who Will Sing For Me (Stanley) SLP 1493
[03] Downtown Blues (Poffinberger) SLP 1493
[04] The Water's So Cold (Jackson) SLP 1493
[05] Home Sweet Home SLP 1493
[06] Lodi (Fogerty)SLP 1493
[07] A Face From Another Place (McCeney) SLP 1493
[08] Mama's Hungry Eyes (Haggard) SLP 1493

[09] Spanish Grass (Auldridge) SLP 1493
[10] Break My Mind (Hamilton) SLP 1493
[11] Laura's Tune (Auldridge) SLP 1493
[12] I Feel Lonesome Too (Waldron)SLP 1493
Cliff Waldron, guitar, vocals; Bill Emerson, banjo, vocals; John Duffey, mandolin, vocals; Mike Auldridge, Dobro, vocals; Bill Poffinberger, fiddle; Ed Ferris, bass

**Bluegrass 45**
July 22, 1971, Rebel session, "Caravan" album, Producer, John Duffey, Engineer, Roy Homer, Roy Homer and Associates, Clinton, Maryland

[02] New Tokaido Line (Watanabe) SLP 1507
Sab "Watanabe" Inoue, banjo, autoharp; Toshio "Speedy" Watanabe, bass; Gakusei Ryo, fiddle, percussion; Tsuyoshi "Josh" Otsuka, guitar; Akira Otsuka, mandolin, guitar

September 9, 1971, Rebel session, Producer, John Duffey, Engineer, Roy Homer, Roy Homer and Associates, Clinton, Maryland

[03] Kiso (T. Otsuka) SLP 1507
[07] Someday Soon(Tyson) SLP 1507
[10] Smile All The Way (T. Otsuka) SLP 1507
Sab "Watanabe" Inoue, banjo, autoharp; Toshio "Speedy" Watanabe, bass; Gakusei Ryo, fiddle, vocals, percussion; Tsuyoshi "Josh" Otsuka, guitar, vocals; Akira Otsuka, mandolin, guitar, vocals

September 14, 1971, Rebel session, *Caravan* album, Producer, John Duffey, Engineer, Roy Homer, Roy Homer and Associates, Clinton, Maryland

[01] What Am I Doing Hanging Around? (Murphey) SLP 1507
[04] Blues Stay Away From Me (Delmore) SLP 1507
[06] Last Call To Glory (Duffey) SLP 1507
[12] Come Home My Dear One (T. Otsuka) SLP 1507
Sab "Watanabe" Inoue, banjo, autoharp, vocals; Toshio "Speedy" Watanabe, bass; Gakusei Ryo, fiddle, percussion, vocals;

Tsuyoshi "Josh" Otsuka, guitar, vocals; Akira Otsuka, mandolin, guitar, vocals

September 15, 1971, Rebel session, *Caravan* album, Producer, John Duffey, Engineer, Roy Homer, Roy Homer and Associates, Clinton, Maryland
[05] Apartment 1101 (T. Otsuka) SLP 1507
[08] Caravan (Ellington) SLP 1507
[09] Hana (A. Otsuka)SLP 1507
[11] Ronnie Bucke (Watanabe) SLP 1507
Sab "Watanabe" Inoue, banjo, autoharp; Toshio "Speedy" Watanabe, bass; Gakusei Ryo, fiddle, percussion; Tsuyoshi "Josh" Otsuka, guitar; Akira Otsuka, mandolin, guitar; John Duffey, percussion [on 08]

## The Seldom Scene
February 20, 1972, Rebel session, *Act 1* album, Producer, Charles R. "Dick" Freeland, Engineer, Roy Homer, Roy Homer and Associates Studio, Clinton, Maryland
[01] City of New Orleans (Goodman) SLP 1511
[02] Darling Corey (Arr. Duffey) SLP 1511
John Duffey, mandolin, vocals; John Starling, vocals, guitar; Mike Auldridge, Dobro, vocals; Ben Eldridge, banjo; Tom Gray, bass, vocals

March 5, 1972, Rebel session, *Act 1* album, Producer, Charles R. "Dick" Freeland, Engineer, Roy Homer, Roy Homer and Associates Studio, Clinton, Maryland

[12] What Am I Doing Hanging Around? (Murphey) SLP 1511
[11] Cannonball (Arr. Auldridge) SLP 1511
[09] Summertime Is Past And Gone (Monroe) SLP 1511
[08] With Body and Soul (Stauffer) SLP 1511
[05] Joshua (Arr. Auldridge) SLP 1511
[10] 500 Miles (West)SLP 1511
John Duffey, mandolin, vocals; John Starling, vocals, guitar; Mike Auldridge, Dobro, vocals; Ben Eldridge, banjo; Tom Gray, bass, vocals

March 26, 1972, Rebel session, *Act 1* album, Producer, Charles R. "Dick" Freeland, Engineer, Roy Homer. Roy Homer and Associates Studio, Clinton, Maryland
[04] Sweet Baby James (Taylor) SLP 1511
[03] Want of a Woman (Craft) SLP 1511
[01] Raised By The Railroad Line (Craft) SLP 1511
[06] Will There Be Any Starts In My Crown (Arr. Duffey)SLP 1511
John Duffey, mandolin, vocals; John Starling, vocals, guitar; Mike Auldridge, Dobro, vocals; Ben Eldridge, banjo; Tom Gray, bass, vocals

**Mike Auldridge**
1972, Takoma sessions, *Dobro* album, 284 Third Avenue, New York, New York. Various studios in New York, Maryland and Virginia. Engineer, George Motion (Massenburg), David Hewitt, Corey Pearson, Producer, Jim McGuire, Mike Auldridge
[01] Hillbilly Hula D-1033TAK 7033
[02] Tennessee Stud D-1033TAK 7033
[03] It's Over D-1033TAK 7033
[04] Dobro Island D-1033TAK 7033
[05] Train 45½ D-1033TAK 7033
[06] Take Me D-1033TAK 7033
[07] Rock Bottom D-1033TAK 7033
[08] Jamboree D-1033TAK 7033
[09] House of the Rising Sun D-1033TAK 7033
[10] Rolling Fog D-1033TAK 7033
[11] Greensleeves D-1033TAK 7033
[12] Silver Threads Among The GoldD-1033TAK 7033
Mike Auldridge. Dobro, vocals; Ben Eldridge, banjo, guitar; David Bromberg, guitar; Vassar Clements, fiddle; Buck Graves, Dobro; Doyle Lawson, guitar, mandolin; Steve Burgh, bass; Bill Emerson, banjo; Charlie Waller, guitar; Tom Gray, bass; John Duffey, mandolin, guitar; Bill Yates, bass; Ed Ferris, bass]

**The Seldom Scene**
November 2, 1972, Rebel session, *Act Two* album, Producer, Charles R. "Dick" Freeland, Engineer, Bill McElroy, Bob Dawson, Bias Studios, 115 Hillwood Avenue, Suite 200, Falls Church, Virginia 22046
[01] Last Train from Poor Valley (Blake) SLP 1520

[02] Gardens And Memories (Starling) SLP 1520
[03] Paradise (Prine) SLP 1520
[04] Small Exception of Me (Hatch, Trent) SLP 1520
[05] Train Leaves Here This Morning (Clark, Leadon) SLP 1520
[06] Keep Me From Blowin' Away (Craft) SLP 1520
John Duffey, mandolin, guitar, vocals; John Starling, vocals, guitar; Mike Auldridge, Dobro, vocals; Ben Eldridge, banjo, guitar; Tom Gray, bass, vocals

November 11, 1972, Rebel session, *Act Two* album, Producer, Charles R. "Dick" Freeland, Engineer, Bill McElroy, Bob Dawson, Bias Studios, 115 Hillwood Avenue, Suite 200, Falls Church, Virginia 22046
[07] Hello Mary Lou (Pitney, Mangiaracina)SLP 1520
[08] Lara's Theme (Jaree)SLP 1520
[09] I've Lost You (Scruggs)SLP 1520
[10] The Sweetest Gift (Cain, Burke)SLP 1520
[11] Reason For Being (Duffey, Hill)SLP 1520
[12] Smokin' Hickory (Eldridge)SLP 1520
[13] House of Gold (Williams)SLP 1520
John Duffey, mandolin, guitar, vocals; John Starling, vocals, guitar; Mike Auldridge, Dobro, vocals; Ben Eldridge, banjo, guitar; Tom Gray, bass, vocals

**Ralph Stanley**
March 22, 1973, Rebel session, Producer, Charles R. "Dick" Freeland, Engineer, Roy Homer, Roy Homer and Associates Studio, Clinton, Maryland
[07] Lonesome River (Stanley)SLP 1530
[08] The Fields Have Turned Brown (Stanley)SLP 1522
Ralph Stanley, banjo, vocals; Roy Lee Centers, guitar, vocals; Ricky Lee, guitar; John Duffey, mandolin, vocals; Curly Ray Cline, fiddle; Jack Cooke, bass

**The Seldom Scene**
July 15, 1973, Rebel session, *Act 3* album, ITI-Recordings Inc, Towson, Maryland., Producer, Charles R. "Dick" Freeland, Engineer, George Motion (Massenburg)
[01] Chim-Chim-Cher-Ee (Sherman, Sherman) SLP 1528

John Duffey, mandolin, guitar, vocals; John Starling, vocals, guitar; Mike Auldridge, Dobro, vocals; Ben Eldridge, banjo, guitar; Tom Gray, bass, vocals

July 21, 1973, Rebel session, *Act 3* album, ITI-Recordings Inc, Towson, Maryland., Producer, Charles R. "Dick" Freeland Engineer, George Motion (Massenburg)
[02] Little Georgia Rose (Monroe) SLP 1528
[03] Another Lonesome Day (Thatcher) SLP 1528
[04] Willie Boy (Rosenthal) SLP 1528
[05] Faded Love (Wills) SLP 1528
[06] Rider (Arr. Eldridge, Duffey, Starling, Auldridge, Gray)
[07] Muddy Water (Rosenthal) SLP 1528
[08] Mean Mother Blues (Starling) SLP 1528
[09] Sing Me Back Home (Haggard) SLP 1528
[10] Hail To The Redskins (Breeskin, Griffith) SLP 1528
[11] Don't Bother With White Satin (Duffey, Hill) SLP 1528
[12] Heaven (McSpadden, McSpadden) SLP 1528
John Duffey, mandolin, guitar, vocals; John Starling, vocals, guitar; Mike Auldridge, Dobro, vocals; Ben Eldridge, banjo, guitar, vocals; Tom Gray, bass, vocals; Clayton Hambrick, guitar [on 08]; Ricky Skaggs, fiddle, viola

**The Seldom Scene**
September 12, 1973, NBC TV documentary session, *When The Past Dries Up – The Story of the C&O Canal album*, Wash. D.C.
[01] Lock Ready (C & O Canal) (Starling)Perspective 42073
[02] Muddy Waters (Rosenthal)Perspective 42073
[03] Salty Dog BluesPerspective 42073

This album was the soundtrack for a WRC/NBC-TV *Perspective* television documentary on the C&O Canal, entitled, *When The Past Dries Up*. 1,000 albums were made and sold at the Great Falls park visitor center.
John Duffey, mandolin, vocals; John Starling, vocals, guitar; Mike Auldridge, Dobro; Ben Eldridge, banjo; Tom Gray, bass, vocals; Robert "Bob" Williams, harmonica

## The Seldom Scene

March 10 and 24, 1974, Rebel session, *Old Train* album, Track Recorders Inc., 8226 Georgia Avenue, Silver Spring, Maryland, Producer, Charles R. "Dick" Freeland, Engineer, George Motion (Massenburg)

[01] Appalachia Rain (Craft)SLP 1536
[02] Wait a Minute (Pedersen)SLP 1536
[03] Different Roads (Starling)SLP 1536
[04] Old Train (Pedersen, Pedersen)SLP 1536
[05] Through The Bottom of The Glass (Craft)SLP 1536
[06] Old Crossroads (Arr. Eldridge, Duffey, Starling, Auldridge, Gray)SLP 1536
[07] Pan American (Williams)SLP 1536
[08] Working On a Building (Arr. E, D, S, A, G)SLP 1536
[09] Walk Through This World with Me (Savage, Seamons) SLP
[10] Maybe You Will Change Your Mind (Reno)SLP 1536
[11] Traveling On and On (Arr. E, D, S, A, G) SLP 1536
[12] C & O Canal (Starling)SLP 1536

John Duffey, mandolin, guitar, vocals; John Starling, vocals, guitar; Mike Auldridge, Dobro, vocals; Ben Eldridge, banjo, guitar, vocals; Tom Gray, bass, vocals; Ricky Skaggs, fiddle, viola; Paul Craft, guitar; Bob Williams, harmonica; Linda Ronstadt, vocals

## Mike Auldridge

March, 1974, Takoma session, Track Recorders Inc., 8226 Georgia Avenue, Silver Spring, Maryland, Producer, Jim McGuire, Mike Auldridge, Engineer, George Motion (Massenburg)

[04] This Ain't Grass (Taylor)D-1041 TAK-8914-2
[05] Eight More Miles To LouisvilleD-1041 TAK-8914-2
[09] Panhandle CountryD-1041 TAK-8914-2
[10]SummertimeD-1041 TAK-8914-2

Mike Auldridge, Dobro, guitar; Ben Eldridge, banjo [on 04, 05, and 09]; John Duffey, mandolin, vocals on [09]; Gery Mulé, lead guitar [on 10], Tom Gray, bass, vocals [on 09]; John Starling, guitar [on 04], vocals [on 09] Vassar Clements, fiddle [on 04, 09, and 10]

## Bill Clifton
June 4, 5, and 18, 1974, "Come By The Hills" album, David Freeman, Producer, Roy D. Homer Studio, Camp Springs, Maryland

| | |
|---|---|
| 203 Come By The Hills County 751 BCD | 16425 |
| 204 Fast Express County 751 BCD | 16425 |
| 205 Going Down The Valley County 751 BCD | 16425 |
| 206 Going To Scotland County 751 BCD | 16425 |
| 207 Honey I'm Ramblin' Away County 751 BCD | 16425 |
| 208 I Love You Best County 751 BCD | 16425 |
| 209 Little Poplar Log House On The Hill County 751 BCD | 16425 |
| 210 Mark's Tune County 751 BCD | 16425 |
| 211 There's a Little Pine Log Cabin County 751 BCD | 16425 |
| 212 This World Can't Stand Long County 751 BCD | 16425 |
| 213 Pretty Flowers UnissuedBCD | 16425 |
| 214 Blue Eyed Elaine County 751 BCD | 16425 |

215 I've Got My One Way Ticket County 751 BCD 16425
Bill Clifton, guitar, vocals; Red Rector, mandolin, vocals; John Duffey, mandolin, guitar, vocals; Walter Hensley, banjo; Tom Gray, bass, vocals; Kenny Baker, fiddle, guitar; Mike Seeger, autoharp, guitar, fiddle, vocals

## The Seldom Scene
December 27 and 28, 1974, Rebel session, "Live At The Cellar Door album, Cellar Door, Washington, D.C., Engineers Bill McElroy, Norm Rowland. Live Concert recording
[01] Doing My Time (Skinner) SLP 1547/48
[02] California Cottonfields (Frazier, Montgomery) SLP 1547/48
[03] Band Introductions SLP 1547/48
[04] Panhandle Country (Monroe)SLP 1547/48
[05] Muddy Water (Rosenthal)SLP 1547/48
[06] Rawhide (Monroe)SLP 1547/48
[07] Baby Blue (Dylan)SLP 1547/48
[08] City of New Orleans (Goodman)SLP 1547/48
[09] Grandfather's Clock (Arr. D, G, S, E, A) SLP 1547/48
[10] The Fields Have Turned Brown (Stanley) SLP 1547/48
[11] Hit Parade of Love (Martin) SLP 1547/48
[12] Will The Circle Be Unbroken (Arr. D, G, S, E, A)
[13] Pickaway (Flatt, Jordan)SLP 1547/48

[14] Dark Hollow (Arr. Duffey, Gray, Starling, Eldridge, Auldridge) SLP 1547/48
[15] Small Exception of Me (Hatch, Tent) SLP 1547/48
[16] If I Were a Carpenter (Hardin) SLP 1547/48
[17] Old Gray Bonnet (Arr. (Arr. D, G, S, E, A) SLP 1547/48
[18] C & O Canal (Starling)SLP 1547/48
[19] Georgia Rose (Monroe)SLP 1547/48
[20] Colorado Turnaround (Graves) SLP 1547/48
[21] He Rode All The Way To Texas (Starling) SLP 1547/48
[22] White Line (Bennett)SLP 1547/48
[23] Rider (Arr. Duffey, Gray, Starling, Eldridge, Auldridge)
John Duffey, mandolin, guitar, vocals; John Starling, vocals, guitar; Mike Auldridge, Dobro, vocals; Ben Eldridge, banjo, guitar, vocals; Tom Gray, bass, vocals

**Various Artists**
1976, National Geographic Society, *Steamboat's A-Comin'* album
[04]Georgia Camp Meeting NG    07787Ben    Eldridge,    banjo; Michael Cooney, banjo; Tom Gray, bass; Paul Gorski, guitar; Saul Broudy, harmonica; John Duffey, mandolin; Jack Grochmal, tambourine

**The Seldom Scene**
April 14 and 17, 1976, Rebel session, *The New Seldom Scene Album* Producer, The Seldom Scene, Engineer, Bill McElroy, Bias Studios, 115 Hillwood Avenue, Suite 200, Falls Church, Virginia 22046
[01] Big Rig (Taylor) SLP 1561
[02] If That's The Way You Feel (Stanley, Stanley)SLP 1561
[03] Easy Ride From Good Times To The Blues (Pedersen)
[04] Paradise Valley (Arr. Gray) SLP 1561
[05] California Earthquake (Crowell) SLP 1561
[06] Railroad Man (Traditional) SLP 1561
[07] Answer Your Call (Starling) SLP 1561
[08] I Haven't Got The Right To Love You (Buchanan, Claude)
[09] Song For Life (Crowell) SLP 1561
[10] Rebels Ye Rest (Beauchamp) SLP 1561
[11] Pictures From Life's Other Side (Arr. Duffey)SLP 1561
John Duffey, mandolin, guitar, vocals; John Starling, vocals, guitar; Mike Auldridge, Dobro, pedal steel, vocals; Ben Eldridge,

banjo, guitar; Tom Gray, bass, vocals; Linda Ronstadt, vocals [on 05]; Mark Cuff, drums, percussion

## Jaime Brockett

January and February, 1977, *North Mountain Velvet* album, Engineer, Jack Conners, Flite Three Studios, 1140 East Cold Spring Lane, Baltimore, Maryland
[01] No Spare Parts (Gritzbach) AD 1028
[03] Second Hand Cowboy (Rubino) AD 1028
[07] North Mountain Window Song (Brockett)AD 1028
[11] Just Stopped By To Git a Cup of Coffee (Elliott)AD 1028
Jaime Brockett, guitar, vocals; Mike Auldridge, Dobro; Ben Eldridge, banjo [on 01, 03, and 11]; Ricky Skaggs, fiddle [01 and 03]; John Starling, guitar [03, 07 and 11]; Tom Gray, bass; Ralph Fisher, drums [on 01, 03 and 07]; Dimitrius Mims, jawharp [01]; Scott Johnson, piano [03 and 07], Pat Petteway, vocals [07], Jan Davis, vocals [07]; A.J. Rubino, pedal steel, guitar [07]; Ramblin' Jack Elliott, guitar, vocals [11]

## Saul Broudy

January, 1977, *Travels With Broudy* album, Producer, Steve Burgh, Flite Three Studios, 1140 East Cold Spring Lane, Baltimore, Maryland
[01] Old Home Place (Webb, Jayne)AD 2011
[04] Alone and Forsaken (Williams)AD 2011
[05] I Ain't Got No Home (Guthrie)AD 2011
Saul Broudy, guitar, harmonica, vocals; Steve Burgh, electric guitar [on 04]; Winnie Winston, pedal steel [on 04], Lew London, mandolin [01 and 05], Dobro [04]; Dennis Gormley, bass [on 01 and 05]; Wannamaker Lewis, banjo [01 and 05]; Hugh McDonald, bass [on 04]; Steve Mosley, drums [04]; Jay Ungar fiddle [on 05], John Duffey, vocals; Mike Auldridge, vocals

## The Seldom Scene

April, August, December 1977, Rebel session, *Baptizing* album, Bias Studios, 115 Hillwood Avenue, Suite 200, Falls Church, Virginia 22046
[01] By The Side of The Road (Brumley) SLP 1573
[02] Brother John (Rosenthal) SLP 1573
[03] Dreaming of a Little Cabin (Brumley) SLP 1573

[04] Fallen Leaves (Jones) SLP 1573
[05] He Took Your Place (Flatt, Scruggs) SLP 1573
[06] Take Him In (Rosenthal) SLP 1573
[07] Hobo On a Freight Train To Heaven (Weideman) SLP 1573
[08] Will You Be Ready To Go Home (Williams) SLP 1573
[09] Were You There? (Arr. Duffey) SLP 1573
[10] Walk With Him Again (Rosenthal) SLP 1573
[11] Gospel Medley (Arr. Duffey) SLP 1573
John Duffey, mandolin, guitar, vocals; John Starling, vocals, guitar; Phil Rosenthal, guitar, vocals; Mike Auldridge, Dobro, vocals; Ben Eldridge, banjo, guitar; Tom Gray, bass, vocals; Ricky Skaggs, fiddle, mandolin rhythm

**Bob Devlin**
February 23, 1979, Pot Luck records session, *String Rambler* album, Producer, Bob Devlin, Executive Producer, Harvey Fernebok, Engineer & Co-Producer, Bill McElroy, Bias Studios, 115 Hillwood Avenue, Suite 200, Falls Church, Virginia 22046
[01] A Day in the Life of Bluegrass Bill's America (Devlin) PL-003
John Duffey, vocals; Bob Devlin, guitar, vocals; Steve Dennis, drums; Steuart Smith, guitar; Jeff Wisor, violin; Akira Otsuka, guitar; Mike Auldridge, Dobro; Phil Rosenthal, vocals; Tom Gray, bass

**The Seldom Scene**
March 3, April 13, 1979, Sugar Hill session, *Act Four* album, Engineer, Bill McElroy, Bias Studios, 115 Hillwood Avenue, Suite 200, Falls Church, Virginia 22046
[01] Something In The Wind SH-3709
[02] Girl in the Night (Thompson) SH-3709
[03] Ride Me Down Easy (Shaver) SH-3709
[04] Leaving Harlan (Rosenthal) SH-3709
[05] Tennessee Blues (Monroe) SH-3709
[06] Life Is Like a Mountain Railway (Arr. Duffey, Auldridge)
[07] I Don't Know You (Black, Moreno) SH-3709
[08] California Blues (Rodgers, Terry) SH-3709
[09] San Antonio Rose (Wills) SH-3709
[10] Daddy Was a Railroad Man (Rosenthal) SH-3709
[11] Walking the Blues (Gray) SH-3709
[12] This Weary Heart You Stole Away (Stanley)SH-3709

John Duffey, mandolin, guitar, vocals; Phil Rosenthal, guitar, vocals; Mike Auldridge, Dobro, pedal steel, vocals; Ben Eldridge, banjo, guitar; Tom Gray, bass, vocals

**Bryan Bowers**
1980, Flying Fish session, *Home, Home On The Road* album
[01]Dixie (Arr. Milt Kramer) FF 091
Bryan Bowers, autoharp, vocals; Sam Bush, mandolin; Howard Levy, tin whistle; Adele Welland cello; Dave Derge, drum; John Duffey, vocals; Mike Auldridge; vocals; Phil Rosenthal, guitar

**John Starling**
1980, Sugar Hill session, Producer, Audie Ashworth, Lowell George, Engineer, Mark Ritter, Lowell George, Blue Seas, Baltimore, Maryland
[01]He Rode All The Way To Texas (Starling) SH-3714
John Starling, guitar, vocals; Mike Auldridge, Dobro, vocals; John Duffey, vocals; Ben Eldridge, banjo; Tom Gray, bass; Scott Johnson, piano

**The Original Country Gentlemen**
February 17, 1980, Sugar Hill session, *Bluegrass: The World's Greatest Show* album, Lisner Auditorium, George Washington University, Washington, D.C. Live Concert Recording. (several sites list this incorrectly as February 27, 1983)
[01] Two Little Boys (Duffey, Davis )SH 2201
[02] Today Has Been a Lonesome Day SH 2201
[03] Bringing Mary Home (Duffey, Mank, Kingston)SH 2201
Charlie Waller, guitar, vocals; John Duffey, mandolin, vocals; Eddie Adcock, banjo, vocals; Tom Gray, bass

**The Seldom Scene**
February 17, 1980, Sugar Hill session, *Bluegrass: The World's Greatest Show* album, Lisner Auditorium, George Washington University, Washington, D.C. Live Concert Recording. (several sites list this incorrectly as February 27, 1983)
[01 ]When Someone Wants To Leave (Parton) SH 2201
[02] The House of The Rising Sun SH 2201
[03] Hickory Wind (Parsons, Buchanan) SH 2201
[04] Wild Kentucky Roan (Rosenthal) SH 2201

[05] Alabama Jubilee (Yellen, Cobb) SH 2201
John Duffey, mandolin, guitar, vocals; Phil Rosenthal, guitar, vocals; Mike Auldridge, Dobro, vocals; Ben Eldridge, banjo, guitar; Tom Gray, bass, vocals

**The Original Seldom Scene**
February 17, 1980, Sugar Hill session, *Bluegrass: The World's Greatest Show* album, Lisner Auditorium, George Washington University, Washington, D.C. Live Concert Recording. (several sites list this incorrectly as February 27, 1983)
[01] Old Train (Pedersen) SH 2201
[02] Through The Bottom of The Glass (Craft)SH 2201
[03] Out Among The Stars (Mitchell)SH 2201
John Duffey, mandolin, guitar, vocals; John Starling, guitar, vocals; Mike Auldridge, Dobro, vocals; Ben Eldridge, banjo; Tom Gray, bass, vocals

**Bill Clifton**
October 21, 1980, *Autoharp Centennial Celebration* album, Producer, Bill Clifton, Bias Recording Co. Inc., 115 Hillwood Avenue, Suite 200, Falls Church, Virginia 22046
257 Silver Bell (Traditional P.D.) ELF 101 BCD          16425
258 Darling Nellie Gray (Traditional P.D.) ELF 101 BCD          16425
259 Plumtree Cakewalk (Clifton) ELF 101 BCD          16425
Bill Clifton, autoharp; Tony Williamson, guitar, mandolin [on 258]; Mike Auldridge, Dobro; John Duffey, mandolin; Tom Gray, bass

October 22, 1980, *Autoharp Centennial Celebration* album, Producer, Bill Clifton, Bias Recording Co. Inc., 115 Hillwood Avenue, Suite 200, Falls Church, Virginia 22046
260 Gray Dawn (Clifton) ELF 101 BCD 16425
261 Liberty (Traditional P.D.) ELF 101 BCD 16425
262 This Land Is Your Land (Guthrie) ELF 101 BCD 16425
263 Under The Double Eagle (Wagner) ELF 101 BCD 6425
264 Mist Over Poor Valley (Clifton) ELF 101 BCD 16425
Bill Clifton, autoharp; Tony Williamson, guitar; Mike Auldridge, Dobro; John Duffey, mandolin; Tom Gray, bass; Mike Seeger, autoharp

October 23, 1980, *Autoharp Centennial Celebration* album, Producer, Bill Clifton, Bias Recording Co. Inc., 115 Hillwood Avenue, Suite 200, Falls Church, Virginia 22046
265 Celebration (Clifton) ELF 101 BCD 16425
266 Tea At Half-Five (Clifton) ELF 101 BCD 16425
267 Wildwood Flower (Carter) ELF 101 BCD 16425
268 Gathering Up The Shells From The Sea-Shore ELF 101
Bill Clifton, autoharp; Tony Williamson, guitar; Mike Auldridge, Dobro; John Duffey, mandolin; Tom Gray, bass; Mike Seeger, autoharp, guitar [on 267]

## The Seldom Scene
January-April 1981, Sugar Hill session, *After Midnight* album, Bias Studios, 115 Hillwood Avenue, Suite 200, Falls Church, Virginia 22046; Track Recorders Inc., 8226 Georgia Avenue, Silver Spring, Maryland, Producer, Bill McElroy and The Seldom Scene
[01] Lay Down Sally (Clapton, Terry, Levy) SH-3721
[02] Hearts Overflowing (Brewer) SH-3721
[03] The Old Home Town (Flatt) SH-3721
[04] Stompin' At The Savoy (Goodman, Sampson, Webb)
[05] The Border Incident (Duffey) SH-3721
[06] Come Early Morning (McDill) SH-3721
[07] After Midnight (Cale) SH-3721
[08] If I Had Left It Up To You (Haggard) SH-3721
[09] Heartsville Pike (McReynolds) SH-3721
[10] Stolen Love (Rosenthal )SH-3721
[11]Let Old Mother Nature Have Her Way (Clark, Southerland) SH-3721
John Duffey, mandolin, guitar, vocals; Phil Rosenthal, guitar, vocals; Mike Auldridge, Dobro, vocals; Ben Eldridge, banjo, guitar, vocals; Tom Gray, bass, vocals; Carl Nelson, fiddle

## Mike Auldridge
November 4, 1981, Sugar Hill session, *Eight-String Swing* album, Bias Recording Studio, 5400 Carolina Place, Springfield, Virginia
[02] Redskin Rag (McAuliffe)SH-3725
[03] Bethesda (Jones)SH-3725
[05] Caravan (Ellington)SH-3725
[07] Bluegrass Boogie (Auldridge)SH-3725

Mike Auldridge, Dobro, guitar; Ben Eldridge, banjo; Tom Gray, bass; John Duffey, mandolin; Phil Rosenthal, guitar; Robbie Magruder, drums; Jimmy Arnold, fiddle; Peter Bonta, piano; Pete Kennedy, guitar

**The Seldom Scene**
May 3, 10, 15 and 20, 1983, Sugar Hill session, *At The Scene* album, Bias Recording Studio, 5400 Carolina Place, Springfield, Virginia, Engineer, Bill McElroy, Produced, The Seldom Scene
[01] A Girl I Know (Rosenthal) (2:48) SH-3736
[02] Jamaica Say You Will (Browne) (3:27) SH-3736
[03] Open Up the Window Noah (Rosenthal) (2:23)SH-3736
[04] Winter Wind (Rosenthal) (2:42)SH-3736
[05] Heal It (Hill, Reid) (3:41) SH-3736
[06] The Weary Pilgrim (Rosenthal) (2:43) SH-3736
[07] It Turns Me Inside Out (Crutchfield) (3:30)SH-3736
[08] The Champion (Landis) (3:32)SH-3736
[09] Born of the Wind (Craft) (2:38)SH-3736
[10] Peaceful Dreams (Handy) (4:30)SH-3736
John Duffey, mandolin, rhythm guitar, vocals; Phil Rosenthal, lead and rhythm guitar, mandolin, vocals; Mike Auldridge, Dobro, high strung guitar, vocals; Ben Eldridge, banjo, second guitar; Tom Gray, bass, vocals; Robbie Magruder, drums; Jimmy Arnold, fiddle, harmonica

**Phil Rosenthal**
1983, Sierra Records session, *A Matter of Time* album, Bias Recording Studio, 5400 Carolina Place, Springfield, Virginia, Engineer, Bill McElroy, Producer, Phil Rosenthal
[01] What the Old Folks Know (Rosenthal)Sierra GA-1983
[03] Wild Flowers (Rosenthal)Sierra GA-1983
[04] Around the Horn (Rosenthal)Sierra GA-1983
[12] I Want To Be That Way (Rosenthal, Sommers Rosenthal) Sierra GA-1983
Phil Rosenthal, guitar, mandolin, banjo, vocals; John Duffey, mandolin, vocals; Ben Eldridge, banjo, vocals; Tom Gray Bass [on 01,03, 04]; Bryon Berline, fiddle [on 12]; Mike Auldridge, Dobro, guitar, vocals [on 01 and 03]; Robbie Magruder, percussion

**Bryan Bowers**
March 1984, Flying Fish session, *By Heart* album, Bias
Recording Studio, 5400 Carolina Place, Springfield, Virginia,
Engineer, Bill McElroy
[01] Hot Buttered Rum (Thompson)FF-313
[02] Zen Gospel Singing (Graham)FF-313
[03] Blackheart (Bowers)FF-313
Bryan Bowers, autoharp, vocals; Mike Auldridge, Dobro [on 01
and 03], vocals [on 02]; Tom Gray, bass [on 01 and 03], vocals
[on 02[; Ben Eldridge, banjo [on 01 and 03]; John Duffey,
mandolin [on 01 and 03], vocals [on 02]; Sam Bush, fiddle [on
01]; Phil Rosenthal, guitar [on 01 and 03]

**Jonathan Edwards and The Seldom Scene**
February 1985, Sugar Hill session, *Blue Ridge* album, Bias
Recording Studio, 5400 Carolina Place, Springfield, Virginia,
Engineer, Bill McElroy
[01] Don't This Road Look Rough and Rocky (Flatt, Scruggs)
[02] How Long Have I Been Waiting For You (Edwards) SH-3747
[03] Blue Ridge (Artis, Mallis) SH-3747
[04] Seven Daffodils (Moseley, Hays) SH-3747
[05] Sunshine (Edwards)SH-3747
[06] Back To Where I Don't Belong (Rosenthal) SH-3747
[07] If I Gave To You (Martin, Gray) SH-3747
[08] Honey, I Won't Be Around (Rosenthal) SH-3747
[09] Only a Hobo (Dylan) SH-3747
[10] God Gave You To Me (Stanley) SH-3747
[11] Little Hands (Edwards) SH-3747
[12] I Don't Believe I'll Stay Here Anymore (Anderson) SH-3747
[13] Don't Crawfish Me Baby (Emerson, Emerson)SH-3747
John Duffey, mandolin, vocals; Phil Rosenthal, lead and rhythm
guitar, vocals; Mike Auldridge, Dobro, steel guitar, guitar, vocals;
Ben Eldridge, banjo, guitar; Tom Gray, bass, vocals; Jonathan
Edwards, guitar, harmonica, vocals; Robbie Magruder,
percussion; Kenny White, piano

**Bill Monroe**
May 7, 1985, MCA session, *Bill Monroe and Stars of the
Bluegrass Hall of Fame* album, Producer, Emory Gordy Jr.,
Sound Stage Studio, Nashville, Tennessee

MC 18239 Remember The Cross (Monroe, Watts)MCA 5625
Bill Monroe, mandolin, vocals; Wayne Lewis, guitar; Blake
Williams, banjo; John Duffey, mandolin, vocals; Mike Auldridge,
vocals; Glen Duncan fiddle; Tater Tate, bass, vocals

**The Seldom Scene**
November 10, 1986, Sugar Hill session, *15th Anniversary
Celebration* album, John F. Kennedy Center For The Performing
Arts, 2700 F Street, N.W., Washington, D.C., Producer, Billy
Wolf, The Seldom Scene. Live Concert Recording
[01] Sittin' On Top of the World (Traditional)SH 2202
[02] Big Train From Memphis (Fogerty) SH 2202
[03] Lorena( Traditional)SH 2202
[04] Dark As a Dungeon (Travis) SH 2202
[05] Blue Ridge (Artis, Mallis) SH 2202
[06] Raised By The Railroad Line (Craft) SH 2202
[07] You Don't Know My Mind (Skinner) SH 2202
[08] Drifting Too Far From the Shore (Traditional) SH 2202
[09] Those Memories of You (O'Bryant) SH 2202
[10] Keep Me From Blowing Away(Craft) SH 2202
[11] Wheels (Hillman, Parsons) SH 2202
[12] Carolyn At the Broken Wheel Inn (Rushing, McDill)
[13] If I Needed You (Van Zandt) SH 2202
[14] Rose of Old Kentucky (Monroe) SH 2202
[15] I Couldn't Find My Walking Shoes (Overstreet, Brown)
[16] Working On a Building (Traditional) SH 2202
[17] Say You Lied (Smith) SH 2202
[18] High On a Hilltop (Collins) SH 2202
[19] The Sweetest Gift (Coats)SH 2202
[20] Take Me In a Lifeboat(Traditional)SH 2202
John Duffey, mandolin, vocals; Lou Reid, guitar, fiddle, bass,
mandolin, vocals; Mike Auldridge, Dobro, steel guitar, vocals;
Ben Eldridge, banjo, guitar; Tom Gray, bass, vocals; John
Starling, guitar, vocals; Linda Ronstadt, vocals; Emmylou Harris,
guitar, vocals; Ricky Skaggs, mandolin, fiddle, guitar, vocals;
Sharon White, vocals; Jonathan Edwards, guitar; Charlie Waller,
guitar, vocals; Tony Rice, guitar, vocals; Alan O'Bryant, banjo;
Peter Bonta, piano; Paul Craft, vocal, guitar; Bobby Hicks, fiddle;
Stuart Duncan, fiddle; Robbie Magruder, drums

## The Seldom Scene

1988, Sugar Hill session, *A Change of Scenery* album, Bias Recording, 5400 Carolina Place, Springfield, Virginia, Engineer, Billy Wolf, Producer, Billy Wolf, The Seldom Scene

[01] Breaking New Ground (Jackson, Salley) SH 3763
[02] Casting My Shadow In the Road (Rushing, Scruggs)
[03] Settin' Me Up (Knopfler) SH 3763
[04] Alabama Clay (Cordle, Scaife) SH 3763
[05] I'll Be No Stranger There (Sebron, Alcorn, Combs) SH 3763
[06] West Texas Wind (Ims) SH 3763
[07] Satan's Choir (Campbell) SH 3763
[08] In Despair (Pennington, Ahr) SH 3763
[09] What Goes On (Lennon, McCartney) SH 3763
[10] Brand New Walking ShoesSH 3763
[11] One Way Rider (Crowell)SH 3763

John Duffey, mandolin, vocals; Lou Reid, guitar, fiddle, mandolin, vocals; Mike Auldridge, Dobro, steel guitar, vocals; Ben Eldridge, banjo, guitar; T. Michael Coleman, bass, vocals; Robbie Magraduer, percussion

## Classic Country Gentlemen, Duffey, Waller, Adcock & Gray

February 20 and 21 1989, Sugar Hill session, *Classic Country Gents Reunion* album, Masterworks, Fairfax, Virginia. Producer: Penny Parsons

[01] Fare Thee Well (Dylan) SH 3772
[02] Stewball (Traditional) SH 3772
[03] I'll Be Here In the Morning (Van Zandt) SH 3772
[04] Champagne Breakdown (Adcock) SH 3772
[05] Here Today and Gone Tomorrow (Fowler) SH 3772
[06] Gonna Get There Soon (M. Adcock) SH 3772
[07] Hey Lala (McBride) SH 3772
[08] Casey's Last Ride (Kristofferson) SH 3772
[09] Wild Side of Life (Warren, Carter) SH 3772
[10] Wait a Little Longer (Houser) SH 3772
[11] Back Home In Indiana SH 3772
[12] Say Won't You Be Mine (Stanley) SH 3772
[13] Thinking of You SH 3772

Charlie Waller, guitar, vocals; John Duffey, mandolin, vocals; Eddie Adcock, banjo, vocals; Tom Gray, bass, vocals; Mike Auldridge, Dobro

**The Seldom Scene**
1990, Sugar Hill session, *Scenic Roots* album, Bias Recording, 5400 Carolina Place, Springfield, Virginia
[01] If You Ever Change Your Mind (Jackson, Stuart) SH 3785
[02] Lost In a Memory (Golding) SH 3785
[03] The Wrath of God (Delmore, Delmore) SH 3785
[04] Before I Met You (Lewis, Rader, Seitz) SH 3785
[05] Red Georgia Clay (Coleman, Reid) SH 3785
[06] I've Cried My Last Tear Over You (Delmore, Jackson)
[07] Not In My Arms (Coleman, Reid) SH 3785
[08] Highway of Heartache (Jackson, Rushing)SH 3785
[09] Long Black Veil (Dill, Wilkin)SH 3785
[10] Last Call To Glory (Duffey)SH 3785
[11] Distant Train (Coleman, Reid)SH 3785
[12] How Mountain Girls Can Love (Rakes)SH 3785
John Duffey, mandolin, vocals; Lou Reid, guitar, fiddle, mandolin, vocals; Mike Auldridge, Dobro, steel guitar, vocals; Ben Eldridge, banjo, guitar; T. Michael Coleman, bass, vocals

**The Seldom Scene**
1991, Sugar Hill session, "Sugar Plums (Holiday Treats From Sugar Hill)" album, Engineer Billy Wolf
[01] Silent Night (Gruber, Mohr)SH 3796
John Duffey, mandolin, vocals; Lou Reid, guitar, vocals; Mike Auldridge, Dobro, vocals; Ben Eldridge, guitar; T. Michael Coleman, bass

**The Seldom Scene**
November 29 and 30, 1991, *Scene 20* album, The Birchmere, 3701 Mount Vernon Avenue, Alexandria, Virginia. Live Concert recording
[01] Introduction SH 3926
[02] I Haven't Got the Right to Love You (Buchanan, Claude, Acuff) SH 3926
[03] Gardens and Memories (Starling) SH 3926
[04] House of Gold (Williams) SH 3926
[05] Pictures From Life's Other Side (Arr. Duffey) SH 3926
[06] Satan's Jeweled Crown (Edens) SH 3926
[07] Will You Be Ready To Go Home (Willaims) SH 3926
[08] Mean Mother Blues (Starling) SH 3926

[09] Were You There? (Arr. Duffey) SH 3926
[10] The Weary Pilgrim (Rosenthal) SH 3926
[11] Leavin' Harlan (Rosenthal) SH 3926
[12] Take Him In (Rosenthal) SH 3926
[13] Stompin' At The Savoy (Goodman, Sampson, Webb)
[14] Something In The Wind (Rosenthal) SH 3926
[15] Muddy Water (Rosenthal) SH 3926
[16] Open Up The Window Noah (Rosenthal) SH 3926
John Duffey, mandolin, vocals; John Starling, guitar, vocals;
Phil Rosenthal, guitar, vocals; Mike Auldridge, Dobro, vocals;
Ben Eldridge, banjo, guitar; Tom Gray, bass, vocals; T. Michael
Coleman, bass, vocals; Emmylou Harris, vocals

**The Seldom Scene**
November 29 and 30, 1991, The Birchmere, 3701 Mount Vernon
Avenue, Alexandria, Virginia. Live Concert recording
[01] Breaking New Ground (Jackson, Salley)SH 3926
[02] Old Train (Pedersen, Pedersen)SH 3926
[03] Wait a Minute (Pedersen)SH 3926
[04 ]Blue Ridge Cabin Home (Certain, Stacey)SH 3926
[05] Gypsy Moon (Coleman, Reid)SH 3926
[06] Walk Through This World With Me (Savage, Seamens)
[07] In the Pines (Traditional)SH 3926
[08] And on Bass (Coleman)SH 3926
[09] Another Lonesome Day (Thatcher)SH 3926
[10] Have Mercy on My Soul (Coleman, Reid)SH 3926
[11] The House of the Rising Sun/Walk Don't Run (Trad., Smith)
[12] In the Midnight Hour (Pickett, Cropper) SH 3926
John Duffey, mandolin, vocals; Lou Reid, guitar, vocals; Mike
Auldridge, Dobro, vocals; Ben Eldridge, banjo, guitar; T. Michael
Coleman, bass, vocals

The same performance was given both nights, including all
former and current members. Then the best recordings of each
tunes were put on one double album celebrating the 20th
anniversary of The Seldom Scene

## The Seldom Scene

1993, Sugar Hill session, *Like We Used To Be* album. Producer Billy Wolf, The Seldom Scene, Bias Recording, 5400 Carolina Place, Springfield, Virginia

[01] Grandpa Get Your Guitar (McCullough, Rushing)SH 3822
[02] Let Me Be Your Friend (Stanley)SH 3822
[03] Like I Used To Do (Alger, O'Brien)SH 3822
[04] Highway of Pain (Dauphin)SH 3822
[05] Cheap Whiskey (Gordy, Rushing)SH 3822
[06] Philadelphia Lawyer (Guthrie)SH 3822
[07] Almost Threw Your Love Away (Germino, Hylton) SH 3822
[08] The Other Side of Town (Clark, Williams, Williams)SH 3822
[09] She's More To Be Pitied (Rakes) SH 3822
[10] Heaven's Green Fields (Rushing, Shamblin) SH 3822
[11] I've Come To Take You Home (Coleman, Duffey) SH 3822
[12] I'll Remember Your Love In My Prayers SH 3822
[13] Some Morning Soon (Lynch, Lynch)SH 3822
John Duffey, mandolin, vocals; John Starling, guitar, vocals; Mike Auldridge, Dobro, vocals; Ben Eldridge, banjo, guitar; T. Michael Coleman, bass, vocals

## Tony Rice

1993, Rounder Records session, *Plays and Sings Bluegrass* album, Producer Billy Wolf, Tony Rice, Bias Recording, 5400 Carolina Place, Springfield, Virginia

[07] This Morning At Nine (Campbell) CD-0253
[09] Galveston Flood (Rush, Duffey, Adcock) CD-0253
Tony Rice, guitar, vocals; Mike Auldridge, Dobro, vocals; John Duffey, mandolin, vocals; Mark Schatz, bass; Bill Emerson, banjo

## Liz Meyer

1994, Producer, Liz Meyer, *Womanly Arts*
[07]*No Curb Service* (Norman, Novello) SCR 37
Liz Meyer, guitar, vocals; John Duffey, mandolin, vocals; Jerry Douglas, Dobro; Jeff Wisor, fiddle; Danny Gatton, guitar; Dick Smith, banjo; Larry Paxton, bass

"Thank you to John Duffey for coming to do a session in my absence, and leaving me with a flawless vocal that makes "No

Curb Service" really fly. I don't think I want to sing this one without you anymore, John." Liz Meyer from liner notes on album

## The Seldom Scene
1996, Sugar Hill session, *Dream Scene* album, Bias Recording, 5400 Carolina Place, Springfield, Virginia
[01] Dry Run Creek (McPeak) SH 3858
[02] Going Up On The Mountain (Gamble, Huff) SH 3858
[03] Willie Roy (Williams) SH 3858
[04] Tulsa Chili Bop (Pennington) SH 3858
[05] When I Get My Rewards (Kennerley) SH 3858
[06] They're At Rest Together (Traditional P.D.) SH 3858
[07] The Boatman (Hylton) SH 3858
[08] Love of The Mountains (Mills) SH 3858
[09] The Little Sparrow (Fair And Tender Ladies)
[10] The Shape I'm In (Connell) SH 3858
[11] Blue Diamond Mines (Ritchie) SH 3858
[12] Bad Moon Rising (Fogerty) SH 3858
John Duffey, mandolin, vocals; Dudley Connell, guitar, vocals; Fred Travers, Dobro, vocals; Ben Eldridge, banjo, guitar; Ronnie Simpkins, bass, vocals

# Index

Casey, Laurie Williams,
vi
Cash, Johnny, 32, 49,
96, 195, 234
Cerri, Dick, vi, 100, 102,
329
Chatman, Lewis "Lucky",
26, 28, 34, 65
Clapton, Eric, 119, 269
Clark, Charles Badger,
43
Clark, Johnny, 69
Clark, Roy, 13, 14, 16,
32, 42, 94
Clement, Jack, 32
Clifton, Bill, 68, 69, 70,
98, 111, 200
Coleman, T. Michael,
123, 314, 328, 332,
341
Connell, Dudley, vi, 126,
314, 333, 334, 352
Cooper, Stoney, 10, 208
Corbitt, Jerry, 48, 49
Cornett, Bob, 319
Cornett, Charles, vi, 319
Cornett, Jean, 319
Cox, Jim, 35, 40, 66, 98
Craft, Paul, 182, 183,
194, 266
Daley, Katy, 184, 352
Dean, James, 233
Dean, Jimmy, 13, 14,
334

Demsey, Lee Michael, vi,
184
Dopera Brothers, 160
Dress, Richard, 165
Duffey Sr., John, 3, 5, 6
Duffey, Florence, 3, 7,
15, 108, 110
Duffey, Jefferson, 5, 359,
360
Duffey, Nancy, 84, 108,
110, 121, 122, 123,
124, 127, 151, 152,
242, 246, 284, 287,
350
Dylan, Bob, 38, 95, 99,
139, 253
Eanes, Jim, 69, 171
Edwards, Jonathan, vi,
175, 267, 297, 325
Eldridge, Barbara, vi
Eldridge, Ben, vi, 70,
126, 128, 129, 148,
157, 160, 161, 181,
182, 192, 202, 237,
242, 253, 266, 281,
285, 307, 310, 314,
328, 333, 341
Eldridge, Chris, 237
Ellington, Duke, 1, 244
Ellsworth, Sterling, vi,
16, 17, 23
Emerson, Bill, vi, 21, 22,
26, 31, 33, 35, 36, 38,
39, 40, 41, 48, 74, 81,

CPSIA information can be obtained
at www.ICGtesting.com
Printed in the USA
BVHW041218260323
660937BV00010B/47